CHILDREN IN COURT

CHILDREN IN COURT

PUBLIC POLICYMAKING
AND FEDERAL COURT DECISIONS

SUSAN GLUCK MEZEY

STATE UNIVERSITY OF NEW YORK PRESS

Chapter 1 is a revised version based on an article originally published in the *Family Law Quarterly*, Copyright (1993) American Bar Association.

Published by
State University of New York Press, Albany

For information, address State University of New York Press,
State University Plaza, Albany, N.Y. 12246

Production by M. R. Mulholland
Marketing by Nancy Farrell

Library of Congress Cataloging-in-Publication Data

Mezey, Susan Gluck, 1944–
    Children in court : public policymaking and federal court decisions / Susan Gluck Mezey.
        p.   cm.
    Includes bibliographical references and index.
    ISBN 0-7914-2961-X (HC : acid-free). — ISBN 0-7914-2962-8 (PB : acid-free)
    1. Children—Legal status, laws, etc. —United States. 2. Judicial process—United States.   I. Title.
    KF479.M46   1996
    346.7301'35—dc20
    [347.306135]   95-21045
                                                                    CIP

10 9 8 7 6 5 4 3 2 1

For Jennifer and Jason

CONTENTS

TABLES

ACKNOWLEDGMENTS

I wrote this book during a time when society appeared to be turning away from its commitment to protect its most vulnerable citizens, its children. By the time the book was completed in 1995, most of the nation's political leaders had demonstrated their unwillingness to hear the voices of the children, especially poor and abused ones, and seemed to be abandoning them to a future with little legal protection and uncertain financial resources.

Despite the often depressing subject matter I was dealing with, writing this book was an enjoyable experience in many ways, and I want to thank the people who helped me. Lynn Cox generously contributed her time and energies to gathering most of the research on congressional policymaking for the WIC and Head Start programs. Scott Yenor checked my citations and read several versions of the manuscript, searching for any remaining errors in the text. Gary Gordon and Heidi Barth provided research assistance.

Loyola University Chicago provided me with yet another semester-long research leave of absence to allow me to work on the book full-time. I was also awarded a University research grant that permitted me to conduct the interviews with the representatives of children's advocacy groups. I want to thank Diane Geraghty and Rich Cozzola of Loyola's Civitas ChildLaw Center for their interest in this project, and Rich for reading and commenting on the child welfare chapter. Clay Morgan, editor at SUNY Press, encouraged me from the start and was willing to offer me a contract on the basis of a brief prospectus. The American Bar Association allowed me to reprint material written for an ABA publication; chapter one is a revised version of an article originally published in the *Family Law Quarterly*, Copyright (1993) American Bar Association.

I especially want to express my appreciation to the people who took time out of their busy schedules to respond to my lengthy questions about their work as children's advocates and their views on the efficacy of federal court litigation. In no particular order, they are: Ira Burnim, Rhoda Schulzinger, Judith Meltzer, Margaret Campbell Haynes, John O'Toole, Carole Shauffer, Marcia Robinson Lowry, Robert Lehrer, MaryLee Allen, Howard Davidson, James Weill, Adele Blong, Benjamin Wolf, Paula Roberts, and Diane Redleaf. Wendell Primus and other officials at HHS were instrumental in helping me to understand the complexity of the attempted "*Suter* Fix." Naturally, however, I bear sole responsibility for any errors contained in these pages.

xii *Acknowledgments*

Last, but certainly not least, I want to thank my family—the three people in my life who make it all worthwhile. To Michael, who has always provided me with as much love and support as I could ever want, and who, despite his heavy administrative responsibilities, remains one of the best scholars I know. To Jennifer and Jason, clearly the two best children a parent could wish to have. They have made, and continue to make, parenthood the joy of my life; they are unusual also in that I can discuss my work with them and rely on them to react with thoughtful comments and criticism. It is to them that I dedicate this book.

PREFACE

A recent effort to combat the powerlessness of children's voices led to the creation of the National Commission on Children, a group intended "to serve as a forum on behalf of the children of the nation." Established by an act of Congress on December 22, 1987, the commission was bipartisan, consisting of thirty-four members, and was chaired by Senator John D. Rockefeller IV of West Virginia. Reflecting almost four years of deliberation, it issued a report entitled *Beyond Rhetoric: A New American Agenda for Children and Families* on June 24, 1991.[1]

The lengthy document included proposals to impose a federal tax credit to replace the existing child tax exemption and to create a program of government-assured child support payments. The commission also recommended a renewed commitment to education through expansion of early childhood programs; greater emphasis on family preservation through programs designed to help troubled families; less reliance on foster care; and improved health care services for pregnant women and children. It acknowledged the substantial price tag of such programs and argued for the expenditure of public funds to improve the lives of children and their families, and ultimately, it claimed, the nation.

The much-heralded report merely reiterated what many people already knew: that the news about the nation's children is not good. Many exist at a subsistence level; one out of five lives in poverty.

The commission underscored another piece of common knowledge, namely, that children are poor because they live in families headed by poor, primarily minority, women. Noting that the problems of many children are inextricably linked to their economic and social status, the report stressed that programs aimed more generally at ending poverty and racial discrimination are an essential prerequisite to improving the quality of children's lives.

The nation's approach to children, arguably its most powerless group of citizens, as demonstrated by this brief summary of the findings of the National Commission on Children, has become part of a highly contentious political debate. The topic of children and family life loomed large in the 1992 presidential campaign and will certainly play a role in election campaigns to follow, including the 1996 presidential race. The changes in congressional leadership as a result of the 1994 elections and the new leadership's proposals to radically restructure the delivery of social services to the poor and the weak makes the national debate over the issue of policymaking for children even more crucial.

If the proposed changes in federal policy are enacted, state and local governments will be called upon to provide more support for children and families with reduced funding from the federal government. These governments have already indicated their inability and, in some cases, unwillingness to take up the slack entirely. Indeed, encouraged by the rhetoric from Washington, many state and local governments have been taking their cues from the federal government and cutting funds from programs that serve children and their families as well as restricting rules of eligibility. And although popular opinion does not respond well to the image of suffering children, it fervently supports cutting taxes, balancing the budget, and shrinking the authority of the federal government.

Based on their role in the political system and their history of providing redress for grievances suffered by minorities, the federal courts are an obvious target for groups attempting to derail many of these projected policy changes. Assessing the likelihood of success in litigation efforts on behalf of children depends, to a large extent, on the court's record of decisionmaking in children's policy issues in the past. One of the goals of this book is to explicate that record.

Notes

1. National Commission on Children, *Beyond Rhetoric: A New American Agenda for Children and Families* (Washington, D.C.: National Commission on Children, 1991).

INTRODUCTION

In enacting the Claude Pepper Young Americans Act of 1990, Congress proclaimed that "children and youth are inherently the most valuable resource of the United States." The act declared that all levels of government have a responsibility to assist children in securing "full and free access" to good health, safe shelter, and educational opportunity.

For the preponderance of the nation's history, these were largely empty sentiments; with the exception of brief intermittent periods, the national government had paid scarce attention to the status of children in society. In the 1960s and 1970s the efforts of the federal government to combat poverty and discrimination assumed a larger place on the national political agenda and the plight of children, especially poor children, captured the attention of national policymakers. In these two decades the federal government created a variety of programs for children whose poverty, disability, or family circumstances required society's protection. These programs marked a change in the locus of decisionmaking for children's policy from the state and local level to the national level.

One of Congress's first attempts to legislate on behalf of children was unsuccessful. Reflecting the influence of the Progressive Era in the early part of the twentieth century, Congress began an assault on the use of child labor in industry.[1] In 1935, when Congress included a program for needy dependent children within the Social Security Act, the federal government started on the path toward a meaningful role in policymaking for children. Following the model of the Social Security Act of 1935, Congress created a number of federal grant-in-aid programs in which the federal government underwrote a substantial part of the costs and entrusted the implementation of these programs largely to state and local authorities; such legislation often left the boundaries between state and federal jurisdiction unclear.

With the growth of federal programs affecting children conditioning state funding on compliance with federal mandates, the federal courts were increasingly drawn into the children's policymaking arena to determine the limits of federal and state decisionmaking. The bulk of cases, revolving around suits brought against state or local government agencies for violating federal law, were brought by children's advocates seeking to further the legislative aims through judicial decrees. Such litigation frequently required the federal courts to settle controversies over the distribution of welfare claims and benefits for children.

Beginning in the late 1960s the federal courts also assumed a more significant role in children's policymaking through the adjudication of children's constitutional claims against the state and federal governments. In many of their early opinions, reflecting the Warren Court's perspective on individual rights, the courts demonstrated a willingness to expand adult constitutional rights to children. Thus, in addition to refereeing conflicts between the state and federal governments, the federal courts also played an important role in policymaking for children by settling disputes over the limits of their autonomy.

Marked by the landmark decision of *In re Gault* in 1967, the Supreme Court began to take seriously the notion that constitutional rights were not limited to adults alone. Gradually, in accepting an increasing number of constitutional challenges to state and federal policies, brought by, or on behalf of, children, the federal courts assumed a greater share of responsibility for determining the outcome of children's lives. Constitutional policymaking eventually encompassed decisions ranging from determining the adequacy of procedural safeguards in the juvenile justice system and the outer limits of freedom of expression and privacy, to fixing the extent of governmental responsibility for protection from parental abuse, to resolving demands for educational equity and the elimination of classifications by birth status.

Taken as a whole, the rise in lawsuits filed on behalf of children, variously embodying claims for an expansion of governmental benefits, greater independence from authority in personal decisionmaking, as well as demands for protection from unfair and arbitrary government action, enlarged the federal court's role in policymaking for children.

The Benefits of Federal Court Policymaking

"Americans have always resorted to the courts to challenge the action of government, but only from the late 1950s on has the use of litigation as an instrument of social reform become so widespread that it can be called a movement."[2]

Since the 1930s the federal courts have offered an opportunity to represent the interests of those less able to make political demands on elected policymakers, and consequently social reformers have sought to enlist the aid of the federal judiciary in their battles for social change. Reflecting on the contribution made by federal courts to the rise of modern public interest liberalism, Michael McCann stresses that "the role judicial victories played in granting dignity and nurturing political action among many long-powerless groups cannot be ignored."[3]

The role of federal court litigation in contributing to political and social change has been well documented. Frequently, litigation is viewed as a "social process," with studies focusing on "details of organizational politics and the imperatives of practical litigation."[4] In this context some scholars examine the participation of a variety of political actors in the litigation process, particularly concerning themselves with the behavior of interest groups.[5] Unlike this "interest group" approach which often centers on the internal dynamics of the organization, this study focuses on the *outcome* of lawsuits affecting the status of children by examining the opinions of the courts in a wide variety of matters.

Earlier studies of litigation examined the efforts of the "disadvantaged" who sought to influence the policymaking process through judicial decision-making because they were unable to achieve their ends through "normal" political means.[6] The most well-known studies of social reform litigation were based on the school desegregation lawsuits under the direction of the National Association for the Advancement of Colored People (NAACP) Legal Defense and Educational Fund, Inc. (LDF).[7] Other studies investigated the effects of judicial policymaking on the status of women and the disabled.[8]

Although other studies have shown the federal courts are not the exclusive reserve of the underprivileged,[9] federal court decisionmaking has often been depicted as advantaging those unable to pursue their goals in representative institutions. For example, surveying the efforts of a variety of public interest law organizations in the two decades between *Brown v. Board of Education* and the mid-1970s, Aryeh Neier concludes that "cause litigation," that is, litigation seeking to advance a cause rather than to pursue an individual remedy, has irrevocably altered the nation's political landscape. By helping "disadvantaged minorities compete fairly in our pluralist democracy," in his view, litigation performs an invaluable service to the nation by rectifying the imbalance of political power.[10]

While generally agreeing that litigation by itself may fail to produce direct results, a number of scholars believe it is a useful tactic within a multi-faceted approach to seeking political change. In their view litigation can mobilize and energize groups as well as publicize their cause; in combination with such activities as legislative and administrative lobbying and public education, litigation can be used to gather support from other political institutions. Recognizing that courts lack the institutional capacity to enforce their decisions, they believe that litigation can play a useful role as part of a broader effort to achieve social reform.[11]

Notwithstanding the benefits secured through litigation, a number of scholars express caution about the use of the courts to attain social reform. They question the extent to which the federal courts have effected meaningful social and economic change.[12]

Appraising the effects of litigation, Marc Galanter concludes that the legal system systematically favors the "haves" and that even with substantive changes in the rules, "litigation . . . is unlikely to shape decisively the distribution of power in society."[13] Surveying litigation efforts on behalf of the poor, Susan Lawrence finds the Court amenable to accepting poverty law cases brought by the Legal Services Program, but unwilling to exert judicial authority to reform America's class and wealth system by endorsing fundamental change in economic and social relationships.[14] The Supreme Court's reluctance to ratify changes in social roles is also noted by Wendy Williams and Sylvia Law.[15] In assessing the role of the Supreme Court in sex discrimination law, they assert that the Court's gender equality decisions refrained from endorsing significant social and cultural role changes for women and men.

Looking specifically at litigation on behalf of children, Robert Mnookin reports mixed results on five test cases brought to vindicate children's constitutional rights of equality, due process, and privacy. In his view, "the remedies [imposed by the courts] appear to be quite modest. The hopes of legal child advocates, who believe courts can achieve broad reform, and the fears of conservatives, who see judicial activism as pernicious, seem equally inflated."[16] He offers a luke-warm endorsement of test-case litigation: its effectiveness is questionable, but perhaps no less questionable than activities in other policy-making forums.

In an attempt to disaggregate the broad category of children's rights and, in part, to determine the degree to which the courts are an appropriate forum for resolution of issues involving children, Michael Wald groups children's claims into four classifications:

(A) generalized claims against the world, e.g., the right of freedom from discrimination and poverty; (B) the right to greater protection from abuse, neglect or exploitation by adults; (C) the right to be treated in the same manner as an adult, with the same constitutional protections, in relation to state actions; (D) the right to act independently of parental control and/or guidance.[17]

Wald differentiates the first group of claims from the others; although important to the child's well-being, in his view, these "generalized claims" are more properly thought of as protections rather than legal rights. For the most part, he believes the judiciary is incapable of granting these needed protections, that is, ordering an end to poverty or deprivation, and argues that such claims should be presented to legislatures rather than courts.

Together these scholars maintain that courts are often unwilling to address fundamental inequities in American society, and even if willing, they cannot. They argue that even during the more activist Warren Court, litigation efforts were thwarted by the Supreme Court's unwillingness to promote role changes and redistributive policies, and that litigation has not significantly altered the maldistribution of economic or social resources in society.

Thus, a mixed picture of the role of the courts in social reform emerges. Using the "disadvantaged" theory, the courts have been depicted as compensating for the deficiencies of the pluralist system by adjudicating on behalf of those with less influence in the political arena. From this perspective, for children who have little clout and few political action committees devoted to furthering their goals, the courts would be a suitable arena in which to articulate their demands.

Yet, because of the nature of their legal claims, litigation in which the rights and interests of children are involved uniquely challenges established economic and social constraints. First, it raises questions about the proper degree of authority over the child by the state. Second, it forces the courts to intervene in disputes over cultural norms involving the role of children in the family. And third, it seeks relief for an inadequate commitment of government resources in child welfare policymaking.

Thus, despite children's status as a "disadvantaged" group, it remains uncertain how sympathetic the federal courts will be to their claims for equality, for improved well-being, for freedom from the constraints of state and/or parental control, and for protection from harm.

The Federal Courts and Children's Issues

Federal court litigation on behalf of children began in earnest in the mid-1960s. First presenting demands for constitutional equality with adults, especially in the criminal justice system, gradually children's advocates began to press the courts to resolve disputes in a myriad of issues affecting children's lives. The federal courts became involved in controversies over the sufficiency of public welfare assistance, the legitimacy of interstate child support enforcement, and the adequacy of the performance of state child welfare agencies.

Much of the federal court litigation affecting children was instigated, or at least aided, by a number of public interest law groups, typically organized as separate units of their parent organizations. The groups, whose involvement ranges from direct sponsorship of cases to submission of amici curiae briefs, are the Children's Defense Fund (CDF), the Children's Rights Project of the American Civil Liberties Union (ACLU), the Center for Mental Health Law, the Center for Law and Social Policy (CLASP), the Center on Social Welfare Policy and Law (CSWPL), the American Bar Association (ABA) Center on Children and the Law, the Children's Rights Project of the Legal Assistance Foundation of Chicago (LAF), the Youth Law Center (YLC), the National Center for Youth Law (NCYL), and the Children's and Institutionalized Persons

Project of the Roger Baldwin Foundation of the ACLU. As part of the research for this book, I interviewed senior staffers (most of them attorneys) of these organizations to ascertain their views on the effects of federal court adjudication in the children's policy arena.[18]

Headquartered in Washington, D.C., San Francisco, Chicago, and New York, these organizations are linked to a substantial number of the federal court decisions affecting children over the last three to four decades. Although the plaintiffs in these cases are not exclusively poor children, much of the litigation is brought on behalf of children living in families at or near the poverty level. The CSWPL, for example, reflecting its origins in the community activism of the 1960s, almost exclusively represents the interests of poor people—both children and adults.

Children's rights claims have involved a mix of constitutional and statutory challenges to government policies relating to the distribution of public welfare benefits, autonomy in speech and reproductive decisionmaking, conditions of confinement and sentencing in the juvenile justice system, treatment of children in mental health facilities and schools, and the ineffectiveness of child welfare systems.

Often seen as the area where they can have the greatest impact, based in large part on several successes in the lower federal courts, most of the groups focus their attention on litigation in pursuit of child welfare reform, encompassing issues of foster care, child abuse and neglect, and adoption.[19] Some, such as the Children's Rights Project of the ACLU, are devoted entirely to child welfare litigation in state and federal courts.[20] Such lawsuits, typically involving class actions against state or county child welfare agencies, are a relatively recent phenomenon, arising out of legal theories formulated in suits brought by prison inmates and adult mental patients. And despite some setbacks, notably two recent Supreme Court rulings, the children's advocates remain convinced that child welfare systems are amenable to change through litigation.

When asked to assess the results of the litigation efforts as a whole, a number of the children's advocates reflected that they had had some successes; they had mandated due process hearings in the denial of government benefits and were often able to persuade courts to grant children greater freedom and self-determination over their lives, especially in school. While they were encouraged by the initial results of the constitutional litigation, they also hoped the federal courts would adopt their legal theory that the Fourteenth Amendment guarantees children adequate nutrition, shelter, education, and freedom from abuse. They expressed disappointment that the Supreme Court was unwilling to accept their arguments about relying on constitutional authority to create a more equitable distribution of societal resources.

While many recognized that litigation by itself is incapable of producing the desired public policy changes (and indeed some stress it should be used only as a last resort in influencing public policy), there was unanimous agreement that federal court litigation had been an important vehicle for social reform in the 1970s, particularly in the areas of juvenile justice, public welfare assistance, and treatment of juveniles in mental hospitals. This feeling of optimism about the court's role in public policymaking was generated by the fact that the federal courts had been receptive to some of the novel constitutional theories proposed by children's rights advocates. However, as John O'Toole, executive director of the NCYL, put it, "those days are over."[21]

Underscoring the growing disaffection with the current posture of the federal courts, Adele Blong, associate director of CSWPL, stated "there's a clear feeling it's not like it was."[22] And James Weill, general counsel of the CDF, similarly noted that over time the positive results of federal court litigation had become "thinner and less frequent."[23]

Thus, there was common accord that the federal bench had become less hospitable to claims brought on behalf of children. Additionally, as some pointed out, whereas their initial efforts to secure judicial support for enforcing legislative mandates had often succeeded in the past, more recently the courts have been more likely to interpret such statutes narrowly and to defer to restrictive executive branch interpretations of the law.

Although the children's advocates were disenchanted with the current occupants of the federal bench, many were reluctant to abandon their efforts entirely and indicated their continued belief that federal court litigation is still a worthwhile enterprise. In their view, the federal courts remain a desirable forum for presentation of federal claims because the federal judiciary (no matter the ideological persuasion of the judge) is accustomed to the complexities of large-scale reform litigation; moreover, some noted, the federal rules of civil procedure (especially the rules of discovery) tend to favor plaintiffs.

Several attorneys underscored the value of litigation as an integral part of social reform change. Diane Redleaf, supervisory attorney of the Children's Rights Project of the Chicago-based Legal Assistance Foundation, described it as a requisite accompaniment to other forms of advocacy.[24] O'Toole emphasized that "litigation is a crucial part of advocacy for poor children." Moreover, in his view, even "a credible threat of litigation works wonders."[25] Margaret Campbell Haynes, director of the Child Support Project of the ABA Center on Children and the Law similarly believed that litigation is advantageous because even the threat of a lawsuit enhances an agency's efforts to obtain a greater share of the state's resources to enable it to fulfil its responsibilities.[26] Referring specifically to the child welfare system litigation, Carole Shauffer, executive director of the YLC, noted that litigation serves as an "attention getter," playing an important role in bringing the parties to the bargaining table to negotiate.[27]

Benjamin Wolf, director of the Children's Rights Project of the Chicago office of the ACLU, echoing the disadvantaged theory, explained that litigation is an essential weapon for poor children, a politically powerless group who lack access to other institutions of power. He stressed that litigation often leads to consent decrees that force states to restructure their child welfare bureaucracies and improve the technology and training that is crucial to the reform needed in all states. The effects of litigation are not immediately apparent, he said, for it may take a significant amount of time to remove the systemic barriers to providing children with good care.[28]

A number of the child advocates pointed out the irony that litigation was frequently welcomed by state agencies (the defendants) because it often compelled legislative bodies to allocate higher amounts of funding than agencies could secure on their own. Shauffer noted that the agencies themselves often felt empowered by the litigation against them, using it as a device for attracting greater resources.[29] Wolf added that the child welfare litigation serves to create a structure of accountability for state child welfare agencies as well as to increase their budgets.[30]

A somewhat contrary view was represented by the staffers of the CDF. In part because of its disenchantment with the effectiveness of federal court litigation in advancing children's interests, the CDF—the group probably most closely identified in the public's mind as the prototypical children's advocacy group—has virtually abandoned litigation since the mid-1980s, limiting itself to an occasional filing of a friend-of-the-court brief. According to MaryLee Allen, head of the Child Welfare Division of the CDF, the organization now devotes most of its resources to public education and legislative and administrative advocacy at the state and federal levels.[31] Its efforts include assistance in drafting state and federal legislation, as well as lobbying Congress and federal administrative agencies. While the CDF is not alone in reducing reliance on litigation to achieve social reform—a number of the groups reported shifting personnel and financial resources to legislative and administrative advocacy—it represents perhaps the most extreme case.

A number of the children's rights advocates have recently become convinced that the state courts may offer a better environment for litigating children's issues than the federal courts, and that some state court judges are more amenable to imposing large-scale judicial remedies than are federal court judges. Thus, they expressed cautious optimism about filing lawsuits in the state courts, especially if the courts appeared willing to espouse expansive principles of state constitutional law. Paula Roberts, senior staff attorney of CLASP, argued that state courts are often more "friendly" and filing a lawsuit there avoids the problem of constitutional immunity from suit enjoyed by the states in the federal courts.[32] Blong similarly believed that state courts are more open to arguments on behalf of social reform litigants than in the past and provide a greater array of remedies than they once did.[33]

As a group, these children's advocates have not renounced litigation; to varying degrees, they remain convinced it has an important role to play in improving the lives of children. Not surprisingly, however, given the current judicial scene, they see their task as a daunting one. Undoubtedly, the children's advocates would have spoken differently had the interviews taken place in the midst of the dynamic, and more successful, litigation battles of the 1960s and early 1970s.

The experiences of these public interest attorneys suggest that federal court decisions have been useful in advancing the cause of social reform on behalf of children. And although they acknowledge the federal courts were more amenable to claims brought on behalf of children in the past, for the most part, they refuse to abandon their litigation efforts, convinced that the federal courts still have an important role to play in improving the lives of children.

Plan of the Book

This book undertakes a systematic investigation of federal court decision-making in cases related to the legal, political, economic, and social status of children. Its purpose is to assess the degree to which the federal courts have shaped the contours of children's public policymaking over the several decades.

For the most part the existing literature on children's legal rights is devoted to analysis of federal court cases involving conflicts among the state, parents, and children over the degree to which constitutional guarantees of equal protection, due process, the right of privacy, and freedom of expression should be extended to children.[34] Because such litigation typically seeks to impose limits on government action rather than evoking affirmative relief from the courts, observing litigation from a constitutional perspective alone presents a myopic view of the activities of the federal courts. To convey the magnitude of the federal court's role in policymaking for children, this study presents federal court decisions arising from disputes over an array of government programs and policies affecting the welfare and rights of children. In part, I also adopt this approach because the court's function in statutory construction is less familiar, though certainly no less important, than its function as constitutional adjudicator, and thus needs to be explicated more fully.

The analysis is based on federal court decisions identified by computer searches in five major areas of federal policymaking for children: public welfare assistance, preschool education, early childhood nutrition, child welfare, and child support. These policy areas represent a range of policymaking activity at all levels of government and by all branches of the federal government. More important, they represent a mix of constitutional and statutory litigation claims involving children and illustrate the reaches of federal court policymaking. To understand the role of the courts in public policymaking for children, each chapter begins by discussing the legal and political context in which the federal courts decided the cases.

The analysis of cases is primarily confined to Supreme Court opinions; although lower courts resolve disputes about details of the Supreme Court opinions and apply the high court rulings, the Supreme Court sets the parameters of national public policy. In selecting cases for analysis, all Supreme Court decisions directly or indirectly involving adjudication of children's rights or interests in these five policy areas are included; when there are no Supreme Court opinions, lower court cases are examined. Most of the cases in the analysis were initially brought by, or on behalf of, a child; some originated as a challenge to a law benefiting a child. Some cases feature the child in opposition to the state, some the child in opposition to the parent and the state, and some the state in opposition to the parent.

Notes

1. See Joseph M. Hawes, *The Children's Rights Movement: A History of Advocacy and Protection* (Boston: Twayne Publishers, 1991), chapter 4, for discussion of the movement to end child labor. The 1916 Keating-Owens bill was challenged by manufacturers and declared unconstitutional by the Supreme Court two years later. A second law to tax products produced with child labor was also struck by the Supreme Court shortly after its passage. Several later attempts to regulate child labor by constitutional amendment also failed. Ultimately, the Fair Labor Standards Act, prohibiting children under sixteen from working in interstate commerce activities, was enacted in 1938 and validated by the Supreme Court in 1941.

2. Joel F. Handler, *Social Movements and the Legal System* (New York: Academic Press, 1978), p. 1.

3. Michael W. McCann, *Taking Reform Seriously: Perspectives on Public Interest Liberalism* (Ithaca, N.Y.: Cornell University Press, 1986), p. 108.

4. Mark Tushnet, *The NAACP's Legal Strategy against Segregated Education, 1925-1950* (Chapel Hill: University of North Carolina Press, 1987), p. xii.

5. There is a long line of scholarship on the role of organized interest groups in litigation activity. See, for example, Donald R. Songer and Reginald S. Sheehan, "Interest Group Success in the Courts: Amicus Participation in the Supreme Court," *Political Research Quarterly* 46 (1993): 339–354; Lee Epstein and C. K. Rowland, "Debunking the Myth of Interest Group Invincibility in the Courts," *American Political Science Review* 85 (1991): 205–217; Gregory A. Caldeira and John R. Wright, "Amici Curiae Before the Supreme Court: Who Participates, When, and How Much?" *Journal*

of Politics 52 (1990): 782–806; Joseph Kobylka, "A Court-Created Context for Group Litigation: Libertarian Groups and Obscenity," *Journal of Politics* 49 (1987): 1061–1078.

6. The "disadvantaged" theory was first presented in Richard Cortner, "Strategies and Tactics of Litigants in Constitutional Cases," *Journal of Public Law* 17 (1968): 287–307.

7. The LDF, first known as the Inc. Fund, was established under its own charter as a spin-off from the NAACP in 1940. For a variety of reasons, including the possibility of revocation of the LDF's tax exempt status, the boards of the two organizations were officially separated in 1957. There was friction between the two organizations thereafter. See Jack Greenberg, *Crusaders in the Courts* (New York: Basic Books, 1994).

8. Studies of litigation for racial equality include Clement Vose, *Caucasians Only* (Berkeley: University of California Press, 1959); Richard Kluger, *Simple Justice* (New York: Alfred A. Knopf, 1976); Cortner, "Strategies and Tactics of Litigants in Constitutional Cases"; Tushnet, *The NAACP's Legal Strategy Against Segregated Education*. For studies of litigation on behalf of women and the disabled, see Karen O'Connor, *Women's Organizations' Use of the Courts* (Lexington, Mass.: Lexington Books, 1980); Ruth Cowan, "Women's Rights Through Litigation: An Examination of the American Civil Liberties Union Women's Rights Project, 1971–1976," *Columbia Human Rights Law Review* 8 (1976): 373–412; Robert Katzman, *Institutional Disability: The Saga of Transportation Policy for the Disabled* (Washington, D.C.: Brookings Institute, 1986); Susan Gluck Mezey, *No Longer Disabled: The Federal Courts and the Politics of Social Security Disability* (Westport, Conn.: Greenwood Press, 1988).

9. See Lee Epstein, *Conservatives in Court* (Knoxville, Tenn.: University of Tennessee Press, 1985); Karen O'Connor and Lee Epstein, "The Rise of Conservative Interest Group Litigation," *Journal of Politics* 45 (1983): 479–489; and Susan Olson, "Interest-Group Litigation in Federal District Court: Beyond the Political Disadvantage Theory," *Journal of Politics* 52 (1990): 854–882, who show that litigation is also used by the "haves."

10. Aryeh Neier, *Only Judgment: The Limits of Litigation in Social Change* (Middletown, Conn.: Wesleyan University Press, 1982), p. 236.

11. Gerald Rosenberg, *The Hollow Hope: Can Courts Bring About Social Change?* (Chicago: University of Chicago Press, 1991), presents one of the most extended arguments against the view that courts are capable of producing significant social change. He maintains that Supreme Court decisions have often led to results opposite to those intended by the litigants and that the Court is able to effect public policy changes only when other branches of government come to its aid.

This analysis is based on an unrealistic image of the Court's authority. Not even the most committed judicial activist would argue that the Supreme Court can, on its own, bring about significant social change. A more reasonable assessment of judicial power is that it has limitations, not that the Court's decisions have had little or no impact on public policy.

12. For discussion of litigation activities in social reform movements, see Stuart Scheingold, "The Politics of Rights Revisited," in Richard Gambitta, Marlynn May, and James Foster, eds., *Governing Through Courts* (Beverly Hills: Sage, 1981); Handler, *Social Movements and the Legal System*; Michael W. McCann, *Rights at Work: Pay Equity Reform and the Politics of Legal Mobilization* (Chicago: University of Chicago Press, 1994); Robert Mnookin, ed., *In the Interest of Children* (New York: W. H. Freeman, 1985).

13. Marc Galanter, "Why the 'Haves' Come Out Ahead: Speculations on the Limits of Legal Change," *Law and Society* (1974): 150.

14. Susan E. Lawrence, *The Poor in Court* (Princeton: Princeton University Press, 1990).

15. Wendy Williams, "The Equality Crisis: Some Reflections on Culture, Courts, and Feminism," *Women's Rights Law Reporter* 7 (1982): 175–200; Sylvia A. Law, "Rethinking Sex and the Constitution," *University of Pennsylvania Law Review* 132 (1984): 955–1040.

16. Mnookin, *In the Interest of Children*, p. 521.

17. Michael Wald, "Children's Rights: A Framework for Analysis," *University of California Davis Law Review* 12 (1979): 260.

18. Three non-attorneys were also interviewed: a senior associate of the Center for the Study of Social Policy who was involved in child welfare policy through her appointment by the court as a monitor following a class action suit against the Washington, D.C. child welfare agency; the director of the Child Welfare Division of the CDF; and the deputy assistant secretary for human services policy in the Office of the Assistant Secretary for Planning and Evaluation of the Department of Health and Human Services.

19. The ABA Center on Children and the Law does not take part in litigation involving children. It may, on very rare occasions, file an amicus curiae brief in a case before the United States Supreme Court. Howard Davidson, personal interview.

20. Marcia Lowry, personal interview.

21. John O'Toole, personal interview.

22. Adele Blong, personal interview.

23. James Weill, personal interview.

24. Diane Redleaf, personal interview.

25. John O'Toole, personal interview.

26. Margaret Campbell Haynes, personal interview.

27. Carole Shauffer, personal interview.

28. Benjamin Wolf, personal interview.

29. Carole Shauffer, personal interview.

30. Benjamin Wolf, personal interview.

31. MaryLee Allen, personal interview.

32. Paula Roberts, personal interview.

33. Adele Blong, personal interview.

34. See, for example, Samuel M. Davis and Mortimer D. Schwartz, *Children's Rights and the Law* (Lexington, Mass.: Lexington Books, 1987); Mnookin, *In the Interest of Children*; Willard Gaylin and Ruth Macklin, eds., *Who Speaks for the Child: The Problems of Proxy Consent* (New York: Plenum Press, 1982); Paul R. Kfoury, *Children Before the Court: Reflections on Legal Issues Affecting Minors*, 2d ed. (Salem, N.H.: Butterworth Legal Publishers, 1991); Wald, "Children's Rights"; Sharon E. Rush, "The Warren and Burger Courts on State, Parent, and Child Conflict Resolution: A Comparative Analysis and Proposed Methodology," *Hastings Law Journal* 36 (1985): 461–513.

1

CONSTITUTIONAL RIGHTS LITIGATION

In 1977 Peter Edelman, then head of the New York State Division for Youth, described the goal of the children's rights movement as seeking "to extend some adult rights and improve government programs so that children will be assured protection and dignity and the chance to develop their maximum potential."[1]

The history of children's rights in the United States can be traced back to the colonial era as limits were established on the degree to which children could be subjected to physical punishment, and institutions were created to care for children abandoned by their parents because of death or desertion.[2] Aside from this scant protection offered by the state, the notion that children had separate rights and interests was hardly apparent during the eighteenth and nineteenth centuries. Throughout, with rare exception, the state's position was that the family had preeminent authority over the child and that interference was permitted only under extreme circumstances. In sum, children had few, if any, enforceable rights at this time.

The evolution of the common law doctrine of *parens patriae* ("the state is the ultimate parent of every child") during the 1800s provided the legal rationale for the state to intervene on the child's behalf. By the end of this century the belief that children were entitled to protection from harm was receiving increasing rhetorical support. But despite the government's attempts to improve the quality of children's lives through the development of social services, especially to counteract the effects of the Great Depression, there was no real voice for children's rights until the 1960s, when the children's rights movement emerged.

Children's Rights Litigation

Following the example of civil rights and feminist movement leaders, children's rights advocates turned to the federal courts with demands for increased constitutional guarantees of freedom of expression, due process, and privacy.

The difficulty of shaping the contours of children's constitutional rights stems from their anomalous status as neither wholly free of, nor wholly subordinate to, their elders.[3] Complicating the clarity of children's demands for greater autonomy have been cases involving children's demands for greater protection from hardships inflicted on them. In these cases, rather than seeking to enhance their autonomy, children seek the government's assistance in improving their lives. The legal issues in such cases are characterized by challenges to classifications on the basis of birth or economic status as well as demands for an expansion of substantive due process rights.

Litigation on behalf of children typically involves claims against an array of institutions, often becoming enmeshed in the tangled relationship between parent and child.[4] Most of the disputes involving children feature the state, alone or in concert with the parent, contesting the child's claims while professing to be acting in his or her best interests.[5] Thus, despite the appearance of broad public support for children's rights, there is little consensus over the extent to which they should prevail over the competing interests of the state or the family.

Children's constitutional litigation, which seeks to advance the rights of children under eighteen, primarily revolves around three sets of issues: challenges to state and/or parental dominion over the child; challenges to legal classifications based on birth and social class; and demands for procedural fairness and protection from harm.

The totality of children's legal claims represents a unique set of challenges for courts, forcing them to delve into, and devise solutions for, some of society's most intractable conflicts. In weighing children's constitutional claims, courts must decide when children should be treated as adults and when their physical and economic dependence and vulnerability require special societal protection. Children's rights advocates emphasize the need to formulate a theory to guide courts in adjudicating children's constitutional rights.[6] They argue that the phrase "children's rights" subsumes a multitude of issues and demands and that courts need to achieve a proper balance among the interests involved.[7] Expecting the courts to arrive at an appropriate balance is made more difficult by the fact that children's advocates are themselves often divided about the degree of control children should have over their own lives.[8]

Most would agree, however, that the courts should attempt to adhere to the following principle of decisionmaking: to maximize the child's independence and well-being, while offering the greatest opportunity for development and protection from physical harm. Although children's best interests may not always be apparent and these precepts will not resolve every controversy involving children's legal claims, they can provide a basis for judging whether the courts have furthered the interests of the minors or not.[9]

To assess the results of constitutional litigation on behalf of children, this chapter examines the last forty years of Supreme Court decisionmaking in children's rights litigation. The analysis includes all Supreme Court opinions *adjudicated* on the basis of a child's constitutional claim.[10] Decisions grounded on more than one principle are classified on the basis of the first, or primary one, used in the opinion. The cases were divided into the terms of the chief justice: the Warren Court beginning in October 1953, the Burger Court in October 1969, and the Rehnquist Court in October 1986. The appendices lists the cases decided as well as the year of the decision and the issue and constitutional principle in each case.

There were fifty-three children's rights cases decided by the Court from October 1953 through July 1993. Table 1 shows the total number of cases in each chief justice's term as well as the average number of decisions during the tenure of each chief justice.

TABLE 1

Children's Rights Cases by Chief Justice

Chief Justice	Total # of Cases	Average # of Cases Per Term
Warren (1953–1969)	6	.37
Burger (1969–1986)	36	2.11
Rehnquist (1986–1993)	11	1.57
1953–1993	53	1.32

As shown in table 1, children's rights litigation did not occupy a great deal of the Court's docket over the last forty years; the Court averaged only about one opinion a term. And despite the expansion of civil liberties during the Warren Court era, only six cases were decided in the time Earl Warren served as chief justice, an average of less than one case every two terms. There was a marked increase in decisions on children's rights claims during the Burger Court, with the Court issuing thirty-six opinions for an average of slightly more than two cases per term. There were eleven children's rights cases decided from October 1986—the beginning of the Rehnquist Court—to July 1993, for an average of about one and a half cases per term.

Constitutional Principles in Children's Rights Cases

The first step in determining the success of children's constitutional litigation during these four decades was to classify the opinions by the constitutional principles used to decide the case: due process, equal protection, freedom of expression, privacy, and free exercise of religion. Table 2 shows the number of decisions handed down within each chief justice's term.

As table 2 shows, the equal protection and due process clauses of the Fourteenth Amendment were the two most frequently invoked constitutional guarantees in the children's rights cases, with seventeen and twenty decisions

TABLE 2

Constitutional Issues in Children's Rights Cases 1953–1993

Constitutional Issue

Chief Justice	Eql. Prot.	Due Proc.*	Privacy	Free Exp.	Free Exer.	Total
Warren	1	3	**	2	**	6
Burger	14	13	6	2	1	36
Rehnquist	2	4	3	2	**	11
Total	17	20	9	6	1	53

* Includes 4th, 5th, 8th, and 14th Amendments.
** Indicates no decisions in this category.

respectively; together these two areas comprise more than two-thirds of the total number of cases. The Court decided nine cases on the basis of children's privacy rights, and six opinions were based on children's freedom of expression. Only one decision, broadly defined as a children's rights claim, was decided on free exercise grounds.[11]

The extent to which the children's claims prevailed in each of these categories is shown in table 3.

TABLE 3

Percentage of Pro-Child Decisions 1953–1993*

Chief Justice	Eql. Prot.	Due Proc.	Privacy	Free Exp.	Free Exer.	Total
Warren	100 (1)	100 (3)	**	50 (2)	**	83 (6)
Burger	64 (14)	30 (13)	66 (6)	50 (2)	100*** (1)	52 (36)
Rehnquist	50 (2)	25 (4)	0 (3)	0 (2)	**	18 (11)
Total	64 (17)	40 (20)	44 (9)	33 (6)	100 (1)	49 (53)

* Considered pro-child if child's claim was upheld by the Court.
** Indicates no decisions in this category.
*** Considered pro-child based on the Court's assumption of an identity of interests between the parents and children.

Table 3 demonstrates that the Court supported the children's demands for expanded constitutional rights in slightly less than half the cases decided since 1953. The Warren Court decided the least number of cases involving children, and ruled in their favor 83 percent of the time. The Burger Court, which decided the largest number of children's constitutional cases, had a more mixed record, supporting the children's claims in 52 percent of its decisions. The Rehnquist Court was least receptive to children's constitutional demands, upholding their claims in only 18 percent of its decisions.

Table 3 also shows that with the exception of the single free exercise decision, the Court decided 64 percent of the equal protection cases in the children's favor; this was the only category, aside from free exercise, in which the litigants succeeded in over half the cases decided. The next most successful category of cases for litigants was in the area of privacy rights, with a 44 percent success rate, followed by due process claims which succeeded 40 percent of the time. Children's rights advocates fared worst in their demands for greater freedom of expression, with the Court ruling in their favor only 33 percent of the time.

The Child's Right of Privacy

Because the Supreme Court had not formally adopted a constitutional right to privacy until 1965, no children's privacy cases were decided by the Warren Court. The minor's constitutional right to privacy was established in a series of Burger Court decisions that allowed minors access to contraception and abortion, albeit the latter with some restrictions.

In 1977 the Burger Court struck a law prohibiting the distribution of contraceptives to persons under sixteen. With respect to abortion decisions, the Court was more reluctant to loosen the reins over the child's right to sexual privacy but at the same time refused to allow the state absolute control over the minor's reproductive decisionmaking. The Court upheld state laws mandating parental involvement in a minor's abortion decision but conditioned a parental consent requirement on the existence of a judicial by-pass procedure in which the minor must be permitted to demonstrate sufficient maturity to make the decision herself or to show that an abortion would be in her best interests.

The Court struck three of the four parental consent laws for failing to provide an adequate by-pass procedure. In 1981 in *H.L. v. Matheson*, its only ruling on a parental notification requirement, the Burger Court upheld a Utah law requiring physicians to notify parents of their daughter's decision to have an abortion.[12] In deciding this case, the Court made it clear that the law was constitutional as it applied to the child who brought the challenge, a fifteen year old living at home and dependent on her parents.

The three privacy cases decided by the Rehnquist Court all involved challenges to parental consent and notification laws, including, in one case, a Minnesota two-parent notice requirement. Because these statutes satisfied the judicial by-pass requirement established in the earlier cases, they were upheld.

The numbers do not tell the entire story, however. Despite the Court's continued commitment to the judicial by-pass provision in abortion consent and notice laws, the minor's protection against the state's invasion of privacy became more tenuous during the Rehnquist Court era. In their separate opinion on the Minnesota law in *Hodgson v. Minnesota*, decided in 1990, four justices agreed that the state could require notice to both parents even absent a by-pass procedure.[13]

The Child's Right to Freedom of Expression

The Court's limited support for children's freedom of expression claims stems from the reluctance of the Warren and Burger Courts to allow minors unrestricted access to sexually explicit language or reading material. Each Court decided two freedom of expression cases, affirming the minor's right in the one case involving political rights and freedom.

In *Tinker v. Des Moines School District*, a 1969 decision, the Warren Court upheld the minor's First Amendment right, establishing the principle that students do not "shed their rights to freedom of speech or expression at the schoolhouse door."[14] Based on this tenet, the Court barred school officials from suspending students for wearing black armbands to protest the Vietnam War unless the school authorities could prove that the students had substantially interfered with the educational process.

One of the Burger Court cases involved a challenge to a decision by the Island Trees Board of Education to remove books from the school library because they were " 'anti-American, anti-Christian, anti-[Semitic], and just plain filthy.' "[15] Committed to supporting the child's right to freedom of access to educational reading material, the Court held that, although school authorities had discretion over curricula, Board members could not remove books from the school library merely because they disliked their content.

Though committed to the belief that children merited a degree of First Amendment protection, neither Court was prepared to extend the protection to speech related to sexuality. They justified rejecting students' First Amendment claims by pointing to the state's *parens patriae* role of protecting children from exposure to speech or writings with pornographic content.

On these grounds, the Warren Court upheld a law prohibiting the sale of magazines containing "harmful" material to minors under seventeen despite the fact that the pictures in question would not have been considered obscene for adults.

The Burger Court upheld the suspension of a student who made a "lewd" speech in the school auditorium. The Court based its decision on the sexual nature of the speech, distinguishing between it and the political message inherent in the *Tinker* students' armbands. And although there was not much evidence to support it, the Court also distinguished these facts from the facts in *Tinker* by pointing to the disruption of school activities resulting from the speech.

The Rehnquist Court moved further away from the precedent set by the Warren and Burger Courts for speech involving political and social issues in *Hazelwood School District v. Kuhlmeier*.[16] In this 1988 opinion, the Court justified the censorship of a high school newspaper, despite the fact that there was no showing of indecency or obscenity in the material in question, because the principal determined that the stories were inappropriate for a high school audience.

In a later First Amendment decision, the Rehnquist Court also upheld a Dallas ordinance requiring separate dance facilities for children, ostensibly to protect them from the potentially harmful effects of older teenagers and adults. The Court ruled that the ordinance did not infringe on the children's freedom of association.

The Child's Right to Equal Protection and Due Process

Children's high rate of success in the Court's equal protection decisions was somewhat surprising. Because of the deferential review normally applied to social and economic legislation, one would not have expected the Court to look favorably on challenges to laws classifying on the basis of wealth or social status. Similarly, the substantially lower rate of success in the due process decisions was also unanticipated. Due process claims, for the most part, do not demand sweeping changes in state policy, rather they are typically limited to challenging the way in which the policy is implemented, often simply calling for an end to arbitrary treatment by law enforcement authorities.

To explain the results in these two categories, the cases in each group were examined in greater detail and the outcomes shown in table 4.

TABLE 4

Percentage of Pro-Child Equal Protection and Due Process Decisions 1953–1993*

| Chief Justice | Equal Protection | | Due Process | |
	Illegitimacy	Status	Criminal	Procedure
Warren	100 (1)	**	100 (3)	**
Burger	72 (11)	33 (3)	42 (7)	16 (6)
Rehnquist	100 (1)	0 (1)	50 (2)	0 (2)
Total	76 (13)	25 (4)	58 (12)	12 (8)

* Considered pro-child if child's claim was upheld by the Court.
** Indicates no cases in this category.

The equal protection cases consist of two types of claims: challenges to laws based on a child's birth status (thirteen cases) and challenges to laws based on income or wealth (four cases).[17] The table shows that the Warren Court's only equal protection decision involved a challenge to an illegitimacy classification, with the Court ruling in favor of the child.[18] Of the fourteen equal protection decisions made by the Burger Court, eleven revolved around legal distinctions among children on the basis of their birth status, and in most, litigants persuaded the Court that the laws were discriminatory. Of the two equal protection cases decided by the Rehnquist Court in its seven terms, children's rights advocates succeeded only when challenging an illegitimacy classification. Obviously, therefore, the overall success of the equal protection litigation over the four decades is attributable to the Court's antipathy to laws classifying on the basis of birth.

Illegitimacy laws began to be viewed with disfavor in 1968 when the Warren Court struck a Louisiana law barring children born out of wedlock from suing for the wrongful death of their mother. More importantly, in this case, *Levy v. Louisiana*, the Court suggested that the judiciary display greater sensitivity to laws affecting "the intimate, familial relationship between a child and his own mother," and that states refrain from punishing children on the basis of their out-of-wedlock births.[19]

Although never according them the status of a suspect category that would require application of the highest form of scrutiny, the Burger Court also looked more critically at birth classifications, striking them 72 percent of the time. In *Trimble v. Gordon*, a landmark 1977 decision, the Court applied intermediate equal protection scrutiny to an Illinois statute preventing nonmarital children from inheriting intestate from their putative fathers.[20] In striking the Illinois law, the Court refused to hold that birth classifications are inherently suspect like race but put states on notice that they must present a more persuasive justification for such laws in the future.

The Rehnquist Court's only ruling on the rights of nonmarital children was one in which the Court struck a Pennsylvania law establishing a six-year statute of limitations for bringing a paternity action against the child's putative father. Following precedent set by the Burger Court, a unanimous Court held that six years did not constitute sufficient time in which to bring a paternity claim.

Thus, on the whole, all three Courts believed the Constitution disfavored differential treatment of children born out of wedlock. With the heightened review conferred on laws creating birth classifications, states were placed at a disadvantage, and not surprisingly, 76 percent of the rulings were decided in favor of the child. Moreover, since absent parents often took advantage of restrictive illegitimacy laws to evade their financial obligations to their children, striking an illegitimacy law troubled neither liberal nor conservative justices.

The remaining equal protection cases contested the state's distribution of educational resources on the basis of family income or economic status. Specifically, plaintiffs challenged laws that imposed fees for busing students, mandated residency requirements for neighborhood schools, created a school financing structure that relied on local property taxes, and charged tuition to the children of undocumented workers attending public schools.

Although it seemed that the Warren Court had taken steps toward adopting a more rigorous standard of review for wealth and income classifications, both the Burger and Rehnquist Courts made it clear that they were not similarly inclined; that the Supreme Court decided only four such cases over the forty-year period suggests a lack of enthusiasm for involving itself in educational policymaking, especially when redistribution of resources was at issue.

For the most part, these cases were characterized by litigants' attempts to convince the Court to subject wealth or income classifications to the same heightened scrutiny as birth classifications and to require greater justification from the state for the inequitable distribution of educational benefits. In *San Antonio School District v. Rodriguez*, a watershed case decided in 1973, the Court rejected plaintiffs' argument that the Texas method of financing schools through local property taxes violated the Constitution by creating inequality in educational facilities.[21] In upholding the state's authority over educational policymaking, the Court applied the deferential approach normally used in economic and social legislation, not the heightened scrutiny demanded by children's rights advocates.

The only victory in an equal protection case involving educational benefits was in the narrowly written opinion in *Plyler v. Doe*, decided in 1982.[22] Here, a five to four majority struck a Texas law requiring the children of undocumented immigrants to pay public school tuition. The decision was based in large part on the Court's aversion to making "innocent" children suffer for the illegal activities of their parents. However, although the law was struck, the Court based its ruling squarely on the facts of the case rather than on the larger principle of redistribution of economic resources or allocation of educational benefits.

Table 4 shows that the due process issues also comprise two kinds of constitutional claims: demands for expansion of the juvenile defendant's rights (twelve cases) and demands for greater fairness in state regulatory procedures regarding the child (eight cases). These cases were more evenly divided over the years than the equal protection cases.

As the table indicates, the Warren Court decided three due process cases, all revolving around a challenge to criminal justice procedures involving juveniles. The Burger Court decided seven criminal procedure cases and six non-criminal procedure cases; the Rehnquist Court decided two cases in each category.

The Warren Court upheld the child's claim in all three cases and, in at least two of them, based on its decisions involving the rights of accused adults, established far-reaching constitutional protections to juveniles charged with criminal offenses.

The constitutional rights of the accused were expanded in 1961 when the Warren Court began to place restrictions on the state's conduct in the investigation and prosecution of criminal cases. Specifically, the Court gave new life to constitutional protections for the accused by extending the guarantees of the Fourth, Fifth, and Sixth Amendments to state criminal justice systems; these limitations resulted in barring most illegally seized evidence from trial.[23]

As with the adult accused, the Warren Court also instituted a far-reaching new approach to minors' rights in court, beginning with the 1966 decision of *Kent v. United States*.[24] Although not its first decision involving a juvenile offender, *Kent* marked the Court's new approach to juvenile justice procedures.[25] Proclaiming that juveniles were entitled to due process and fairness, the Court required a more formal basis for a juvenile court judge's decision to waive jurisdiction over the juvenile and transfer the case to adult criminal court. While the Court did not agree that all protections afforded adults must be made available to juveniles, it recognized that the juvenile justice system fell short of its sponsors' expectations: juveniles were often punished more severely than adults, with few of the protections afforded adults.

In the 1967 ruling of *In re Gault*, the Warren Court found the existing juvenile justice system inadequate to protect the juvenile's constitutional rights and created a panoply of new rights for juveniles facing criminal charges: the right to adequate notice of the charges, the right of confrontation, the right to the assistance of counsel, and the right to remain silent.[26]

The Burger and Rehnquist Courts were more constrained in their support for juvenile rights. In three instances, the Burger Court followed the lead of the Warren Court in conforming juvenile court procedures to adult court by requiring a juvenile's guilt to be proved beyond a reasonable doubt, providing protection against double jeopardy, and restricting the use of the death penalty for juveniles. In its four remaining juvenile justice cases, the Burger Court took the opposite tack and allowed states to detain juveniles without bail before trial, denied that states must provide the juvenile with a jury trial, held that a request for a probation officer does not constitute an invocation of the Fifth Amendment right to remain silent, and refused to strike a state statute allowing the state to file exceptions to a not guilty finding made by a master of the juvenile court.

The Rehnquist Court's two juvenile justice opinions solely involved determination of the constitutionality of the death penalty for juveniles. In a

1982 decision, the Burger Court had held that a defendant's youth must be considered a mitigating factor in death penalty sentencing. Continuing the trend of treating the juvenile as a special defendant, in *Thompson v. Oklahoma*, decided in 1988, the Rehnquist Court narrowly held that juveniles who commit crimes when they are younger than sixteen cannot be executed unless the relevant state statute specifically provides for this punishment.[27] But a year later, in *Stanford v. Kentucky*, the Court made it clear that it would not block death sentences for juveniles by announcing that states may constitutionally put offenders as young as sixteen to death.[28]

Table 4 also illustrates that both Burger and Rehnquist Courts were even more reluctant to curtail the state's authority over the child in the non-criminal setting. Of the eight due process cases in this category, only one Burger Court opinion favored the child. Thus, the low rate of success in due process cases overall stems from the approach of the Burger and Rehnquist Courts to the rights of non-offenders; both Courts demonstrated a greater willingness to defer to state officials in disputes over educational policy and civil commitment.

Specifically, the Burger Court applied a narrow definition of due process in matters of school searches and discipline, including corporal punishment, and committing juveniles to state institutions for the mentally ill or developmentally disabled. In each case in which the child's freedom of action or liberty was restrained in some way, the Court assumed the state or parent acted in the child's best interests and that the procedure for confinement or punishment was constitutionally adequate. The only exception to this was *Goss v. Lopez* when, in this 1975 decision, the Court held that school authorities were constitutionally required to provide students with notice of the charges against them and an opportunity to be heard in an informal hearing before suspending them from school for more than a brief length of time.[29]

The Rehnquist Court gave states even more latitude in determining their responsibility to, and for, the child. In 1989, in *DeShaney v. Winnebago County Department of Social Services*, the Rehnquist Court held that the state had no obligation to protect a four-year-old victim from the child abuse that had led to profound retardation caused by severe brain damage.[30] In ruling that the due process clause placed no affirmative obligation on the state to protect a child not formally within its custody, the Court declined to hold the state liable for his injuries. Though the state had been aware of the father's abuse and had even taken some half-hearted measures to protect the child, the Court believed that the state child protection laws were not constitutionally enforceable in federal court. In the Court's view, despite the state's knowledge and failure to perform, only the father was responsible for the child's injuries.

The Rehnquist Court's restrictive interpretation of due process was again evident in the 1993 decision of *Reno v. Flores*.[31] In a seven to two opinion, the Court rejected a challenge to the Immigration and Naturalization Service (INS) policy of detaining undocumented juvenile immigrants awaiting a deportation hearing. Narrowly defining the scope of the due process clause, the Court ruled that the INS policy was rationally related to the government's interest in the welfare of the child, and that it need not hold individualized hearings to justify each child's detention.

Conclusion

In the late 1960s the Supreme Court adopted the position that "neither the Fourteenth Amendment nor the Bill of Rights is for adults alone."[32] Yet, in many of its following decisions, the Court manifested an ambivalence over the extent to which children are entitled to adult guarantees of due process, free expression, and privacy. And although the Court relied on principles of equality when striking most state laws limiting the rights of nonmarital children, it refused to expand the constitutional parameters of the equal protection clause to state education policies based on wealth or income criteria.

The decisions show that over time the Court has tended to assign a lower priority to the child's interests than to the competing interests of the state and the family. But most of the Court's rulings can be explained by traditional principles of constitutional law rather than by the Court's adherence to principles of child protectionism over child autonomy. Supreme Court decisionmaking in children's rights cases has followed the pattern of decisionmaking for adults; that is, there has been decreasing support for individual rights claims in the evolution from the Warren Court to the Rehnquist Court, with the declining rate of success in children's rights claims largely attributable to the Court's reluctance to interfere with state autonomy in matters of social and economic policy.[33]

Such decisionmaking has yielded incoherent results at times: with the Court "protecting" children from the dangers of inappropriate speech, yet failing to protect them from abusive parents; allowing states to limit the reproductive decisionmaking of minors on the grounds of immaturity, yet at the same time, permitting states to subject minors to the death penalty. While few would want the Court to adopt either a wholly protectionist or wholly autonomous view of children, it is reasonable to require the Court to explain how a decision like *DeShaney* can be reconciled with the principle of the best interests of the child. The cases show that the best explanation for the Court's decisionmaking is that increasingly, under the leadership of Warren Burger and William Rehnquist, the Court has been reluctant to interfere with the state's authority over policymaking for children.

Notes

1. Peter B. Edelman, "The Children's Rights Movement," in Beatrice Gross and Ronald Gross, eds., *The Children's Rights Movement: Overcoming the Oppression of Young People* (Garden City, N.Y.: Anchor Books, 1977), pp. 203–204.

2. See Joseph M. Hawes, *The Children's Rights Movement: A History of Advocacy and Protection* (Boston: Twayne Publishers, 1991), which chronicles the development of children's rights in the United States.

3. Michael Wald, "Children's Rights: A Framework for Analysis," *University of California Davis Law Review* 12 (1979): 255–282.

4. Robert Lehrer, personal interview.

5. In their book on children's legal status, Davis and Schwartz address the difficulties of generalizing about children's rights and the relationship between children and the state. Samuel M. Davis and Mortimer D. Schwartz, *Children's Rights and the Law* (Lexington, Mass.: Lexington Books, 1987).

6. See, for example, Stuart J. Baskin, "State Intrusion into Family Affairs: Justifications and Limitations," *Stanford Law Review* 26 (1974): 1383–1409; Sharon E. Rush, "The Warren and Burger Courts on State, Parent, and Child Conflict Resolution: A Comparative Analysis and Proposed Methodology," *Hastings Law Journal* 36 (1985): 461–513; Robin Paul Malloy, "Market Philosophy in the Legal Tension between Children's Autonomy and Parental Authority," *Indiana Law Review* 21 (1988): 889–900.

7. For differing views on the meaning of children's rights, see, for example, Hillary Rodham, "Children under the Law," *Harvard Educational Review* 43 (1973): 487–514; Wald, "Children's Rights"; Jonathan O. Hafen, "Children's Rights and Legal Representation—the Proper Role of Children, Parents, and Attorneys," *Notre Dame Journal of Law, Ethics and Public Policy* 7 (1993): 423–463.

8. See Hawes, *The Children's Rights Movement*, chapter 8, for a discussion of the views of "child protectors" and "child liberationists."

9. Establishing such a benchmark, moreover, provides additional evidence that the children's advocates represent their best interests.

10. To ensure discovery of all Supreme Court opinions relating to children between 1953 and 1993, a Lexis search of the GENFED library, US file, was conducted, using "child! or student" and "equal protection," "due process," "privacy," and "First Amendment" respectively as the search terms. The search yielded over a thousand cases, with substantial duplication among the searches. Two categories of cases, challenges to racial discrimination in public schools and challenges to prayer in public schools, were excluded because first, these issues involve adjudication of conflicts *among* children; and second, the Court does not frame its decisions in these areas within the context of the children's rights involved, but on the basis of constitutional doctrines that have an independent legal and political meaning that transcend children's rights. Of the remaining cases, there were fifty-three opinions in which the Court resolved disputes over children's constitutional rights.

11. At first glance, *Wisconsin v. Yoder*, 406 U.S. 205 (1972), should be considered a children's rights case because it challenged a Wisconsin law that restricted the religious freedom of a group of Amish children. There is some doubt, however, whether it is

actually a children's rights case because the Court decided it on the basis of the parents' free exercise rights and failed to explore any potential conflict of interest between the children and the parents. Only Justice Douglas's separate opinion noted that the parents' decisions to remove their children from school at the age of fourteen might not be in the children's best interests.

12. 450 U.S. 398 (1981).

13. 497 U.S. 417 (1990).

14. 393 U.S. 503, 506 (1969).

15. *Board of Education, Island Trees Union Free School District v. Pico*, 457 U.S. 853, 857 (1982).

16. 484 U.S. 260 (1988).

17. The illegitimacy cases do not include challenges to laws brought by the fathers of children born out of wedlock.

18. To avoid the use of the pejorative term "illegitimate child," I use the phrase "nonmarital child" to describe a child whose parents are not married. The Uniform Parentage Act, adopted by almost half the states, attempted to remove the stigma associated with illegitimacy by recognizing that a parent-child relationship does not depend on marital status. However, because "illegitimacy" remains a legal classification in most states, it is necessary to continue to use this term when referring to state laws and judicial decisions.

19. 391 U.S. 68, 71 (1968).

20. 430 U.S. 762 (1977).

21. 411 U.S. 1 (1973).

22. 457 U.S. 202 (1982).

23. Subsequently, some of these guarantees were narrowed by the Burger and Rehnquist Courts, but not eliminated outright; with a few notable exceptions, the Warren Court innovations in criminal procedure cases were largely maintained. See Vincent Blasi, ed., *The Burger Court* (New Haven: Yale University Press, 1983).

24. 383 U.S. 541 (1966).

25. In *Gallegos v. Colorado*, 370 U.S. 49 (1962), the Court overturned the conviction of a fourteen-year-old boy whose confession was extracted from him after five days of interrogation during which he was not allowed to see his mother. The case was decided on the "totality of circumstances" test rather than on a per se rule about juvenile confessions.

26. 387 U.S. 1 (1967).

27. 487 U.S. 815 (1988).

28. 492 U.S. 361 (1989).

29. 419 U.S. 565 (1975).

30. 489 U.S. 19 (1989).

31. 113 S.Ct. 1439 (1993).

32. *Gault*, 387 U.S. at 13.

33. The Court has recently been more supportive of individual rights claims involving private property.

2

AID TO FAMILIES WITH DEPENDENT CHILDREN

It has become commonplace to observe that children comprise the single largest group of poor people in the United States. Perhaps even more disturbing is the fact that the number of very young children who are homeless is rapidly increasing.[1]

The poor have many faces but children have a greater likelihood of living in poverty if they are members of a racial minority group or live in a single-parent family headed by a woman. In 1991, 45.9 percent of all African American children, 16.8 percent of all white children, and 40.4 percent of all Hispanic children lived below the poverty line of $10,860 for a non-farm family of three, $13,924 for a family of four. And although a substantial number of poor children live in two-parent families, children living in female-headed households comprised more than half (59 percent) of the childhood poverty population.[2]

In the 1980s the percentage of children living in poverty had risen to its highest level since the early 1960s when poverty was "discovered" in the United States.[3] In 1987, for example, the childhood poverty rate was 20.6 percent, an increase of almost 50 percent over its 1969 rate of 14 percent.[4] By 1991 there were over fourteen (14.3) million children living in poverty, 21.8 percent of all children or more than one child in five; the number was higher (one in four) for children under six.[5] The CDF attributes the increase in childhood poverty to cuts in government income-support programs and the failure of wages to keep up with inflation.[6]

Sylvia Ann Hewlett echoes the view of the CDF that declining wages have contributed to the increase in childhood poverty. But she also holds the government responsible for the deterioration in children's lives; and in her view, government policies marked by "inadequate (and in some instances, declining) public investments in day care, housing, medical care, and other social supports . . ." exacerbate the effects of poverty.[7] That the United States has become increasingly indifferent, if not hostile, to the plight of so many of its children is demonstrated in its approach to the program ostensibly intended to alleviate the effects of poverty on children—the Aid to Families With Dependent Children (AFDC) program.

Children in Poverty

To the extent that government had concerned itself with the plight of poor children throughout the nation's history, it was left to state, or more typically, local public officials. The federal government began to take a more active role in poverty policymaking in the 1930s, with the emergence of the welfare state as part of Franklin Roosevelt's New Deal.

The roots of the New Deal's efforts on behalf of children can be traced back to the early nineteen hundreds when, influenced by the Progressive movement, states began to provide limited financial support to certain classes of widows and their children.[8] As part of a nationwide effort to deter child labor and reduce reliance on orphanages, reformers gathered at the first White House Conference on Children in 1909, convened by President Theodore Roosevelt. Within the next ten years, states began to provide public assistance to widows, termed "Mothers' Pensions," to allow children to remain within the family as an alternative to being bound out or placed in the poorhouse. Thus, considered part of the "deserving poor," poor widows and their children were excused from the workforce.[9]

Local officials retained broad discretion over eligibility for public assistance, leading to a wide disparity in the distribution of benefits. Most African American, Hispanic, and Native American families were excluded on racial grounds: in 1931, African American families constituted only 3 percent of Mothers' Pensions caseloads. Additionally, women believed to have violated notions of propriety for reasons that included working outside the home, having children out of wedlock, or even, in some states, failing to keep their homes tidy, were also denied aid. Thus, despite its rationale, the support was neither generous enough, nor secure enough, to ensure survival of large numbers of poor children and their mothers.[10] Moreover, by introducing fitness and suitability as tests for assistance, public officials were authorized to enter homes to inspect conditions and make judgments about the character of the recipient.[11]

The Origins of the AFDC Program

As part of the federal government's reaction to the Great Depression, Congress enacted the Social Security Act of 1935, consisting of two social insurance programs, Old Age/Retirement Insurance and Unemployment Insurance, and three public assistance programs, Old Age Assistance (for needy persons over sixty-five), Aid to the Blind (for the needy adult blind), and Aid to Dependent Children (for needy children).[12]

The public assistance programs, commonly known as welfare, comprised varying degrees of federal-state involvement; they are jointly funded by the state and federal governments and administered by state and local governments. In 1972 Congress established the means-tested Supplemental Security Income (SSI) program, combining the Old Age Assistance and Aid to the Blind programs; it also included a means-tested component for the disabled poor.

The Aid to Dependent Children (ADC) program, its name changed to AFDC in 1962, was established in Title IV-A of the Social Security Act "for the purpose of encouraging the care of dependent children in their own homes." Founded on the philosophy of the state Mothers' Pensions programs, the law was designed to provide aid to a needy child "who has been deprived of parental support or care by reason of the death, continued absence from the home, or physical or mental incapacity of the parent."[13]

Title IV-A, establishing the framework for national public welfare assistance for children, began as a program to allow the "deserving poor," mostly white widows, to remain out of the workforce and stay home to rear their children.[14] Thus, from its inception, Title IV-A excused certain types of people from work without castigating them as immoral or unworthy.

Joel Handler, an advocate of social welfare reform, argues that welfare policy must be seen in the context of the interaction of race, class, and gender ideologies. In his view "the heart of poverty policy [in the United States] centers on the question of who is excused from work. Those who are excused are the 'deserving poor'; those who must work, the 'undeserving.' "[15]

Because of the southern states' insistence on retaining control over eligibility requirements, stemming primarily from racial motivations, states were given the authority to determine suitability for benefits. As with the Mothers' Pensions program, local officials used their discretion to exclude children in minority families as well as those in families headed by never-married or divorced women.

Eligibility for AFDC

Throughout the 1950s and 1960s, with the acquiescence of the federal government, states increasingly adopted rules restricting eligibility on the basis of "suitability." A number of states, particularly in the South, relied on such rules to remove thousands of children (predominantly African Americans) from the AFDC rolls.

In 1961 Secretary of Health, Education, and Welfare Arthur Flemming issued a rule to bar states from the practice of withdrawing aid to "unsuitable" families while allowing the children to remain within the home; if the homes were considered unsuitable, he maintained, the children should be removed from them. The Social Security Amendments of 1961 and 1962 put the Flemming rule into effect, but many state officials continued to deny public assistance to women whom they claimed were immoral or "unsuitable."[16] Thus, like the Mothers' Pensions programs, the primary beneficiaries of the early ADC program were families headed by white widows. Lacking means of support, poor non-white women with children were forced into the labor market to survive as best as they could.[17]

Throughout the 1960s, as benefits became more available to families headed by minority women, concern over government aid to the "undeserving poor" rose and led to a reevaluation of the AFDC mother's role in the workforce. The rise in the number of AFDC families headed by never-married or divorced women also fueled the campaign to impose work requirements on AFDC beneficiaries. That the government would move toward a policy of conditioning AFDC benefits on work when the number of minority families on AFDC increased was not surprising. The cash benefits that had allowed mothers to remain at home with their children had generally been unavailable to poor minority women for whom not working was never a real option. Indeed, as Frances Fox Piven and Richard Cloward argue, welfare policies had been designed to keep African American women in the labor pool, especially in the South. During periods of seasonal employment, for example, a number of southern states simply refused to accept their AFDC applications; for the same reason, they also provided lower levels of benefits to African American women than to white women.[18]

As AFDC policymakers became more preoccupied with the issue of work and the extent to which welfare benefits should be contingent on employability and employment, they created programs aimed at encouraging welfare recipients to work; however, these were largely unsuccessful and had little effect on the size of the welfare rolls because there was little or no federal funding for training programs or child care services.[19] Between 1962 and 1967, the AFDC caseload grew by 36 percent.[20] By the late 1960s, welfare began to be viewed as a national "crisis." And as a consequence of the growing number of non-white beneficiaries, support for AFDC became increasingly divided along racial lines.

Concern with rising AFDC rolls led to passage of the 1967 Social Security Amendments that created a Work Incentive program (WIN) to encourage the acquisition of work skills or experience.[21] WIN was based on the belief that the economy offered sufficient work for those who wanted to work, and that continued receipt of AFDC benefits was contrary to the interests of the beneficiaries as well as the larger society.

Qualified AFDC beneficiaries were required to accept jobs or register for work-training programs. As it turned out compulsion was unnecessary in most cases; more volunteered for training than the system was able to accommodate.[22]

Between 1967 and 1972 the welfare rolls more than doubled.[23] With a growing sense of alarm at continually climbing welfare costs, Congress created WIN II, also known as the Talmadge Amendments, in 1971. Emphasizing

Congress's commitment to welfare reform, the Talmadge Amendments ended WIN's exemption for mothers with preschool children.

The Talmadge Amendments shifted emphasis from education and training to immediate employment at any available job. Although states were required to allocate funds for training and employment services, for the most part these were underfunded and inadequate, with no provisions for child care expenses. According to Irwin Garfinkel and Sara McLanahan, there were many more AFDC volunteers for work services than the states were financially able to provide. Thus, the work requirements were never effectively implemented.[24]

Overall, the lack of funding for the states' efforts, the dearth of available jobs, and the low wages of the available jobs contributed to the failure of both WIN I and its successor WIN II to accomplish their stated goals of significantly reducing the AFDC rolls or decreasing welfare "dependency" in any meaningful sense.[25]

Debate over welfare policy continued throughout the 1970s. The welfare initiative in the Nixon administration, entitled the Family Assistance Plan (FAP), was designed to provide a guaranteed annual income for families with dependent children.[26] Also termed a "negative income tax," the plan called for the federal government to provide cash assistance to raise people up to the poverty line; for a variety of reasons, the FAP failed to gain enough support to pass out of Congress.

A version of the negative income tax, the Earned Income Tax Credit (EITC) was added to the Internal Revenue Code during the Ford administration in 1975; it was designed to offset a simultaneous increase in the social security payroll tax. The EITC, a mechanism for effectively increasing the earnings of low income working families, is a refundable tax credit (that is, if the tax owed is less than the credit, the government will refund a specified amount to the taxpayer).[27]

AFDC and the Reagan Administration

In 1981, President Ronald Reagan, aided by Democratic Senator Russell Long of Louisiana, a consistent foe of the AFDC program, began to fulfil his campaign promise to cut down on federal spending by reducing federal funding for AFDC and the food stamp program, among others. In his budget message to Congress in February 1981, the president vowed to preserve a "social safety net of programs," such as retirement and survivors' benefits, veterans' compensation and pensions, and Supplemental Security Income for "all those with true need." Although "true need" was never defined, Secretary of Health and Human Services (HHS) Richard Schweiker later characterized "the truly needy" as those who "wouldn't have any other alternative to economic survival."[28] Yet, despite this promise, it was estimated that of the eleven million entitlement program dollars slashed by the 1981 budget, 60 percent represented cuts in spending for the poor.[29]

The Reagan welfare policy was codified in the Omnibus Budget Reconciliation Act of 1981 (OBRA). Ironically, although it was intended to increase employment among welfare recipients, the changes instituted in OBRA often had the opposite effect of penalizing them for working and ultimately discouraging employment.

One of the most significant changes occasioned by OBRA was the placement of an overall income cap on eligibility in which no family with a gross income above 150 percent of the state-determined standard of need could receive AFDC benefits, regardless of work expenses.[30] Additionally, OBRA revised the rule exempting the first thirty dollars of the recipient's earnings and one-third of all additional earnings, the so-called "30 and 1/3" rule, from the recipient's income.[31] Under the provisions of OBRA the exemption was limited to the first four months of employment; after that time, AFDC checks were reduced dollar-for-dollar by the amount of the wages. The law also changed the existing rule that allowed recipients to "disregard" all reasonable expenses related to employment. The new policy permitted only a standard $75 deduction for work-related expenses (raised to $90 in 1988) and a standard child (or dependent) care deduction of $160 a month (raised to $175 in 1988).[32] Thus, by virtually eliminating the "disregards" for earned income, OBRA placed many working AFDC mothers beyond the level of eligibility, ignoring the recommendations of economists and welfare professionals who had been urging the AFDC policymakers to allow higher income deductions as an incentive to work.[33]

Taking a much broader approach to the notion of "available income," OBRA and subsequent AFDC rule changes also created new accounting procedures, such as the "lump sum" rule, the "filing unit" rule, and the "income deeming" rule, in which states charged certain kinds of income against benefit awards without regard for whether the money was actually available to the child. Other changes during the 1980s included revisions in the amount of assets permitted to AFDC families, more stringent overpayment policies, and calculations of the value of food stamp and housing assistance as part of income.[34]

These rules, allowing states to include an increased share of a family's income in determining eligibility, eliminated roughly four million people, including over a million and a half children, from the AFDC rolls for exceeding the income level. In thirteen states, families of four with incomes over $3,000 were denied AFDC benefits. More than half the states dropped families of three with incomes of $5,000. Not surprisingly, the percentage of poor families covered by the AFDC program fell from an average of 83 percent in 1970 to 62.9 percent in 1983. Seventy-five percent of poor children received AFDC benefits in the

1970s, by 1983, only 53.3 percent of poor children were covered by the AFDC program.[35]

The Reagan administration also committed itself to link work efforts to welfare. Tom Joe and Cheryl Rogers argue that these cuts represented a shift in the nation's approach to public welfare assistance, and that many of the new policies were ill-conceived and produced contradictory results. In their view, these policies created a greater disincentive to work because, by increasing the "marginal tax rate" on benefits, AFDC recipients were better off not working than working.[36] The administration's solution for this disincentive was to create work programs in which women would be required to work for their families' benefits.

The administration unsuccessfully urged states to adopt mandatory work programs for welfare recipients. Collectively entitled "workfare," these programs included "work relief" projects in which AFDC recipients would be required to work in public sector jobs in exchange for AFDC benefits. In states with such policies, women had to absorb the costs of child care and transportation in exchange for their AFDC check, thus forcing them to work for less than they received as AFDC benefits.[37]

The demonstration job training and/or work relief programs instituted by state and local governments had only a "modest" impact on saving welfare dollars or reducing welfare caseloads.[38] In general, the programs depended on the economy's ability to absorb low-skilled and marginally educated job applicants as well as the state's willingness to provide the necessary funds for training, education, and child care.[39]

The Family Support Act

In the latter part of 1980, a bipartisan consensus over welfare reform led to passage of the Family Support Act (FSA) of 1988. Supporters of the FSA argued that it was reasonable to expect AFDC mothers to work because most women with children did. They also maintained that the government's demand for work was a fair trade in exchange for assistance in the form of education, job training, child care, and health benefits.

The reality of women's work, however, is that most single women cannot lift themselves out of poverty by full-time work. As David Ellwood noted in his book, *Poor Support*, in 1984 approximately a quarter of working mothers worked full-time the entire year; most had only part-time jobs, and mothers of small children worked less than others. Because the AFDC program does not allow part-time work, by eliminating welfare assistance the mothers of AFDC children will be forced to exhibit work patterns unlike those of other women in the nation. Moreover, in order to lift themselves out of poverty, they will need to find jobs that pay above the minimum wage, a remote prospect for most welfare recipients.[40]

On October 13, 1988, Reagan signed the FSA, requiring states to create job opportunities and basic skills (JOBS) programs to assist AFDC recipients to find employment and leave the welfare rolls. The law also provided for transitional medical and child care benefits to women leaving welfare for work—up to twelve months in some cases. Beginning in 1990, states were required to institute either work, training, or education programs for AFDC recipients. However, although the federal government offered increased matching dollars to states for JOBS programs (about $1 billion a year), state budgets were severely strained and many states have not been able to come up with the funds to draw down their share of federal dollars.[41] By 1992, the states were only registering about 7 percent of adult AFDC recipients in their JOBS programs; the best performing states reached only 15 percent.[42]

Although there was widespread support for the FSA, Handler argues that reducing federal authority and allowing states greater discretion in determining the balance between education, training, and work relief led to negative consequences for AFDC recipients, especially those in less economically developed and more rural states. In his view the FSA accomplished one of Reagan's major goals of sharply diminishing the federal government's responsibility for the poor by devolving much authority over participation and spending to the states.[43]

One of the most important effects of the Reagan years was that the debate over welfare reform became detached from, and superseded, the debate over how to end poverty.[44] Little attention was paid to the dramatic impact the changes in the law would have on the children in AFDC families. Proponents of reduced federal welfare spending framed the debate in terms of the mother's welfare dependency, refusing to acknowledge that denying welfare assistance to the mother has a detrimental effect on the well-being of her dependent children.[45]

Society's willingness to diminish its support of children in this way raises a question about whether it has also consigned them to the status of "undeserving poor." Peter Edelman believes this to be the case, arguing that despite the rhetoric to the contrary, the poverty rate among children indicates that "what we actually do for particular children depends upon what we think of their parents."[46] Thus, in his view, when their parents are classified as undeserving, so are the children.

AFDC Benefits

Over the last two decades the number of AFDC recipients almost doubled from 7.4 million in 1970 (5.5 million children) to 13.6 million in 1992 (9.2 million children); similarly the number of families more than doubled from 1.9 million in 1970 to 4.8 million in 1992.

Today's AFDC is a joint federal-state cash grant program in which the federal government defrays from 50 to 80 percent of the costs; the federal share rises as the state's per capita income falls. As an entitlement program, established by an open-ended congressional authorization of funds, AFDC recipients have a legal right to benefits if they meet the statutory eligibility requirements.

States are given the option of participating in the AFDC program; currently all fifty states, plus the District of Columbia, Guam, Puerto Rico, and the Virgin Islands provide AFDC benefits.[47] States determine the size of the cash benefit, and although federal law prohibits distinctions *within* states, there is wide variation in benefit levels *among* states. Under federal law, each state must file a "state plan" with the Department of Health and Human Services that must include the state's "standard of need," based on items considered essential for minimal living conditions. Each state calculates a benefit award, up to 100 percent of the need level. States differ widely in their determination of "basic need," and only thirteen states have maximum AFDC grants that comprise 100 percent of the need standard. The "basic need" becomes the ceiling for eligibility within the state; families with income higher than this amount are ineligible for benefits.

Based on data compiled by the federal government in January 1993, monthly AFDC benefits ranged from a high of $923 (for a one-parent family of three in Alaska) to a low of $120 (for a one-parent family of three in Mississippi). According to these figures the median maximum AFDC monthly benefit for the fifty states and the District of Columbia was $367, amounting to 39 percent of the 1992 poverty level. No state's AFDC benefits alone placed recipients above the poverty level; only Alaska and Hawaii provided benefits that brought recipients up to 100 percent of the 1992 poverty threshold by combining food stamp and AFDC benefits.[48]

Because AFDC benefits are not indexed to the rate of inflation, their value has steadily declined. "After accounting for inflation, the average monthly AFDC benefit per family was $644 in 1970 and $388 in 1992, a 40 percent reduction."[49] Surveying these two decades of welfare policymaking, Peter Edelman grimly states "the poor have taken it on the chin since 1973."[50]

Thus, participation in the AFDC program does not guarantee an end to poverty. Unlike Old Age Insurance benefits which have moved a good portion of the elderly out of poverty, AFDC leaves its recipients below the poverty line.[51] Overall, comparing the rate of federal expenditures aimed at the elderly and at children in the decade between the late 1970s and 1980s shows that the former increased by 52 percent, while the latter declined by 4 percent.[52] This should not be taken as a criticism of the nation's more generous approach toward the elderly; rather, it suggests that, with political will, policymakers can affect the rate of poverty in the Unites States.

Aid to Families with Dependent Children costs have risen from $14.8 billion in 1970 to $22.2 billion in 1992, with the federal share about $12 billion. Although critics attack the amount of money committed to AFDC, federal spending for AFDC consumes a very small percentage (since 1980, less than 1 1/2 percent) of total federal spending. Indeed, following a period of growth from the middle 1960s to the middle 1970s, despite the continual increase in the number of recipients, federal AFDC spending as a percentage of total federal spending has declined.[53]

Welfare "Reform"

The growing number of children living below the poverty line is testimony to the fact that welfare has not cured the problem of poverty in the United States. Paradoxically, when poverty rates go up, and there is a greater need for welfare, there is a mounting public perception that welfare is getting "out of control" and consequently, public resistance to it grows.[54]

The election of Bill Clinton in 1992 was accompanied by promises to "end welfare as we know it" by imposing a two-year limit on public aid and moving welfare recipients into private or public sector jobs within that time. The problems of the welfare system are not insoluble but changes, other than complete termination of benefits to large numbers of recipients, require a commitment of resources that governments have so far been unwilling to make. Clinton's approach in part reflects the strategies of welfare reformers such as David Ellwood, who served as the Assistant Secretary for Planning and Evaluation in HHS. Ellwood and others have argued that time limits must be conditioned on the availability of jobs and other types of financial support for families, including child care. They have expressed doubt about whether it is realistic to impose a full-time work requirement on single mothers, especially those with young children and little or no work experience or education.[55]

Although there is disagreement over the conditions under which the government should terminate support for AFDC families, the consensus over reducing welfare spending and trimming the welfare rolls that guided the passage of the FSA persists. What appears to be missing, however, is any consensus on how these ends should be accomplished.

Amid growing public support for restricting the reach of AFDC, the Clinton administration unveiled its proposal to revamp the welfare system on June 14, 1994. The plan would have required beneficiaries born after 1971 to work within two years of receiving assistance. After two years those unable to find work would be given federally subsidized jobs. The cost of education, job training, and child care to implement the program was estimated at $9.3 billion over five years. When the administration proposal reached Congress, it joined a number of bills submitted by members of both parties; these bills ranged from more drastic measures such as eliminating all public assistance, including AFDC and food stamps, to all unwed mothers under twenty-one, to increased spending on job training and education. When the 103d Congress adjourned at the end of 1994, hearings had been held but no bill had been reported out of committee.

The Clinton administration's drive to alter the welfare system was reinforced by the results of the 1994 elections. The new 104th Congress, dominated by the Republican Party in the House and Senate, promised a welfare proposal within the first hundred days as part of the House Republican's "Contract with America."[56] Called the Personal Responsibility Act, the House-passed bill would deny public assistance to large numbers of children, with estimates varying from 1.5 million to over 5 million. Most important, the House bill eliminated the entitlement status of AFDC; states would receive federal funding under a block grant that would specify rules for denying AFDC assistance to certain groups of beneficiaries and leave other questions of eligibility to the states. By transforming AFDC from an entitlement into a block grant, there would be no guarantee that funds would be sufficient to provide for eligible families in times of greater need, or even under current levels of need. In September 1995 the Senate passed a bill that, while not as draconian as the House bill, also ended AFDC as an entitlement program.

Welfare Rights Litigation

As the AFDC program grew in size and occupied a larger place on the national agenda, state officials sought ways to restrict eligibility and limit benefits. Welfare recipients increasingly turned to the federal courts to resolve controversies over the distribution of benefits and rules of eligibility, primarily the latter.[57] Stemming from this litigation, the courts had a significant impact on the national debate over welfare policy. As an entitlement program, anyone meeting the eligibility criteria for AFDC has a legally enforceable right to benefits.[58] Not surprisingly, therefore, much of the litigation related to the AFDC program has centered on interpretation of the eligibility rules.

Federal court litigation helped contribute to the growth of the AFDC program in the 1960s. The creation of an active welfare rights movement and the appearance of initial judicial receptivity to the idea that welfare constituted a right was instrumental in preventing state welfare authorities from excluding eligible beneficiaries on the basis of race or other arbitrary criteria.[59] During this time the number of AFDC applicants rose dramatically, expanding the AFDC rolls.[60]

Welfare Reformers

Ironically, Lyndon Johnson's Great Society and War on Poverty of the 1960s had only a minimal direct effect on the AFDC program. There was an important indirect effect, however. The Office of Economic Opportunity (OEO) provided grants to the newly created Legal Services Program (LSP) attorneys to represent indigents in civil cases. The community activism arising from the War on Poverty also led to the formation of the National Welfare Rights Organization (NWRO), a group that played an important role in agitating for welfare reform. Composed primarily of African American welfare recipients, the NWRO attempted to flood the courts with welfare issues, as well as sponsor street demonstrations and apply political pressure.[61]

Following a strategy of combining individual client representation with law reform activity, the LSP staff attorneys played an important role in representing welfare clients in challenging restrictive AFDC policies in the lower federal courts, and ultimately in the Supreme Court.[62] In addition to direct representation by legal service programs, AFDC litigants, especially in the earlier cases, were supported by amici curiae briefs filed on their behalf by a variety of public interest groups such as the National Lawyers Guild, the ACLU, the United Way, and People for Adequate Welfare, and occasionally, by attorneys in legal service programs around the nation.

The CSWPL viewed litigation as part of an overall effort to achieve social policy reform. Serving as a model for the development of the LSP, the CSWPL had been originally funded by the Mobilization for Youth, operating in New York City with Ford Foundation funds.[63] Unlike the more narrowly focused traditional legal aid approach, the LSP and the CSWPL adopted a multi-faceted strategy for fighting poverty.[64] As part of this effort the CSWPL, headed by Edward Sparer as executive director, sought to persuade the Court to invoke the equal protection clause to expand the rights of the poor by recognizing a federally guaranteed "right to life."[65]

The Constitutional Era

Welfare reform litigation can be divided into three eras, largely following chronological order but characterized by differing types of claims as well. In the first, welfare reformers, primarily relying on constitutional arguments, challenged restrictive state AFDC policies.[66] The Supreme Court's rulings in *King v. Smith* (1968), *Shapiro v. Thompson* (1969), and *Goldberg v. Kelly* (1970) signalled its apparent willingness to set limits on the state's authority over AFDC eligibility policy.

King was the Supreme Court's first welfare rights case. The issue here was a 1964 Alabama regulation disqualifying children whose mothers had "frequent or continuing" sexual relations with an "able-bodied man," in the home or away.[67] Based on the state's authority to condition welfare aid on "suitability," the regulation declared that such a man was the children's "substitute father" and therefore responsible for their support. Relying on this regulation, the state had expunged almost twenty thousand persons, including sixteen thousand children, from the welfare rolls.

The lower court struck the Alabama regulation on constitutional equal protection grounds. The Supreme Court declined to reach the constitutional question, basing its ruling instead on statutory grounds.[68] The Legal Defense (or Inc.) Fund and the Child Welfare League filed amici curiae briefs on behalf of the welfare litigators.

Acknowledging that the state has an important role to play in determining the level of AFDC benefits, the Court insisted that Congress retained the authority to determine eligibility. It rejected the state's argument that it could treat a "substitute father" as the actual father. Without proof of paternity and legal support obligations, the state could not designate a man engaging in sexual relations with the children's mother as a "parent" within the meaning of the act. Doing so breached its duty to provide "aid to families with dependent children . . . to all eligible individuals."[69]

Despite the state's urging, the Court declined to view the regulation as a permissible device to discourage "illicit sexual behavior and illegitimacy." The Court noted that while states had been allowed to condition eligibility on morality in the past, recent legislative action indicated that Congress no longer sanctioned this approach.

Shapiro v. Thompson marked the first time the Court based its opinion on the validity of a state welfare regulation on constitutional grounds.[70] As permitted by federal statute, almost all states conditioned AFDC benefits on the length of residency in the state. *Shapiro* arose when Vivian Thompson, a nineteen-year-old single mother, applied for Connecticut welfare benefits. She was denied eligibility because she had not lived in the state for a year; the lower court upheld her challenge to the Connecticut law.[71] Indicating the importance of this case, the ACLU, the American Jewish Congress, the CSWPL, the National Federation for the Blind, and two county-wide legal aid associations filed amici curiae briefs urging the Supreme Court to affirm the lower court.

The high court held that the waiting period created two classes of needy families, different only in the length of time they had lived in the jurisdiction. Stressing the importance of the interest involved, that is, "the ability . . . to obtain the very means to subsist—food, shelter, and other necessities of life," the Court examined the rationale for the distinction. Because the residency requirement implicated the exercise of the fundamental right of interstate travel, the Court adopted the strict scrutiny review reserved for racial classifications and demanded the state produce a compelling reason for its policy.[72]

The Court found neither of the state's proffered justifications—controlling welfare costs or discouraging in-migration to higher-benefit states—sufficiently compelling. Indeed, it underscored the fact that welfare recipients, no less than others, may choose to live in other states to take advantage of whatever benefits were offered, and states were not permitted to "fence [them] out."

Some believed *Shapiro* was a step toward judicial recognition of a constitutional right to welfare. Court documents show, however, that despite some language in the opinion, the majority rejected this position and opted to rest the holding on the constitutional right to travel.[73]

The next step in the welfare rights campaign was a due process attack on New York City's welfare termination procedure.[74] The plaintiffs in *Goldberg v. Kelly* were AFDC and General Assistance beneficiaries who asked the Court to subsume welfare benefits within the growing category of legal entitlements. The theoretical justification for this approach, supplied in part by Yale University Law Professor Charles Reich, was that welfare grants, like other benefits such as drivers' licenses, government contracts, or public employment, should be characterized as "new property," protected from arbitrary governmental deprivation by the due process clause of the Fourteenth Amendment.[75]

Under New York law, welfare officials could remove beneficiaries whose eligibility they questioned from the rolls without allowing them an opportunity to object; recipients could request a "post-termination 'fair hearing' " after they were removed. The state defended its procedure on the basis of its interest in preserving its fiscal integrity.

Characterizing welfare benefits as "statutory entitlements," to which constitutional protections applied, the Court ruled that pre-termination hearings were required. Unlike other forms of governmental entitlements, said the Court, "termination of aid pending resolution of a controversy over eligibility may deprive an *eligible* recipient of the very means by which to live while he waits."[76] To satisfy the due process clause, recipients must be provided with timely notice and an opportunity to be heard prior to removal from the welfare rolls. The state need not, however, conduct a full evidentiary hearing.[77]

Dandridge v. Williams, a 1970 decision, represented another step in carrying out Sparer's "right to life" strategy.[78] In this class action suit plaintiffs hoped to persuade the Court that the equal protection clause of the Fourteenth Amendment guaranteed a child's right to sufficient resources of life, enforceable by judicial decree. They urged the Court to apply the fundamental rights analysis used in *Shapiro* and subject the state's welfare policy to strict scrutiny review.

The plaintiffs challenged the way in which Maryland calculated welfare benefits—the so-called flat grant. Under this plan, benefits for each additional child in the family were gradually diminished until an upper limit of $250 a month was reached. Linda Williams, a single mother of eight, challenged the law, arguing that distinguishing among families on the basis of the number of children contravened the equal protection clause because it was unrelated to the program's purpose of helping needy dependent children. The state countered that the policy encouraged employment, discouraged childbearing, bolstered public support for the welfare system, and rationed scarce resources.

The district court agreed that the flat grant approach violated the equal protection clause and the CSWPL submitted an amicus curiae brief urging the Supreme Court to affirm. Recognizing the state's authority to allocate its limited AFDC funds, the high court found the state plan consistent with the Social Security Act. And when addressing the constitutionality of the Maryland scheme, far from applying a fundamental rights analysis, the Court retreated to minimal scrutiny typically used in reviewing economic and social legislation. The effect of the difference in scrutiny is illustrated by the fact that in *Shapiro* the Court rejected the state's defense of the residency requirement on economic grounds, but in *Dandridge* it accepted the state's justification of the policy for financial reasons.[79] Echoing the principles articulated in *Kelly* and *Shapiro*, the Court agreed with the plaintiffs that "the administration of public welfare assistance . . . involves the most basic economic needs of impoverished human beings." Yet, it nevertheless held that the state was within constitutional bounds in establishing a maximum family benefit.[80]

In *Rosado v. Wyman*, decided on the same day as *Dandridge*, the Court ruled on the state's authority to determine standards of need within the federal government's overall dominion over AFDC policy.[81] *Rosado* arose in response to the 1967 Social Security Amendments requiring states to recalculate their standards of need upward to reflect increases in living expenses. When New York eliminated its "special needs" grants, thus substantially reducing, not raising, the size of its public assistance awards, welfare recipients unsuccessfully challenged the policy in the lower federal courts. Urging the Supreme Court to reverse, the New York Civil Liberties Union, Catholic Charities of New York, and People for Adequate Welfare filed amici curiae briefs.

The Supreme Court found the New York policy inconsistent with the federal mandate, yet was unwilling to order the state to raise its benefit levels. Although the 1967 law required states to recalculate their standards of need, the Court held that they were still free to "pare down payments to accommodate [state] budgetary realities by reducing the percent of benefits paid or switching to a percent reduction system."[82] Thus, the Court ruled that while the federal government could order states to reflect increases in beneficiaries' living costs in their standards of need, the benefits paid by states did not have to reflect these increases. This ruling represents the Court's attempt to chart a course between state and federal responsibilities for the AFDC program: it upheld the state's authority to determine the level of benefits to AFDC beneficiaries within its borders while acknowledging the federal government's role in national AFDC policymaking.

Wyman v. James, decided in 1971 on Fourth Amendment grounds, further illustrates the Court's unwillingness to attach substantive constitutional guarantees to the receipt of public welfare. At issue in *James* was a New York policy under which welfare caseworkers made scheduled home daytime visits every three months as a condition of aid.[83] The welfare litigants argued that state officials had no authority to enter their homes without properly served search warrants. The lower court agreed, and amici curiae briefs filed by the American Federation of State, County, and Municipal Employees and the Legal Aid Society of San Mateo County urged the Supreme Court to affirm.

The high court held that because recipients could refuse the caseworkers permission to enter their home, such visits did not constitute searches within the meaning of the Fourth Amendment. Although they might "appear mandatory," refusing to allow the visits carried no criminal penalty, merely the loss of aid.

Even if the visits were searches, and the Fourth Amendment applied, said the Court, they reasonably furthered the state's interest in protecting the dependent child (there had been reports of suspected child abuse in the house) and ensuring compliance with welfare regulations. Moreover, because they were scheduled in advance and occurred only during the daytime, the visits did not unduly intrude on the welfare family's privacy.

In *Jefferson v. Hackney*, a 1972 case, litigants challenged the system of allocating AFDC benefits in Texas.[84] They argued that Texas violated the Social Security Act and the equal protection clause of the Fourteenth Amendment by differentiating between AFDC recipients and beneficiaries of the state's categorical assistance programs, the aged, blind, and disabled. Specifically, they claimed that the state discriminated against them by awarding them only 75 percent of the state-determined standard of need while awarding the aged, and blind and disabled 100 percent and 95 percent respectively of the standard of need. Viewed in the perspective of welfare theory, the Texas law exemplified the distinction between the "deserving poor" and "undeserving poor." The latter, mostly minority children and their mothers, were allocated fewer resources on the basis of their status, not their need.

The Court was not persuaded, however, ruling that neither the Fourteenth Amendment nor the Social Security Act barred states from distinguishing among public assistance beneficiaries, and that awarding lower benefits to AFDC recipients was neither irrational nor invidious. And absent proof of racial bias, the mere fact that 87 percent of the AFDC recipients were either African American or Hispanic did not indicate that the scheme was racially discriminatory.[85]

Dismissing any evidence of racial motivation, which would have demanded the use of strict scrutiny, the Court followed the minimal scrutiny approach of *Dandridge* and held that "since budgetary constraints do not allow the payment for the full standard of need for all welfare recipients," a state could well decide that certain categories of welfare beneficiaries were more needy than others.[86] As in *Dandridge* the Court emphasized that the state must be allowed to exercise discretion over the allocation of scarce resources. And it expressed little concern that the policy placed minority children in a more disadvantageous position.

The *King-Shapiro-Kelly* trilogy had raised expectations that the Supreme Court might be amenable to the use of judicial authority to expand welfare rights. The opinions in *Dandridge, Rosado, Jefferson*, and *Wyman*, however, demonstrated its unwillingness to classify public assistance as a substantive constitutional right and its decision to limit its role in state welfare policymaking primarily to ensuring the procedural rights of AFDC beneficiaries.

In his assessment of the litigation strategy followed by poverty reformers during these early years, Samuel Krislov asserts that the OEO lawyers were too precipitous in bringing *Dandridge* to the Supreme Court for review; he maintains that the Court was not ready to accept their constitutional theory of the right to welfare.[87] According to Sparer, however, the strategy was a sound one because "a contrary decision in *Dandridge* would have permitted wholesale challenges to the barriers created by state legislators and Congress to deny welfare assistance to groups of needy people." He adds that had the plaintiffs succeeded, "the equal protection clause would have become the vehicle for establishing a constitutional guarantee of human life . . . [and] affirmative judicial scrutiny to guarantee equal protection could have led to a different America."[88] Whether precipitous or not, *Dandridge* clearly established that the Court was not prepared to accept the welfare reformers' vision of a constitutional "right to life."

Statutory Claims

During the second phase of Supreme Court decisionmaking on welfare claims, challenges to state AFDC policies were primarily framed on federal statutory grounds.[89] The issues in most of these cases were whether states exceeded their authority by creating rules of eligibility that were neither expressly allowed nor prohibited by the Social Security Act.[90]

Townsend v. Swank, a 1971 opinion, involved an Illinois welfare provision denying AFDC benefits to eighteen to twenty-year-old college students, while making them available to eighteen to twenty-year-olds attending high school or vocational school.[91] Ruling that the federal statute required participating states to provide AFDC benefits to "all eligible" individuals, the Court held that once the state chose to provide benefits to children over eighteen, it could not arbitrarily limit eligibility only to those attending vocational or technical schools. Justice Brennan underscored the limitations on a state's ability to restrict eligibility by explaining that:

> *King v. Smith* establishes that, at least in the absence of congressional authorization for the exclusion clearly evidenced from the Social Security Act or its legislative history, a state eligibility standard that excludes

persons eligible for assistance under federal AFDC standards violates the Social Security Act and is therefore invalid under the Supremacy Clause.[92]

A year later, in *Carleson v. Remillard*, the Court reviewed a challenge to a California regulation that denied AFDC benefits to dependent children whose fathers were away from home on military duty.[93] The named plaintiffs in this class action suit claimed eligibility for AFDC benefits because their need exceeded the monthly military allotment. The Court held that the regulation violated the Supremacy Clause because the Social Security Act's standard of "continued absence" from the home meant absence for any reason, including military service. Although there was evidence that Congress had not intended to include parents in military service, they had not been expressly excluded in the statute. Again the Court endorsed the principle that states were not permitted to depart from federal eligibility requirements "without express or clearly implied congressional authorization."[94]

Shortly thereafter, however, in *New York State Department of Social Welfare v. Dublino*, a 1973 case, the Court itself departed from the trend toward nationalized AFDC standards.[95] The issue was whether federal law, specifically the WIN provisions of the 1967 Social Security Amendments, pre-empted state work incentive rules. Under New York law AFDC beneficiaries who were considered employable were required to seek jobs, and to appear at the welfare office every two weeks to report on the results of their search; if they failed to do so or refused to accept an available job, the entire family was disqualified for benefits.

In an amicus curiae brief, the NWRO argued that the state had no authority to impose additional work requirements on AFDC recipients. But the Supreme Court held that despite its comprehensiveness, the federal law did not pre-empt the New York Work Rules. Where federal and state policy exist within a "complementary administrative framework," said the Court, the standard for federal pre-emption must be higher. And in this case, there was insufficient evidence that Congress intended to preclude the state from acting; indeed, the Court believed that Congress intended the opposite. Because of limits in funding and coverage, Congress could not have expected the federal program to solve the problem of jobs for welfare recipients on its own.

Dublino appeared to mark a break with the *Townsend-Carleson* line of cases in which the Court emphasized that national standards barred states from restricting AFDC eligibility in the absence of "express or clearly implied congressional authorization." In *Dublino*, the state was permitted to act because there was no "clear" indication of a contrary congressional intent.

In *Shea v. Vialpando*, decided in 1974, the Court resolved a dispute over a state income "disregard" rule.[96] The suit was filed by an AFDC beneficiary whose income exceeded the eligibility threshold because the state did not deduct her transportation expenses. The Court struck the Colorado regulation that limited the work expense disregard to a standard $30 a month on the grounds that it conflicted with the Social Security Act's explicit requirement that states consider "any expenses" reasonably related to earnings. The state's arbitrary limits on work-related expenses, noted the Court, conflicted with Congress's intent of encouraging AFDC beneficiaries to work.

The Court ruled on another state eligibility rule in *Burns v. Alcala*, a 1975 decision.[97] *Burns* revolved around the question of whether states were required to provide AFDC benefits to pregnant women. An amicus curiae brief by the American Association for Maternal and Child Health urged the Court to adopt a generous interpretation of the term "dependent child."

Because the Social Security Act contained no language suggesting otherwise, the Court was persuaded that Congress meant to give the term "child" its ordinary meaning of "already born" and provide AFDC benefits to mothers only after their children were born. The AFDC program was designed to allow women to stay home with their children, said the Court; there were other federal programs that provided assistance to expectant mothers.

In another 1975 decision, *Philbrook v. Glodgett*, the Court delivered an opinion on a state regulation associated with a program that provided AFDC benefits to families in which the father was unemployed, the AFDC–Unemployed Father (UF) program.[98] Federal law barred states from providing AFDC benefits to "unemployed" fathers in the same week they *received* unemployment compensation. Vermont denied benefits to fathers who were merely *eligible* for unemployment benefits. In striking the state law, the Court stated its belief that the federal law only disqualified *actual recipients* of unemployment benefits, and that it found no evidence that Congress intended to allow states to impose additional restrictions on AFDC eligibility.[99]

In *Quern v. Mandley*, decided in 1978, the Court ruled on an Illinois regulation limiting eligibility for its Emergency Assistance to Needy Families with Children (EA) program.[100] Under the 1967 Social Security Amendments, states could receive federal matching funds for providing cash or other forms of emergency relief to families with children, including AFDC beneficiaries. Illinois had abolished the state EA program and created in its stead a "special needs" program that was available only to families who were temporarily without shelter, or who were "presumptively eligible for AFDC" and required immediate assistance for household furnishings and clothing expenses. The lower court held that the Illinois program was inconsistent with federal law and enjoined the state from restricting eligibility more narrowly than the federal statute.

On appeal, despite an amicus curiae brief by the United Way of Metropolitan Chicago, the Supreme Court reversed the lower court. Because participation in the federal EA program is optional, said the Court, the state could devise an alternate emergency funding program and seek federal funds for it.

The Court distinguished between a state's obligation to provide aid to all persons meeting the eligibility criteria specified by federal law and "the well-established principle that the States have 'undisputed power to set the level of benefits and the standard of need for their AFDC programs.' "[101] Congress's failure to specify criteria for EA eligibility, said the Court, meant that it intended to allow states the flexibility to determine their own eligibility standards.

A year later, in *Miller v. Youakim*, the Court issued an opinion on the state's efforts to limit AFDC benefits to certain categories of abused and neglected children.[102] The suit was brought by children who had been removed from their home and sent to live with their sister and her husband. They challenged the provision of Illinois law that denied the higher benefits of the AFDC–Foster Care (FC) program to children placed in foster care with relatives. The United States solicitor general and the American Orthopsychiatric Association submitted amici curiae briefs supporting their claims against the state's restrictive interpretation of the AFDC-FC program.

Relying on the language and legislative history of the Social Security Act, the Court ruled that the children's relationship to their foster caretakers was irrelevant to the purpose of the statute. It held that Congress intended to provide the "best available care" to children placed in foster homes and the Illinois policy frustrated this intent.

In *Blum v. Bacon*, decided in 1982, the Court ruled on another Emergency Assistance program that barred AFDC beneficiaries, but not Social Security and SSI recipients, from receiving cash relief for lost or stolen grants.[103] Ruling on constitutional grounds, the Second Circuit had held that the differential treatment of AFDC beneficiaries violated the equal protection clause.

The Supreme Court declined to reach the constitutional question but held that the New York program was inconsistent with federal policy because it conflicted with a federal regulation requiring equitable treatment for all recipients of the Emergency Assistance program. Its decision in *Mandley* was not controlling, said the Court, because that had not addressed the issue of whether a state could exclude *all* AFDC recipients from its EA program.

Reactions to Changes in Federal Law

The third phase of the Supreme Court's decisionmaking was characterized by challenges to state and federal laws reflecting the changes in AFDC policy enacted during the Reagan administration.

Heckler v. Turner, a 1985 decision, involved a class action suit contesting a federal regulation interpreting the "income and resources" provision of OBRA.[104] Under previous law, most states deducted payroll tax withholdings from any income before determining the family's eligibility for AFDC. When the flat $75 "disregard" was instituted in OBRA, the executive branch advised state agencies to include payroll taxes within the $75. After California implemented regulations to this effect, AFDC beneficiaries filed a class action suit, charging that the state's interpretation of the phrase "earned income" in the federal statute was incorrect. The lower courts agreed.

The Supreme Court reversed, holding that even though OBRA did not precisely define "income," Congress desired states to subsume mandatory payroll taxes within the $75 deduction. The Court concluded that Congress intended to substitute a fixed sum in place of unlimited work expenses, and there was no indication of any intent to allow an additional deduction for payroll taxes. Although the appellate court found that Congress could not have intended to include payroll taxes within the $75 because it would discourage recipients from working, the high court noted that Congress had replaced the policy of providing incentives to work with requiring adult recipients to work. It also pointed out that the 1984 Deficit Reduction Act (DEFRA) defined "earned income" as "gross earned income prior to any deductions for taxes."

Two years later, in 1987, in *Lukhard v. Reed* the Court issued an opinion on how states should treat personal injury awards received by AFDC beneficiaries.[105] Before the passage of OBRA, states would treat lump-sum amounts as income for the first month and resources for the following months. Under the provisions of OBRA states were required to attribute all lump sums to income for as many months as the money would last if spent in an amount equal to the state's standard of need.

Virginia AFDC beneficiaries filed a class action suit, charging that by classifying personal injury awards as income, the state violated the statute and federal regulations. The lower courts upheld their claim, ruling that the meaning of the term "income" did not include personal injury awards and that it was irrational to treat such awards as income while treating property damage awards as resources.

Despite an amicus curiae brief from the North Carolina Legal Services urging affirmance of the lower court decision, the Supreme Court reversed, ruling that personal injury awards were contemplated within the meaning of income as defined by the act and federal regulation.

The plaintiffs had argued that income connotes gain, and personal injury awards were compensatory. Not so, said the Supreme Court; such awards typically compensate for "lost income," and were contemplated within the meaning of income as defined by the act. Moreover, noted the Court, its decision in *Turner*, subsuming taxes within the definition of income, clearly indicated that the act encompassed all "income" without regard to gain. The Court was not persuaded by the fact that other federal statutes excluded personal injury awards from the definition of income, because, it said, by its silence Congress refrained from applying the same principle to the AFDC statute.

In *Bowen v. Gilliard*, another case decided in 1987, the Court was asked to uphold the federal government's expansive interpretation of a "filing unit" in determining the family's eligibility for AFDC benefits.[106] The case had originated in a decade-old class action suit, won by public welfare recipients who were allowed to exclude any child receiving child support from the family unit, while retaining the child support payment.

The 1984 DEFRA expanded the definition of the family, or filing, unit to encompass all family members living in the house, including any child for whom child support payments were received. Under this process, called "income deeming," the state was entitled to assume, without proof, that income is available to the dependent child from all members of the household, including stepparents, grandparents, and half- or step-siblings. Clearly, when stepparents, grandparents, and siblings are considered part of the family unit and their income is calculated as part of the family's income and used to determine eligibility, benefits will be reduced accordingly or eliminated entirely.[107]

When North Carolina adopted the new deeming regulations, the litigants in the 1970 class action suit filed to have the original court order reopened. They challenged the child support provisions of DEFRA, claiming they violated the due process and "takings" clauses of the Fifth Amendment.[108]

Applying strict scrutiny because the law implicated the fundamental right of family autonomy, the district court agreed. And, indicating the importance of this decision, amici curiae briefs supporting the lower court decision were filed by the ACLU, the Juvenile and Family Court Judges, and the National Organization for Women Legal Defense and Education Fund.

The Supreme Court reversed the lower court and applying minimal scrutiny ruled that DEFRA rationally furthered Congress's goal of reducing federal spending and allocating scarce resources among welfare beneficiaries fairly. There is no "takings" violation, said the Court, because Congress could have reasonably concluded that one child's support payments yielded benefits for the entire family, not just the individual child. Also, because social welfare program benefits may be adjusted by Congress, beneficiaries have no protected property interest in a specified level of benefits.

In 1988, in *Gardebring v. Jenkins*, the Court revisited the provisions of OBRA after Minnesota suspended the AFDC benefits of a family whose husband received a lump-sum social security disability payment.[109] The mother claimed that the state violated a federal regulation requiring states to provide "information in written form, and orally as appropriate, about . . . conditions of eligibility." She won in the courts below, and on the state's appeal to the Supreme Court, the Economic Rights Task Force of the National Lawyer's Guild filed an amicus curiae brief urging the high court to affirm.

Interpreting the regulation narrowly, the Court found that the state had satisfied its requirements by distributing two brochures describing the rules and regulations of the AFDC program, including a statement about the obligation to report all income, to all beneficiaries. After OBRA was enacted, recipients were informed of the changes in the program, including the lump-sum rule. Moreover, said the Court, the express terms of the notice provision refers to "applicants," not current recipients, and permits the state agency to decide how to present the information. Additionally, the Court relied on the secretary's belief that the state properly informed the beneficiaries of the consequences of the lump-sum income at the time it was reported to the caseworker.

Finally, in 1990, in *Sullivan v. Stroop* the Court ruled on another provision of DEFRA that allowed a disregard of $50 for child support payments.[110] Because federal regulations referred to child support as financial assistance from absent parents, states did not apply the $50 disregard to child insurance benefits paid to the children of a disabled worker under the Social Security Disability Insurance program; the entire amount of the insurance benefit was used as part of the family's "income and resources" in determining AFDC eligibility.

Relying on the Supreme Court's explanation in *Gilliard* that the $50 disregard had been adopted "to mitigate the burden of the changes wrought by DEFRA," the lower court had found no rational basis for distinguishing between children receiving child support payments and children receiving disability insurance payments.

The Supreme Court disagreed, ruling that the distinction between types of beneficiaries raised no equal protection concerns. It held that Congress could reasonably decide to treat child support payments differently from other payments to children in an effort to encourage parents to support their children. Moreover, the Court found that Congress had consistently defined "child support" as payments from absent parents and there was no evidence that it intended to deviate from the "common usage" of the term.

Conclusion

Joel Handler maintains that although "not our largest or most expensive social welfare program," AFDC is "our most troublesome . . . . It is the program most closely associated with the term 'welfare' in the public's mind, especially when it is combined with 'problem' or 'mess.' "[111]

The turbulent history of the AFDC program bears out this assessment, especially in light of recent efforts to limit the reach of AFDC to needy children. The AFDC program was created with divided responsibilities for policymaking with states exercising a great deal of autonomy over determinations of eligibility and allocation of benefits in the early years. For the most part, decisions over benefits and eligibility, especially in the South, reflected the racial bias of state officials and led to the exclusion of members of minority groups from the program. For the first thirty years of its existence, the AFDC program primarily served white widows and their children.

In the 1960s, as the nation began to pay more attention to the problems of race and poverty, there were increasing efforts to expand the welfare rolls to minority families. During this time, as well, public assistance beneficiaries and applicants turned to the federal courts seeking judicial annulment of state policies that limited enrollment and benefits. Thus, the courts began to play an important role in AFDC policymaking.

Although welfare reformers hoped the Court would accept their claims that the Constitution guaranteed a "right to life," the Court refused to adopt this far-reaching principle that would require states to distribute governmental resources more equitably. Instead the Court based its rulings barring states from denying eligibility through residency requirements and arbitrarily removing beneficiaries from the welfare rolls on non-welfare principles such as the right to travel or due process. When squarely faced with demands for redistribution of economic resources on behalf of children in *Dandridge*, the Court refused to support the litigants' constitutional claims. Moreover, although in *King* it prohibited the state from applying the racially biased "man in the house" rule on the grounds that it was inconsistent with the Social Security Act, the Court rejected the claims of the mostly minority AFDC beneficiaries in *Jefferson*, finding no evidence of racial animus in the state's decision to provide fewer resources to them than to recipients of other need programs.

When the Court made it clear that constitutional challenges to state welfare policies would receive the same level of scrutiny as ordinary state economic and social legislation, litigants increasingly attempted to persuade the Court to strike restrictive state policies on the grounds that they conflicted with federal law. Because AFDC is an entitlement program, this litigation primarily revolved around conflicts between state and federal definitions of eligibility for benefits. Again litigants were successful in the earlier cases as the Court ruled that in the absence of clear authorization from Congress, states were not permitted to restrict AFDC eligibility or contravene the remedial purposes of the statute. The Court's emphasis on a uniform national welfare policy redounded to the benefit of the AFDC recipients and encouraged further litigation. During this time, however, without much explanation, in some opinions the Court rather contradictorily also held that congressional silence allowed states to impose more restrictive eligibility rules than the federal statute specified. These opinions reflected the Burger Court's concern for preserving the state's autonomy in social welfare policymaking.

When viewing the first twenty years of AFDC litigation as a whole, despite some setbacks and the ultimate failure of the "right to life" strategy, litigants won a significant number of victories that opened the AFDC rolls to greater numbers.

Litigants fared least well in attacking the state's authority to determine the level of benefits. After the Court made it clear that it would apply the lowest level of scrutiny to laws allocating state resources, litigants were forced to attack such policies on statutory grounds. This posed great difficulty for the plaintiffs as the Court interpreted the provision of the Social Security Act that authorized states to determine the level of benefits within their borders quite broadly. The Court's reluctance to interfere with state policymaking was most evident here, even extending to its opinion in *Rosado* where it allowed states to reduce actual benefits in the face of congressional action mandating that states raise the standard of need upon which benefits are based.

The changes in AFDC policy that were enacted during the Reagan administration as part of OBRA and DEFRA made the task of challenging welfare policies in the Supreme Court even more daunting. Suits in the third phase of litigation were characterized by challenges to laws that reflected the government's determination to reduce the AFDC rolls. Unlike in the earlier cases, in these cases the federal government, either alone or in concert with the state agency, appeared as defendant. Although the lower courts ruled in favor of the plaintiffs in these cases, finding that the new welfare policies conflicted with the U.S. Constitution as well as with the federal statute, the high court reversed.

Thus, while the Court was not principally responsible for the restrictive AFDC policies of the 1980s, its decisions indicated that the majority had little desire to reverse the results of the federal government's AFDC policymaking. The Court's posture in these cases led Justice Blackmun to denounce its "acquiescence in an administrative effort to cut the costs of the AFDC program by any means that are available."[112]

If the contemplated changes in AFDC policy are enacted into law, that is, the entitlement is abolished and children born into certain types of families are excluded, it is unlikely that the Supreme Court will be able to provide much relief on statutory grounds. It appears that plaintiffs' only possibility for success in challenging such new policies will be if they can persuade the Court to adopt a fundamental rights approach to public welfare assistance; such a possibility is remote at best.

Notes

    1. See Jonathan Kozol, *Rachel and Her Children* (New York: Ballantine Books, 1988).

2. These data were derived from Children's Defense Fund, *The State of America's Children* (Washington, D.C.: Children's Defense Fund, 1992); Committee on Ways and Means, U.S. House of Representatives, *Overview of Entitlement Programs, 1993 Green Book: Background Material and Data on Programs within the Jurisdiction of the Committee on Ways and Means* (Washington, D.C.: Government Printing Office, 1993), pp. 1217–1219; Suzanne M. Bianchi, "Children of Poverty: Why Are They Poor?" in Judith A. Chafel, ed., *Child Poverty and Public Policy* (Washington, D.C.: Urban Institute, 1993), p. 193.

3. Harrell R. Rodgers, Jr., *Poor Women, Poor Families*, 2d ed. (New York: M. E. Sharpe, 1990), pp. 13–14.

4. Timothy J. Casey, "The Family Support Act of 1988: Molehill or Mountain, Retreat or Reform?" *Clearinghouse Review* (December 1989), p. 930.

5. Children's Defense Fund, *The State of America's Children*, pp. 25–26.

6. *New York Times* (July 8, 1992): A20. See William H. Scarbrough, "Who Are the Poor? A Demographic Perspective," in Chafel, ed., *Child Poverty and Public Policy* for a good discussion of the trends in childhood poverty rates over the last three ·decades.

7. Sylvia Ann Hewlett, *When the Bough Breaks: The Cost of Neglecting Our Children* (New York: Free Press, 1991), p. 37.

8. These began to replace the Poor Laws in which families were broken up and most women and children either sent to work or confined to the poorhouse. Sheila B. Kamerman and Alfred J. Kahn, *Mothers Alone: Strategies for a Time of Change* (Dover, Mass.: Auburn House Publishing, 1988), chapter 2; Linda Gordon, *Pitied but Not Entitled: Single Mothers and the History of Welfare* (New York: Free Press, 1994), chapter 3.

9. Sheila B. Kamerman, "Toward a Child Policy Decade," *Child Welfare* 68 (July-August 1989): 375; see Michael Katz, *In the Shadow of the Poorhouse: A Social History of Welfare in America* (New York: Basic Books, 1986).

10. Frances Fox Piven and Richard A. Cloward, *Regulating the Poor: The Functions of Public Welfare*, 2d ed. (New York: Vintage Books, 1993), p. 134 n. 11; Stephanie Coontz, *The Way We Never Were* (New York: Basic Books, 1992), chapter 6; see Mimi Abramovitz, *Regulating the Lives of Women: Social Welfare Policy from Colonial Times to the Present* (Boston: South End Press, 1988).

11. Jeanne M. Giovannoni and Rosina M. Becerra, *Defining Child Abuse* (New York: Free Press, 1979), chapter 2.

12. The Social Security Disability Insurance program, enacted in 1956, provided benefits for totally and permanently disabled workers no longer capable of working.

13. See Theda Skocpol, *Protecting Soldiers and Mothers: The Political Origins of Social Policy in the United States* (Cambridge, Mass.: Belknap Press of Harvard

University, 1992) on Mothers' Pensions programs and their relationship to the AFDC program.

14. Another approach to welfare was to classify the poor as employable and unemployable. Sylvia A. Law, "Women, Work, Welfare, and the Preservation of Patriarchy," *University of Pennsylvania Law Review* 131 (1983): 1249–1339 argues that society derives benefits from placing people into these categories.

15. Joel F. Handler, " 'Constructing the Political Spectacle': The Interpretation of Entitlements, Legalization, and Obligations in Social Welfare History," *Brooklyn Law Review* 56 (1990): 906.

16. Paul A. Levy, "The Durability of Supreme Court Welfare Reforms of the 1960s," *Social Service Review* 66 (June 1992): 215–236; see Winifred Bell, *Aid to Dependent Children* (New York: Columbia University Press, 1965) for a discussion on the manner in which local administrators used "suitability" to determine eligibility for ADC. See also Gordon, *Pitied but Not Entitled.*

17. Handler, "Constructing the Political Spectacle."

18. Piven and Cloward, *Regulating the Poor*, chapter 4.

19. Irwin Garfinkel and Sara S. McLanahan, *Single Mothers and Their Children: A New American Dilemma* (Washington, D.C.: Urban Institute Press, 1986), chapter 4.

20. Thomas J. Kane and Mary Jo Bane, "The Context for Welfare Reform," in Mary Jo Bane and David T. Ellwood, *Welfare Realities: From Rhetoric to Reform* (Cambridge: Harvard University Press, 1994), p. 11.

21. See Piven and Cloward, *Regulating the Poor*, chapter 11, for a discussion of various state and local work programs.

22. Theodore Marmor, Jerry Mashaw, and Philip L. Harvey, *America's Misunderstood Welfare State* (New York: Basic Books, 1990).

23. Kane and Bane, "The Context for Welfare Reform," in Bane and Ellwood, *Welfare Realities*, p. 12.

24. Garfinkel and McLanahan, *Single Mothers and Their Children*, p. 116; see Katherine E. Meiss and Ann VanDePol, "California's GAIN: Greater Avenues or a Narrow Path? The Politics and Policies of Welfare Reform and AFDC Work Programs in the 1980s," *Berkeley Women's Law Journal* 3 (1987/88): 49–95.

25. Joel F. Handler, "The Transformation of Aid to Families with Dependent Children: The Family Support Act in Historical Context," *Review of Law and Social Change* 16 (1987–1988): 491.

26. See Michael Katz, *The Undeserving Poor: From the War on Poverty to the War on Welfare* (New York: Pantheon Books, 1989), chapter 3. For analysis of Nixon's motivation, see Katz, *In the Shadow of the Poorhouse*, chapter 3.

27. The EITC was significantly expanded at the start of the Clinton administration. In 1990 the maximum amount refundable was $953. In the 1993 Omnibus Budget Reconciliation Act the EITC percentage was increased and amounted to $2,038 for a family with one child earning at least $7,750; it increased over time and with the number of children in the family. The cut-off for the EITC was a $23,760 income for families with one child, and $27,000 for families with two children. Childless workers also qualify for a more modest EITC, although the cut-off there is $9,000 a year. Rodgers, *Poor Women, Poor Families*, p. 124; *Congressional Quarterly Weekly* (September 18, 1993): 2490; see Bane and Ellwood, *Welfare Realities*.

28. *New York Times* (March 17, 1981): A1. The Department of Health, Education, and Welfare (HEW) was redesignated as the Department of Health and Human Services (HHS) in 1979.

29. Michael Neuhardt, "The 1981 AFDC Amendments: Rhetoric and Reality," *University of Dayton Law Review* 8 (1982): 81.

30. The standard of need was always below the poverty level.

31. Robert Moffitt, "Work Incentives in the AFDC System: An Analysis of the 1981 Reforms," *American Economic Review* 76 (May 1986): 219–223.

32. Rodgers, *Poor Women, Poor Families*, chapter 4; Marian Wright Edelman, *Families in Peril: An Agenda for Social Change* (Cambridge: Harvard University Press, 1987).

33. See Robert Moffitt, "Work Incentives," for studies of the effect of "disregards" on work incentives.

34. Casey, "The Family Support Act of 1988," p. 934; *Congressional Quarterly Weekly* (August 15, 1981): 1493.

35. Committee on Ways and Means, U.S. House of Representatives, *Overview of Entitlement Programs, 1993 Green Book*, pp. 738–739; Rodgers, *Poor Women, Poor Families*, chapter 4.

36. Tom Joe and Cheryl Rogers, *By the Few for the Few* (Lexington, Mass.: Lexington Books, 1985), chapter 3.

37. Neuhardt, "The 1981 AFDC Amendments."

38. David T. Ellwood, *Poor Support: Poverty in the American Family* (New York: Basic Books, 1988), p. 152.

39. Meiss and VanDePol, "California's GAIN"; Bane and Ellwood, *Welfare Realities*.

40. Ellwood, *Poor Support*, chapter 3.

41. *Congressional Quarterly Weekly* (March 28, 1992): 810.

42. Bane and Ellwood, *Welfare Realities*, p. 25.

43. Handler, "The Transformation of Aid to Families with Dependent Children," p. 515.

44. Sheldon Danziger, "Fighting Poverty and Reducing Welfare Dependency," in Phoebe H. Cottingham and David T. Ellwood, eds., *Welfare Policy for the 1990s* (Cambridge: Harvard University Press, 1989).

45. Andrea Paterson, "Between Helping the Child and Punishing the Mother: Homelessness among AFDC Families," *Harvard Women's Law Journal* 12 (1989): 237–259.

46. Peter B. Edelman, "Toward a Comprehensive Antipoverty Strategy: Getting Beyond the Silver Bullet," *The Georgetown Law Journal* 81 (1993): 1707. Race plays a role in attitudes toward welfare recipients as well. African Americans constitute a disproportionate share of the welfare rolls, but the majority of welfare recipients are white. The public's hostility to welfare stems, in part, from a misperception that AFDC is predominantly a program for racial minorities. See *New York Times* (September 17, 1995): A1.

47. Committee on Ways and Means, U.S. House of Representatives, *Overview of Entitlement Programs, 1993 Green Book*, section 7.

48. Only four states, California, Connecticut, Hawaii, and Vermont (and a portion of a fifth—New York's Suffolk County) allowed maximum monthly benefits of $600 or more. Committee on Ways and Means, U.S. House of Representatives, *Overview of Entitlement Programs, 1993 Green Book*, pp. 655–661; Children's Defense Fund, *The State of America's Children*, pp. 71–121.

49. Committee on Ways and Means, U.S. House of Representatives, *Overview of Entitlement Programs, 1993 Green Book*, p. 615.

50. Edelman, "Toward a Comprehensive Antipoverty Strategy," p. 1722.

51. Sheila B. Kamerman, "Doing Better by Children: Focus on Families," *The Journal of Law and Politics* 8 (Fall 1991): 79.

52. Bianchi, "Children of Poverty," p. 103, citing Sheldon Danziger and Jonathan Stern, "The Causes and Consequences of Child Poverty in the United States," *Innocenti Occasional Papers, Number 10* (Florence: UNICEF International Child Development Centre, 1990).

53. Marmor, Mashaw, and Harvey, *America's Misunderstood Welfare State*, p. 85, table 4.2.

54. Rodgers, *Poor Women, Poor Families,* chapter 4.

55. Bane and Ellwood, *Welfare Realities,* chapter 5; Garfinkel and McLanahan, *Single Mothers and Their Children*, chapter 2, also believe in preferential treatment for single mothers.

56. *Congressional Quarterly Weekly* (November 5, 1994): 3182.

57. To ensure discovery of all Supreme Court opinions relating to the AFDC program between 1935 and 1993, a Lexis search of the GENFED library, US file, was conducted, using "AFDC or Aid w/5 Famil! w/5 Dependent Child! or Title IV-A" as the search terms. This search yielded sixty-three decisions. Of these, there were twenty-seven opinions that were *relevant* to the AFDC program, that is, opinions in which the Court resolved disputes over AFDC policy by interpreting a state or federal law or regulation. Some of these opinions are discussed in the notes.

58. This concept of "entitlement" differs from the definition of statutory entitlement, the deprivation of which may involve a due process violation.

59. Piven and Cloward, *Regulating the Poor*, chapter 10.

60. Barbara Sard, "The Role of the Courts in Welfare Reform," in Elizabeth A. Mulroy, ed., *Women As Single Parents* (Dover, Mass.: Auburn House Publishing, 1988).

61. See Martha F. Davis, *Brutal Need: Lawyers and the Welfare Rights Movement, 1960–1973* (New Haven: Yale University Press, 1993), chapter 8.

62. Susan E. Lawrence, *The Poor in Court* (Princeton: Princeton University Press, 1990), chapter 1. In 1975 the Legal Services Corporation, with a different perspective on appellate litigation, replaced the LSP. See Marie A. Failinger and Larry May, "Litigating against Poverty: Legal Services and Group Representation," *Ohio State Law Journal* 45 (1984): 2–56 for discussion of the LSC.

63. Lawrence, *The Poor in Court*, chapter 3.

64. Legal aid services were underfunded as well. Studies have estimated that only 10 percent of poor people were receiving legal services from legal aid organizations. Sar A. Levitan, *The Great Society's Poor Law: A New Approach to Poverty* (Baltimore: Johns Hopkins University Press, 1969), p. 178.

65. Sparer modeled his campaign for welfare reform on the campaign for racial equality during the 1930s and 1940s. Levy, "The Durability of Supreme Court Welfare Reforms of the 1960s"; Lawrence, *The Poor in Court*, chapter 2. For the differing perspectives of practitioners' legal strategy for welfare reform, compare Davis, *Brutal Need*, with Samuel Krislov, "The OEO Lawyers Fail to Constitutionalize a Right to Welfare: A Study in the Uses and Limits of the Judicial Process," *Minnesota Law Review* 58 (1973): 211–245.

66. See R. Shep Melnick, *Between the Lines: Interpreting Welfare Rights* (Washington, D.C.: Brookings Institute, 1994), chapter 5.

67. 392 U.S. 309 (1968).

68. In his concurring opinion, Justice William Douglas stated he would strike the regulation on constitutional grounds as the lower court had done. He found no "rational connection" between the state policy and the children's need.

69. Two years later, in *Lewis v. Martin*, 397 U.S. 552 (1970), the Court extended *King* by invalidating a California law that presumed the income of a "man assuming

the role of spouse" (MARS) or a non-adopting stepfather was available to AFDC children and deducted his income from the AFDC benefits. The U.S. solicitor general's office and the CSWPL filed amici curiae briefs urging the Supreme Court to reverse the ruling of the court below and declare MARS invalid.

Similarly, in *Engelman v. Amos*, 404 U.S. 23 (1971), in a per curiam opinion, the Court affirmed a lower court ruling, striking a New Jersey regulation that considers a stepfather's income without regard to whether the income is available to the dependent child. And in *Van Lare v. Hurley*, 421 U.S. 338 (1975), the Court struck a state regulation that reduced AFDC shelter allowances solely because the family allowed a non-paying lodger, not responsible for the child's support, to live in the home. Citing *King* and *Martin*, the Court held that states were barred from reducing AFDC benefits on the assumption that "nonlegally responsible persons" contribute to the children's support.

70. 394 U.S. 618 (1969).

71. Plaintiffs in Pennsylvania and the District of Columbia challenged similar laws and also won in the courts below. The Supreme Court consolidated the three cases for review.

72. *Shapiro* was the first case to apply the "compelling state interest" test, or "strict scrutiny," to laws involving fundamental rights. Bernard Schwartz, *The Ascent of Pragmatism: The Burger Court in Action* (Reading, Mass.: Addison-Wesley, 1990), chapter 10.

73. Elizabeth Bussiere, "The Failure of Constitutional Welfare Rights in the Warren Court," *Political Science Quarterly* 109 (1984): 105–131.

74. 397 U.S. 254 (1970).

75. Charles Reich, "Individual Rights and Social Welfare: The Emerging Legal Issues," *Yale Law Journal* 74 (1965): 1245–1257; Charles Reich, "The New Property," *Yale Law Journal* 73 (1964): 733–787.

76. *Kelly*, 397 U.S. at 264 (emphasis in the original).

77. A few years later in *Mathews v. Eldridge*, 424 U.S. 319 (1976), the Supreme Court essentially limited *Kelly* to its facts by holding that states are only required to provide pre-termination hearings for AFDC recipients.

78. 397 U.S. 471 (1970).

79. A decade later, in *Harris v. Rosario*, 446 U.S. 651 (1980), the Court again rejected an equal protection challenge to an AFDC policy. In a per curiam opinion the Court held that Congress's decision to provide a lower level of reimbursement under the AFDC program to Puerto Rico than to the fifty states was justified because it had a "rational basis."

80. *Dandridge*, 397 U.S. at 485.

81. 397 U.S. 397 (1970). *Rosado* played a crucial role in establishing the right of welfare beneficiaries to sue in federal court. The principal issue of concern to the

62 Children in Court

Court in *Rosado* was whether the lower federal court had jurisdiction to decide the case, specifically, whether it should have retained "pendent jurisdiction" over the statutory claim when the constitutional claim that had been the basis of federal jurisdiction was dismissed. After finding the lower court had proper jurisdiction, the Supreme Court questioned whether plaintiffs, as beneficiaries of a federally funded state welfare program, had a right to sue the state in federal court to force it to comply with its statutory obligation to the federal government. Without extended discussion, the Court concluded that they had a right to seek relief in the federal courts because they were unable to intervene in agency reviews of state welfare programs.

82. *Rosado*, 397 U.S. at 413.

83. 400 U.S. 309 (1971).

84. 406 U.S. 535 (1972).

85. *Jefferson*, 406 U.S. at 575 (Marshall, J., dissenting). Justice Marshall noted these facts in his dissent.

86. *Jefferson*, 406 U.S. at 549.

87. Krislov, "The OEO Lawyers Fail to Constitutionalize a Right to Welfare."

88. Quoted in Aryeh Neier, *Only Judgment: The Limits of Litigation in Social Change* (Middletown, Conn.: Wesleyan University Press, 1982), p. 138.

89. *Califano v. Westcott*, 443 U.S. 76 (1979), was the only other AFDC case decided in favor of the beneficiary on constitutional grounds. Using intermediate scrutiny, the Court held that providing AFDC benefits to familes with unemployed fathers, but not unemployed mothers, violated the equal protection clause. An amicus curiae brief filed by the American Civil Liberties Union supported the sex-neutral interpretation of the statute.

90. Fred C. Doolittle, "State-Imposed Nonfinancial Eligibility Conditions in AFDC: Confusion in Supreme Court Decisions and a Need for Congressional Clarification," *Harvard Journal on Legislation* 19 (1982): 1–48.

91. 404 U.S. 282 (1971).

92. *Townsend*, 404 U.S. at 286.

93. 406 U.S. 598 (1972).

94. *Carleson*, 406 U.S. at 601.

95. 413 U.S. 405 (1973).

96. 416 U.S. 251 (1974).

97. 420 U.S. 575 (1975). Doolittle, "State-Imposed Nonfinancial Eligibility Conditions in AFDC."

98. 421 U.S. 707 (1975). This program was initially limited to families with unemployed *fathers* only. In 1981 Congress limited eligibility in this program to families in which the "principle wage earner, that is, the one whose income has been greater for the last two years, is unemployed."

99. Two years later in *Batterton v. Francis*, 432 U.S. 416 (1977), the Court held that a federal regulation authorizing states to deny AFDC-UF benefits to fathers whose unemployment resulted from a labor dispute or other reason that would have disqualified them from receiving unemployment compensation benefits under state law was a valid exercise of the authority of HHS to interpret the Social Security Act.

100. 436 U.S. 725 (1978).

101. *Mandley*, 436 U.S. at 738 (quoting *King*, 392 U.S. at 334).

102. 440 U.S. 125 (1979).

103. 457 U.S. 132 (1982).

104. 470 U.S. 184 (1985).

105. 481 U.S. 368 (1987).

106. 483 U.S. 587 (1987).

107. Amy E. Hirsch, "Income Deeming in the AFDC Program: Using Dual Track Family Law to Make Poor Women Poorer," *Review of Law and Social Change* 16 (1987–1988): 713–740.

108. Case notes, "*Bowen v. Gilliard*, 107 S.Ct. 3008 (1987)," *Journal of Family Law* 26 (1987–1988): 846–851.

109. 485 U.S. 415 (1988).

110. 496 U.S. 478 (1990).

111. Handler, "The Transformation of Aid to Families with Dependent Children," p. 459 n. 4.

112. *Stroop*, 496 U.S. at 496 (Blackmun, J., dissenting).

3

THE WOMEN, INFANTS, AND CHILDREN PROGRAM AND HEAD START

The problems of poverty are manifested in a number of ways: nutritional and educational deficiencies are crucial factors affecting the lives of poor children. Two federal programs aimed at remedying the scarcities caused by poverty in these areas are the Special Supplemental Food Program for Women, Infants, and Children (WIC) and Head Start.

The WIC Program

The U.S. Department of Agriculture (USDA) provides food to needy children under the authority of the National School Lunch Act and the Child Nutrition Act of 1966. Programs funded through these acts include the National School Lunch Program, the Special Milk Program for Children, the School Breakfast Program, the Commodity Supplemental Food Program, the Summer Food Service Program, the Child Care Food Program, and WIC.

WIC furnishes low-income mothers and their children with special vouchers for infant formula and other specified foods.[1] Administered by the Food and Nutrition Service (FNS) of the USDA, by 1979 there were WIC programs in forty-nine states, twenty-seven Native American agencies, and in Puerto Rico and the Virgin Islands. States must submit an annual plan of operation to the secretary of agriculture. Upon approval, the federal government provides cash grants to states that in turn fund local agencies, typically county or municipal departments of health, hospitals, or community action agencies; states are not required to provide matching funds. The local units certify eligibility and provide vouchers or coupons (WIC checks) to allow recipients to purchase designated foods at authorized vendors; in some areas the local agencies distribute the food.[2] In 1988 the mean average cost of a WIC food package was $31.00.[3]

WIC Participants

Unlike AFDC, WIC is not an entitlement program and requires periodic congressional authorizations and appropriations. Because its funding has always fallen short of the need, WIC has never fully served the total eligible population. Applicants are ranked according to priorities established in the federal regulations; under these guidelines, pregnant women and infants are accorded the highest priority.[4]

WIC's average annual participation rate rose from slightly less than eighty-eight thousand in fiscal 1974 to almost two million in fiscal 1980. According to the USDA, however, this number reflects only about one-fifth of those eligible. In 1980 the USDA estimated that almost nine million women and children met the program's criteria for income and nutritional risk.[5]

Participation in WIC continues to grow: by 1988, there were almost three and a half (3.4) million WIC recipients.[6] But participation has not kept apace with the need. In 1989 the Director of the Food Research and Action Center (FRAC), a public interest group, estimated that nearly three million children were being excluded from the WIC program.[7] By 1992, WIC was serving somewhat over five (5.3) million women and children, a figure also estimated to include only about half of those eligible.[8]

WIC has proven effectiveness as a preventive program. According to a 1978 Senate report, "WIC participants demonstrated a substantial reduction in anemia, a reduced incidence of low-birthweight infants, and improvements in achieving proper weight in participants who were underweight or overweight when entering the program."[9] Thus, money for WIC contributes to reductions in federal spending through lower costs for postnatal medical care.[10] Indeed, it has been calculated that every dollar spent on WIC realizes savings of more than three dollars.[11] In 1985 the House Select Committee on Children, Youth, and Families designated WIC "as the first among eight 'cost-effective programs for children': programs that improve children's lives and save money in other programs."[12]

Funding for WIC

The idea for creating a nutrition program for indigent pregnant women arose out of the need to produce more favorable birth outcomes and improve childhood development by "meet[ing] the nutritional needs of young children from low-income families at their most critical stage of development, and . . . provid[ing] extra protein-rich food to their high-risk mothers during pregnancy and while they are nursing."[13]

On September 26, 1972, Congress approved a two-year WIC pilot program, as part of § 17 of the Child Nutrition Act. WIC was created to generate food supplements for low-income pregnant or lactating women and their children under four considered to be at nutritional risk because of "inadequate nutrition or inadequate income."

The program was authorized for the fiscal year beginning July 1, 1972, with the secretary of agriculture directed to spend $20 million a year for each of the two years and to utilize "Section 32" funds if insufficient funds were appropriated.[14] Despite the $20 million authorization, the USDA expended no funds for the WIC program during the first year of its existence, and even failed to promulgate regulations to implement the program.[15]

Over the next few years Congress continued to authorize additional spending for WIC. In 1973 it amended the National School Lunch and Child Nutrition Acts to extend the WIC program until June 30, 1975, and increased its authorization to $40 million. Then on June 30, 1974, Congress authorized $100 million (plus all unspent funds) for the WIC program for the 1975 fiscal year. Despite these authorizations, however, the USDA spent less than $25 million on WIC during the 1974 fiscal year, with fewer than one hundred thousand women and children participating in the program.

In 1975 disagreement between Congress and the executive branch arose over the funding of a number of federal child nutrition programs, including the school lunch and breakfast programs and non-school food programs such as WIC. In vetoing the new spending bill, President Gerald Ford expressed concern about "the steady expansion of Federal child nutrition subsidies to increasing numbers of non-needy children." He characterized the bill to increase authorizations for WIC (and the other child nutrition programs) as fiscally irresponsible and proposed instead to consolidate all child nutrition programs into state block grants beginning in the fiscal 1976 budget.[16]

The Subcommittee on Agricultural Research and General Legislation held hearings during April 1975 to consider several proposed nutrition bills with the only testimony favoring the block grant approach presented by the USDA. Witnesses, consisting of representatives of food programs, food producers, nutrition groups, and medical and dental professionals, all voiced concern that along with other special food programs, WIC would be eliminated if the block grant approach were adopted.[17]

The block grant proposal, known as the Child Food Assistance Act of 1975, would have combined all child nutrition funding into one appropriation. Supporting the administration's bill, the USDA representative, Assistant Secretary of Agriculture Richard Feltner, stressed that by restricting WIC services to the poor only there would be considerable savings (an estimated $4 billion over five years) and food would become available for the 700,000 needy children not now receiving it.[18] Under the administration's proposal, states would not be reimbursed for spending for the non-poor.

Congress rejected the block grant approach and enacted the 1975 National School Lunch and Child Nutrition Amendments, continuing the WIC program through September 30, 1978 (the end of the 1978 fiscal year), and authorizing appropriations of $250 million a year. The secretary of agriculture was ordered to use Section 32 funds to make up the difference in fiscal 1976 and 1977 if the entire $250 million was not appropriated by Congress and to carry over any unspent WIC funds from previous years through the end of the authorized period. Additionally, the secretary was directed to form a National Advisory Council on Maternal, Fetal, and Infant Nutrition and to submit annual reports to Congress and the president.

States were promised increased funds for administrative costs and directed to use part of the funding to provide nutrition education for program recipients; they were also permitted to fund Native American "tribes, bands, or groups" as local WIC agencies. The law also extended eligibility to five year olds.

On October 3, 1975, Ford vetoed the bill. A few days later, in a 397 to 18 vote, the House overrode the veto; the Senate later followed suit in a 79 to 13 vote.[19] On October 7, 1975, the bill to extend the federal food programs, including WIC, became law. However, despite Congress's continuing support for WIC, the executive branch refused to spend the appropriated amount, allocating only about $65 million for WIC by the end of the 1975 fiscal year.

In 1978, with WIC's funding authorization expiring, Congress rejected suggestions to establish WIC as a four-year entitlement. It compromised by creating a capped entitlement with guaranteed funding for the first two years (at $550 million for the first year and $800 million for the second). The yearly authorizations for the last two years would rise to $900 million for fiscal 1981 and $950 million for fiscal 1982.[20] Senator George McGovern, Democrat of South Dakota and sponsor of the bill, agreed to the compromise but argued that WIC was a "special case." In his view, the four-year entitlement would have been more appropriate, given the program's uneven pattern of funding. The compromise bill also mandated a uniform standard of eligibility in place of varying local standards. The new eligibility requirements were designed to eliminate the possibility that non-poor persons would receive WIC program benefits.

Seeking to demonstrate the Carter administration's commitment to the re-authorization bill, Carol Tucker Foreman, assistant secretary of agriculture for food and consumer services, testified before the Senate Committee on Agriculture, Nutrition, and Forestry that WIC was "one of the most effective and successful health and nutrition programs operated by the Federal Government."[21] Notwithstanding this endorsement, however, the Carter White House urged Congress to lower the age of eligibility from five to three.

Rejecting a recommendation from his Office of Management and Budget to veto the bill because of its inflationary influence, Carter signed the Child Nutrition Amendments of 1978 in November, extending the WIC program for another four years (through fiscal 1982). As part of the price of obtaining his signature, however, members of Congress agreed that they would trim WIC funds from $800 million to $750 million in the 1980 fiscal year. The law also required the secretary to facilitate the participation of migratory workers and their families in the program, and to set aside money for nutritional education for WIC recipients; 20 percent of the total funds were earmarked for administrative expenses.[22]

In an effort to preclude cost-cutting by the incoming Reagan administration, in December 1980, Congress extended authorizations for the several child nutrition programs, including WIC, through fiscal 1985.

WIC was nevertheless targeted for cuts by the Reagan White House in the 1980s. In 1981 the administration sought a 30 percent reduction in WIC spending for the 1982 fiscal year—from $927 million to $653 million.[23] Demonstrating its support for WIC, Congress not only rejected the proposal, but for the next three years funded WIC at higher levels than the administration requested.

Despite this strong endorsement, the administration and congressional WIC supporters continued to wage war over funding. In 1982 the administration sought to eliminate WIC as a separate program and place it within the maternal and child health block grant. The administration plan proposed to increase the block grant funds by $650 million, less than the current spending for WIC of almost $1 billion.[24] As part of its assault on WIC, the administration also refused to release a report showing that WIC was successful in combatting fetal and infant mortality, especially among African Americans and the less educated.

Congress again rejected the block grant approach, but although the level of funding increased to over $1 billion by 1984, and there were over three million participants in the program, funds were still inadequate to meet the needs of all eligible beneficiaries.[25]

In 1984 when funding for WIC and other child nutrition programs was about to expire, it was reauthorized in a House Education and Labor Committee bill with increased funding levels through fiscal 1988. Although the bill had originally proposed transforming WIC into a capped entitlement program that would guarantee specified appropriations and preclude administration deferral of spending, this provision was deleted before the final House vote.

Congress adjourned without acting on the measure, and WIC funding was provided in continuing resolutions for the next two years through fiscal 1986.

Finally, late in 1986, Congress extended WIC authorizations through fiscal 1989 and increased its funding levels to $1.58 billion in fiscal 1986, to "such sums as may be necessary" in 1987 and 1988, and to $1.78 billion in 1989. These funding increases were aimed only at retaining the current rate of participation among WIC recipients.[26]

Following the election of George Bush, the White House endorsed proposals to improve the lives of poor children, with increased funding for a variety of child welfare programs, including WIC. At the time of the reauthorization, WIC was reaching approximately four million children and their mothers, estimated to be about half of those eligible. On November 10, 1989, with strong bipartisan support, Congress passed the Child Nutrition and WIC

Reauthorization Act of 1989, reauthorizing the WIC program for five more years—until the end of fiscal 1994—with an authorization of $2.16 billion for fiscal 1990 and "such sums as may be necessary" for the next four fiscal years.

The increased WIC funding was expected to allow an additional 300,000 women and children to receive WIC benefits. Other provisions aimed at raising the participation level, and permitted states, for the first time, to offer WIC benefits to women and infants in state or local prisons and homeless shelters, as well as to children in foster care or otherwise part of the child welfare system. The act also required states to contain program costs, especially the cost of infant formula, to stretch WIC dollars further. In signing the bill, Bush praised the competitive bidding system, already adopted by over half the states, that lowered the costs of infant formula.[27]

During this time Congress entertained a variety of proposals related to WIC. Legislative initiatives such as Colorado Democrat Patricia Schroeder's KIDSNET would have provided full funding for WIC, as well as other children's programs such as childhood immunization. Republican Senator Robert Dole of Kansas and Democratic Senator Patrick Leahy of Vermont sponsored a bill entitled the "Every Fifth Child Act" to increase funding for children's programs including WIC, the name stemming from the statistic of every fifth child in the United States living in poverty and likely hungry. Neither bill was successful, primarily because of the budgetary climate.

By the end of the Bush administration, despite the universal acclaim for WIC, including support for increased funding from both sides of the aisle and both ends of Pennsylvania Avenue, WIC was still underfunded and served only about half of the eligible population. Although still considered by some a candidate for entitlement status, the budget deficit precluded any attempt to establish WIC as an entitlement program and remove it from the annual battles over authorizations and appropriations.

Although it never achieved the status of entitlement, WIC was reauthorized in the Agriculture, Rural Development, Food and Drug Administration, and Related Agencies Appropriation Act of 1994. When signing the bill, on October 21, 1993, President Clinton commended Congress for accepting his "goal to phase in full funding" for WIC.[28] As part of the provisions for child nutrition programs, Title IV of the act authorized $3.2 billion "to remain available" for "necessary expenses to carry out" the WIC program through September 30, 1995.

WIC has always enjoyed bipartisan support in Congress. Indeed, even a WIC critic, who labeled it "an unmitigated disaster," admitted that "few government programs have ever been as popular, not to say sacrosanct" as WIC.[29] Its supporters in the Senate range from Democratic Senator Edward Kennedy of Massachusetts to Republican Senator Alan Simpson of Wyoming. Yet despite its successes and broad appeal across party lines, WIC has never been able to secure the financial support to achieve the goal of feeding all the poor and hungry women and children in the nation. And as with the AFDC program, future funding for WIC remains uncertain with the 104th Congress targeting numerous food programs for spending cuts. Echoing the past, congressional Republicans have renewed proposals to include WIC as part of a nutritional block grant to the states, creating even more uncertainty about its future.

WIC Litigation

With statutes and regulations to interpret, not surprisingly—as in the AFDC program—the federal courts have played a role in WIC policymaking. For the most part, however, because the participants in WIC litigation brought an entirely different set of issues to the courts than did AFDC litigants, the nature of the decisions made with respect to the two programs differed greatly.

The USDA and WIC

In the early 1970s, WIC recipients, aided by a number of public interest groups, including FRAC, enlisted the aid of the federal courts in forcing the executive branch to spend the funds designated for the WIC program. In ruling on these cases, the federal courts were forced to referee between the other two branches of government, a role they are usually reluctant to assume.[30]

Shortly after WIC was implemented, in 1973, in *Dotson v. Butz*, eligible recipients filed a class action suit in federal court to reverse the USDA's refusal to fund the program.[31] They sought an injunction to compel Secretary of Agriculture Earl Butz to spend the funds for WIC that Congress had directed it to. On August 3, 1973, Judge Oliver Gasch of the District of Columbia District Court ordered the USDA to issue regulations and process applications for funding until the entire amount—the full $40 million allocated to fiscal 1973 and 1974—was expended by the end of the 1974 fiscal year. To do otherwise, reasoned the court, would allow the executive branch to withhold an entire year of congressional funding simply by failing to implement the program within the first year.

At the end of June 1974 plaintiffs returned to court, claiming that although Congress authorized and appropriated $100 million for fiscal 1975 (plus any remaining unspent money from previous years), the USDA had spent only $25 million during fiscal 1974. Because of the agency's continued refusal to issue funds for the WIC program, Gasch issued another order on July 29, 1974, requiring the USDA to spend the $100 million for WIC program costs during fiscal 1975 plus any unspent carry-over funds from fiscal 1974. He directed the agency to obligate carry-over funds from 1975 by funding new clinics and/or continuing to fund those in operation.

The executive branch continued to oppose spending for WIC, however, and a few years later, in *Durham v. Butz*, another suit was filed against the secretary of agriculture and the director of the Office of Management and Budget in an attempt to force the expenditure of WIC funds. Plaintiffs sought to require the USDA to spend a total of $285 million during fiscal 1976 (the $250 million authorized in 1975 legislation plus an approximate $35 million of unspent fiscal 1975 funds).

The plaintiffs charged that executive branch officials improperly "impounded" millions of dollars by failing to spend money designated by Congress for the WIC program. Because the funds had been withheld, they claimed, at least half a million potential recipients had been excluded from WIC benefits.[32]

The district court found that the department had only spent about $49 million in the first half of the 1976 fiscal year and would only spend a total of $160 million during the entire fiscal year. Additionally, the judge found that WIC had failed to serve more than 500,000 needy mothers and children because the department had not acted on new applications from over two hundred local health clinics seeking to operate WIC programs and had wrongfully delayed approving existing clinic applications. Nor had the Secretary allocated money for expanding services in existing programs; the only new WIC programs had been created from existing federal supplemental feeding programs that were allowed to "switch over."

On June 22, 1976, Gasch ordered the agriculture secretary to spend all the WIC money that remained unspent since the beginning of the 1975 fiscal year, that is, to spend a total of $687.5 million by June 30, 1978—the end of fiscal 1978.[33] Following the example set in *Dotson*, the judge directed the secretary to add previous unused funds to the amounts spent in subsequent years. He ordered the executive to fund all eligible WIC clinics with applications pending until the amount authorized, including any carry-over funds, was spent.

The rulings in the *Dotson* and *Durham* litigation, although ultimately leading to the court-ordered release of the WIC funds, were relatively short-lived victories. For although the litigants were able to persuade the court that the secretary had wrongfully withheld funds from the WIC program, they were given no opportunity to challenge the inadequate delivery of WIC services.

WIC Vendors

The bulk of the federal court decisions involving the WIC program arose from suits brought by retailers and vendors associated with it.[34] These cases largely revolved around actions brought by store owners to challenge their disqualification as WIC distributors, as well as to contest the subsequent revocation of their more lucrative food stamp contracts by the USDA. Owners, generally unaware that being disqualified as WIC distributors also serves to disqualify them as food stamp distributors, do not typically contest the WIC sanction. They subsequently challenge their disqualification from WIC when they realize its implications for their status in the food stamp program.

For the most part, the courts upheld the actions of the USDA in regulating the WIC program. But while these rulings theoretically affected the distribution of WIC services, they had little or no direct effect on the interests of WIC clientele. Only one retailer case, *Hong Kong Supermarket v. California*, decided in 1987, had the potential of affecting WIC recipients.[35] Hong Kong Supermarket filed suit on behalf of its Southeast Asian WIC customers, claiming that the WIC regulations denied them equal protection of the law. The market argued that because Southeast Asian women and children suffered from lactose intolerance, they were unable to use the prescribed milk and milk products distributed through WIC. The court dismissed the complaint, ruling that because the vendor's interests were not inextricably intertwined with those of the WIC recipients, the market lacked standing to sue on their behalf.

Demonstrating the value of WIC to the food industry, there were two cases involving conflict between corporate litigants and the federal government. In *Chocolate Manufacturer's Association v. Block,* the chocolate industry brought suit over rules related to the distribution of chocolate milk in the WIC program.[36] They claimed the FNS violated the Administrative Procedure Act and WIC regulations by failing to provide adequate notice of a WIC rule change. Reversing the lower court, the Fourth Circuit directed the agency to reopen the public comment period to allow the chocolate manufacturer's group to participate.

The other case was part of an ongoing action by the Federal Trade Commission (FTC) against Abbott Laboratories for allegedly driving up the costs of the WIC program by fixing prices and rigging bids for infant formula.[37] The court granted the FTC a preliminary injunction, in anticipation of a trial on the price-fixing counts. Shortly after the FTC had announced its charges, Congress enacted legislation to fine companies found guilty of anti-competitive practices injurious to the WIC program up to $100 million a year and to bar them from participating in the WIC market for up to two years.[38]

Distribution of WIC Benefits

There was only one reported decision in which WIC beneficiaries challenged the distribution of WIC benefits through litigation. In *Alexander v. Polk*, which resulted in opinions from two lower courts and one appellate court over a seven-year span, WIC recipients charged local authorities with unlawfully restricting WIC eligibility.

The lawsuit began in August 1978 when a group of WIC mothers filed a class action suit against the city of Philadelphia, charging it with violating the 1966 Child Nutrition Act and its regulations as well as the due process clause of the Fourteenth Amendment by terminating the benefits of their four-year-old children.

Philadelphia had contracted with the state to operate the WIC program, with spending limits up to $300,000 a month (plus administrative expenses) and a recommended caseload of fifteen hundred recipients. When it discovered in November 1977 that its caseload exceeded this number by several thousand, the city eliminated postpartum women and children over four with no medical problems from the program. In instituting these cuts, it claimed to be acting in accord with the priorities specified in the federal WIC regulations.

Under this scheme, pregnant and breastfeeding women and infants with documented medical or clinical indicators of need for supplemental food were first in line for benefits; other infants up to six months old were the next highest priority, followed by older children with documented medical need. Pregnant and breastfeeding women and infants under six months with only an "inadequate dietary pattern" rather than clinical or medical indicators of inadequate nutrition were lower in priority. Finally, children over four and postpartum women with "dietary insufficiency" were placed in the lowest priority; they were informed their benefits were terminated when they appeared at the local health facility to obtain their WIC vouchers.

The WIC recipients attempted to stop the city from terminating their benefits, claiming that the statute entitled them to individual determinations of their eligibility by "competent professional authority."[39] Asserting that the city lacked authority to implement the priority program on its own, without a direct order from the state, they argued the regulations prohibited the city from creating a separate priority category of four year olds. They also maintained that the city's caseload was below capacity, thus making their removal unnecessary. Finally, they charged that the city's failure to provide them with written notice of termination prior to their removal violated the statute and the due process clause of the Fourteenth Amendment.

District Court Judge Alfred L. Luongo refused to grant the plaintiffs a preliminary injunction against the city. He pointed out that, with one exception, the children targeted for removal from WIC had exhibited no clinical or medical evidence of malnutrition, that they had been included in the program only because of an "inadequate dietary pattern." He did find, however, that four-year-old Leon Truitt was suffering from anemia and inadequate growth patterns and should not have been removed from the program. However, despite his wrongful termination, the judge did not enjoin the city to reinstate him because by that time, he had reached his fifth birthday and was beyond WIC eligibility.

The judge was persuaded that the priority program was necessary to ensure WIC's survival, and without it, the city would be forced to abandon the entire program. Noting that the city could have decided to terminate benefits to all children with lower priority, Luongo approved its approach of removing the children least likely to suffer nutritional damage; he believed it reasonable to draw the line at four year olds.

In a telling footnote, Luongo added that a state's claim of financial distress does not usually allow it to deny benefits to those statutorily defined as eligible. However, because it is funded by "a flat grant" from the federal government, WIC is different. He said,

> the regulations recognize the limitations implicit in the manner of funding and anticipate the problems inherent in the administration of *a program with more needy people than funds to serve them*. The regulations not only contemplate the possibility of maximum spending but also specifically authorize selective participation according to the priorities [established in the regulations] to meet this contingency.[40]

Five years later, in 1983, following a trial and a decision on the merits, the district court ruled that the class of plaintiffs had a "protectible property interest" in their WIC benefits, and that the city's method of terminating their benefits had violated their due process rights. The city had erred by not providing recipients with written notice of their termination and informing them of their right to a hearing.[41] In a footnote, the judge reaffirmed his belief that the priority program was reasonable.

The judge awarded the plaintiffs damages totaling $89.75: $1 for the entire class of plaintiffs for the due process violation; $87.75 for Leon Truitt, the four year old who had been wrongfully terminated; and $1 for another four year old who was wrongfully terminated from the program after her mother used "abusive language" to a store clerk. The court denied punitive damages because the city officials had not demonstrated "callous indifference" to the plaintiff's rights.

The plaintiffs appealed but the Third Circuit affirmed the lower court on most issues, only remanding the case to allow a reassessment of some of the damages.[42]

Almost seven years of litigation in *Alexander* resulted in a nominal victory for plaintiffs. They were able to show that the city had erred in the manner in which it removed the four year olds from the WIC program, not the fact of their removal. And even this victory was fleeting as well: by the end of 1978 the city discontinued the WIC program entirely, raising anew questions about whether the *Alexander* plaintiffs had achieved anything at all.

The Head Start Program

Head Start, the early childhood program designed to compensate children for educational disadvantages, is arguably the most popular and successful of the federal programs arising out of Lyndon Johnson's War on Poverty.[43]

Head Start is funded by grants from HHS and the Indian and Migrant Program Division of Head Start to local public or private nonprofit agencies which may in turn create "delegate agencies" to implement the program. Most Head Start centers operate out of public schools and neighborhood churches. For school-sponsored programs, additional money may be obtained from funds authorized under Title I of the 1965 Elementary and Secondary Education Act.

From the program's inception in 1965 to its twenty-fifth anniversary in 1990, Head Start had served over 11 million children.[44] But like WIC, Head Start has always been undersubscribed because of insufficient funds. The nearly 500,000 children enrolled in Head Start in its silver anniversary year comprised only about 20 percent of the nation's three to five year olds living in families with incomes below the poverty line.[45] By 1994 a total of nearly 14 million children had attended Head Start, representing only 53 percent of the nation's eligible four year olds and 21 percent of eligible three year olds. Overall, participation in Head Start has been largely restricted to four year olds in half-day programs; only 15 percent of Head Start centers operate on a full school day schedule.[46]

Over the years, Head Start has evolved into a multi-faceted program with a comprehensive approach to family and child development aimed at improving the lives of low-income families. It serves as the core of many innovative programs such as the Follow Through Program, the Child Development Associate Program, and the Child and Family Resource Program.[47] According to Laura Miller, former deputy commissioner of the Administration for Children, Youth, and Families (ACYF), Head Start's strength derives from the fact that it provides a wide array of services to its clientele.[48]

There have been numerous studies on the effects of Head Start on low-income children. And although there is some evidence that early intervention does not have lasting effects unless it is followed by later educational enrichment, the general concensus is that Head Start participation advantages children and their families in a number of ways.[49] Furthermore, there is evidence that both Head Start and non-Head Start families benefit from the increased services accompanying the presence of a Head Start program in the community.[50]

Head Start's principal goal was to raise the educational level of children in poverty. With its emphasis on poor children, a high proportion of Head Start's clientele are from families receiving AFDC.[51] Nearly two-thirds of Head Start children are African American and Hispanic; whites comprise almost one-third and the remaining children served by Head Start are Asian or Native American.[52]

In recent years Head Start has been forced to deliver more comprehensive social and health services to counter the numerous devastating effects of poverty in the home. Having to deal with the increasingly difficult social problems of the poor has meant that the resources of the Head Start program have been stretched very thin.

The Origins of Head Start

The Economic Opportunity Act of 1964 created a multi-faceted attack on poverty, including such programs as Job Corps; VISTA, the domestic Peace Corps; and Community Action Programs (CAP), from which Head Start emerged. One of the driving forces behind the act was the belief that it was preferable to attack poverty by education and job training programs rather than simply continue public welfare assistance and that the poor should be involved in the planning and administration of programs intended for their benefit. The idea of Head Start grew out of this concept. Johnson named Sargent Shriver, the former director of the Peace Corps under John Kennedy, to head the Office of Economic Opportunity (OEO).

The idea for a child development project as part of a community action program had been briefly mentioned in a Senate report during the passage of the Economic Opportunity Act in 1964, but Congress played no role in the creation of Head Start. In February 1965 a panel headed by Dr. Robert Cooke, professor of pediatrics at Johns Hopkins University School of Medicine, and Sargent Shriver's family pediatrician, presented a report to Shriver suggesting a summer program to enrich the education of children in low-income families.

Head Start became known as a "National Emphasis program" of the OEO, a term used to describe federally funded programs administered through local CAP agencies.[53] Community Action Programs were not well received by local governments because involving the poor in poverty program administration deprived state and municipal bureaucracies of control over a significant amount of federal funds. But with its emphasis on education, Head Start was perceived as less threatening to local administrators; indeed, subsuming the Head Start program as a CAP within the War on Poverty was intended to deflect opposition from the other activities funded through the CAPs.[54] In the words of Sargent Shriver, "faced with local and congressional hostility, I felt that . . . Head Start could ameliorate some of this hostility to OEO's CAP efforts by establishing certain national programs that many communities would consider desirable."[55]

On May 18, 1965, Johnson announced that one of the first OEO projects would be an eight-week summer enrichment program for preschool children from low-income families. In launching Head Start Johnson stated that its goal was to put children in poverty "on an even footing with their classmates as they enter school."[56] Although it was originally thought that a summer program could accomplish the results Head Start sponsors had envisioned, it soon became clear that more was necessary. Additionally, because of the perception that Head Start had a crucial role to play in generating support for the larger poverty program, it soon was transformed from a summer program into one that operated year-round, enrolling over 500,000 three to five year olds during the first summer of 1965.

Johnson's statement reflects the optimism with which Head Start was begun: "Thirty million man-years—the combined life span of these youngsters—will be spent productively and rewardedly, rather than wasted in tax-supported institutions or in welfare-supported lethargy."[57]

Because it was seen as experimental, the program expanded to include health and social services; probably the most significant innovation was the decision to involve parents in administration and classroom activity. According to Edward Zigler and Jeanette Valentine, the policy of parental involvement had tremendous political and practical importance:

> As a War on Poverty program, Head Start represented a new attitude on the part of the government towards the poor. Disadvantaged families were no longer seen as passive recipients of services dispensed by professionals. Instead, they were viewed as active, respected participants and decision makers, roles they assumed with an unexpected degree of success.[58]

Funding for Head Start

A year after the first Head Start pilot program in the summer of 1965, Congress amended the Economic Opportunity Act to incorporate Head Start into the War on Poverty and explicitly required the OEO to fund Head Start through CAP, authorizing $352 million. The law also specified the delivery of health care services to children enrolled in Head Start. The Economic Opportunity Amendment of 1967 created the Follow Through program to continue the delivery of Head Start services to elementary school children from low-income families from kindergarten through the third grade. Like Head Start, it provides comprehensive social and medical services as well as educational enrichment.

By this time, however, the nation's interest in fighting poverty had begun to wane. Anti-poverty programs had been under attack from southern Democrats and Republicans since Johnson first announced a "war on poverty" in his State of the Union Message on January 8, 1964. The principal target of the attacks was the OEO, with critics charging it with causing urban riots by inflaming the militant (mostly minority) poor, with invading states' rights, and with creating another layer of federal bureaucracy by needlessly duplicating existing programs. Although Head Start was often caught in the crossfire of these attacks, it generally managed to escape the cuts aimed at other anti-poverty measures.

The future of most of the federal anti-poverty programs, always fragile, became even more uncertain following the election of Richard Nixon in 1968. Even under Johnson, faced with mounting financial pressures from the escalating Vietnam War, appropriation requests for the anti-poverty crusade had begun to diminish by 1967.[59]

Head Start was dealt a blow in 1969 when a study conducted by the Westinghouse Learning Corporation concluded that early gains by Head Start children dissipated within two or three years of attending regular school. The Westinghouse Report came under substantial attack from Head Start supporters who cited its flawed methodology.[60] Taking advantage of the opportunity presented by this report, Head Start advocates pointed to the program's other benefits, such as the delivery of health care services to children in low-income families, to justify its existence. It was also used to substantiate the need for additional programs designed to reinforce the early effects of Head Start.[61]

In 1969 Congress enacted the Economic Opportunity Amendments, authorizing the appropriation of over $2 billion for each of the next two fiscal years (1970 and 1971) for various poverty programs, including Head Start, the Legal Services Program, and the Comprehensive Health Services Program. Of this authorized amount, almost $400 million was allocated for Head Start in fiscal 1970 and just under $600 million for the next fiscal year. The amendments also specified that children from families below the poverty line, required to comprise 90 percent of the classes, were to have priority in registration.[62]

Over the years, local governments had become increasingly irritated at OEO staff and CAP leaders who supported, and at times even orchestrated, citizens' demands on government agencies such as housing authorities, school boards, and welfare departments.[63] Additionally, state and local officials were irritated at their inability to veto anti-poverty projects within their jurisdictions. In part, also, the War on Poverty had become largely identified with urban poverty and with the Civil Rights Movement. And by the middle 1970s there was less sympathy in the nation as a whole for the goals of civil rights/anti-poverty reformers.[64]

The signs of OEO's demise were evident. Precipitating its collapse, in 1970 Congress began to transfer the control of anti-poverty programs from OEO to other federal agencies.[65] Nevertheless, in 1972, Congress authorized about $500 million annually for the Head Start program for fiscal 1973 and 1974, with an additional $70 million a year for the Follow Through program. It also required that at least 10 percent of the enrollment of Head Start in each state be available to children with disabilities.[66]

In January 1973, Nixon appointed Howard Phillips as director of OEO, replacing Donald Rumsfeld, with instructions to disassemble it. The Head Start Economic Opportunity and Community Partnership Act (also called the Community Services Act) of 1973 officially repealed the Economic Opportunity Act of 1964 and created the Community Services Administration as the successor to OEO. This law provided for continuing Head Start and other poverty programs.

Authorizations for Head Start and Follow Through were relatively stable at about $500 million through fiscal 1977. The Economic Opportunity Act Amendments of 1978 extended Head Start for three more years and created a new formula for the distribution of federal Head Start funds to states.

During the Reagan years, despite the reduction in spending generally, funding for the Head Start program increased. Considered part of the "safety net," Head Start was alone among social service programs in avoiding being cut in Reagan's first budget for the Department of Health and Human Services.[67] Indeed, in 1984 Head Start received an increase in appropriations over the 1981 level.[68]

The 1984 Human Services Reauthorization Act extended Head Start's authorization through fiscal 1986 at a little over $1 billion a year. Concerned that some children required at least two years of Head Start activities, Congress expressly authorized multi-year participation at the option of the local program. And in 1986 the Human Services Reauthorization Act provided for $1.1 billion for the 1987 fiscal year to $1.4 billion for the 1990 fiscal year.

Critics have charged that the Reagan administration favored Head Start over other public welfare programs because it allowed it to demonstrate a commitment to the poor at relatively little expense. Additionally, they claim Head Start was preferred because unlike the Legal Services Program, for example, it did not threaten established interests.[69] Despite its position relative to other poverty programs, however, Head Start never achieved the status of an entitlement program, and because of this, like WIC, it also failed to live up to its potential of providing a full array of services for all eligible children. Indeed, although nominal program costs per child grew from 1980 to 1990, after adjusting for inflation, there was a 14 percent drop in the program's annual cost per child—from $3,773 to $3,245.[70]

At the start of the Bush administration in 1989, there were about half a million three and four year olds enrolled in Head Start, less than a fifth of the two and a half million estimated to be eligible.[71] The president's attempt to fulfil his promise of "full funding" for Head Start led to increased visibility for the program. But, despite his campaign pledge, Head Start was never fully funded and fully subscribed, and although Head Start spending rose during his administration, Bush never sought sufficient funds to support full participation for all eligible children.

With its authorization expiring in 1990, its twenty-fifth anniversary year became a time when Head Start moved center stage as all sides of the political spectrum claimed to support the concept of full funding.[72] With the agreeable prospect of funding increases, there were differing views on whether to direct the limited resources toward improving services for the children currently in the program or to include more children in the program and maintain the level of services.

Speaking for the Bush administration, Wade Horn, commissioner of the ACYF, stated: "We think this year our priority is to make a big splash in expanding the program." In contrast, Zigler, one of the founders of Head Start, believed it was more important to improve quality before expanding enrollment.

Zigler saw "a tremendous decline in the quality of Head Start from 25 years ago," he said, and stated that he would "rather serve fewer children well than more children badly."[73]

Congress spoke out on the quality versus quantity debate in the Senate Labor and Human Resources Committee Report accompanying the Human Services Reauthorization Act of 1990. Expressing concern that the quality of the Head Start programs nationally were declining, the report cited increasing class size, inappropriate facilities, reduction in class hours, inadequate transportation, and staff shortages and turnover, the latter primarily attributable to low salaries. Thus, the committee emphasized that Head Start was increasingly unable to meet the needs of the growing number of poor children in the nation. After assessing testimony and available data, the committee was persuaded that "Head Start programs lack the staff resources to give these multiproblem families the intensive attention required to secure comprehensive social services for them."[74]

Bush's 1990 budget request asked Congress to increase Head Start funds by $500 million for the 1991 fiscal year, for a total expenditure of $1.9 billion; this would have allowed Head Start to serve 70 percent of all eligible four year olds for at least one year.[75] Exceeding his request, Congress authorized funds ranging from $2,386,000,000 for fiscal 1991 (five hundred million more than Bush had asked for) to $7,660,000,000 for fiscal 1994. Reflecting a consensus on the need to improve quality before expanding enrollment, Congress targeted 10 percent of the authorized funds (25 percent in subsequent years) to improve the quality of Head Start services, especially staffing.[76]

The authorized funds, representing the largest increase in Head Start spending since its inception in 1965, would allow Head Start to serve all eligible three and four year olds and 30 percent of the five year olds not in kindergarten.[77] Bush signed the bill, notwithstanding objections about its costliness from his secretary of HHS and his budget director. Politically, it would have been difficult for Bush to veto a bill that purported to fulfil one of his 1988 campaign promises.

In a measure that would have ensured adequate funding for Head Start in the future, Kennedy drafted a bill in 1991 to establish Head Start as an entitlement program, with funding estimated to rise to $8 billion by 1997. Under the terms of his bill, all eligible children would be entitled to receive Head Start services. Funding for the program would rise by a billion dollars each year, beginning with $3 billion in fiscal 1992 and climbing to $8 billion in fiscal 1997.

Kennedy's measure was partially motivated by the fact that funds authorized in the 1990 act had not been fully appropriated by Congress. Although Head Start had been singled out in the Senate budget resolution as one of the programs specifically allowed to grow, its sponsors still needed to find revenues to offset the cost of the program.[78] Approved by the Senate Labor and Human

Resources Committee, the Kennedy bill languished, and Head Start was never granted entitlement status.

Head Start became an issue in the 1992 presidential election when, in January 1992, Bush promised to ask Congress for an additional $600 million for Head Start. At the time, 621,000 children were participating in the program, with almost two million more eligible to participate. Calling Head Start "a government program that works," Bush saw the commitment to Head Start as a way of deflecting criticism that he lacked a domestic agenda.[79] He claimed that the new funding level would enable 80 percent of all eligible four year olds below the poverty line to attend Head Start.

Congressional Democrats welcomed the campaign pledge, but questioned whether the promise to serve all four year olds was realistic, especially in light of the provision that 25 percent of new Head Start money must be spent on improving the quality of services. Additionally, they claimed that the 1990 Reauthorization Act had already committed the government to full funding by 1994.

Head Start spending was far below its authorized level, pointed out Democratic Representative Dale Kildee of Michigan, chair of the House Education and Labor Subcommittee on Elementary and Secondary Education. Kildee noted that Head Start spending had been authorized at $6 billion for 1993, and the Bush proposal would only bring spending up to $2.8 billion.[80]

Thus, despite the repeated commitment to Head Start over the years, the funds necessary to allow it to deliver its promise to all eligible children have never been appropriated: Congress authorized $7.7 billion for fiscal 1994, only appropriating $4.2 billion.[81]

Legislation proposed in 1993, and signed into law by Clinton on May, 18, 1994, demonstrated a new consensus between the White House and Congress on improving the quality of Head Start programs while also increasing enrollment. The Head Start Act Amendments of 1994 (Title I of the Human Services Amendments), sponsored by Kennedy and Representative Matthew Martinez, Democrat of California, reauthorized spending at unspecified sums through fiscal 1998. A bipartisan effort, the bill included members of both parties among its cosponsors and was passed by a vote of 393 to 20 in the House and 98 to 1 in the Senate. For his part, Clinton proposed another $700 million increase in Head Start funding, boosting it to a $4 billion program. In a signing ceremony on the twentieth-ninth anniversary of the founding of Head Start, he expressed enthusiasm for Head Start's future, and talked of raising Head Start enrollment to 840,000 children in 1995.[82]

Following the recommendations of a forty-seven–member bipartisan advisory committee, the law continued to set aside 25 percent of funding for improving services. It imposed national performance standards, enforced by the threat of termination for failure to meet them, on all Head Start grantees, including standards set for the provision of family social services with greater oversight of the local programs by the federal government. The bill authorized up to 3 percent of the program's total fiscal 1995 appropriations for a new infant and toddler (newborn to three) initiative; funding for this program was scheduled to rise to 4 percent in fiscal 1996 and 1997, and 5 percent in fiscal 1998. Finally, the law directed the secretary of HHS to conduct a study of the need for full-day and full-year services.[83] Although it is too early to judge, perhaps the federal government's renewed commitment to Head Start can negate a comment made by Zigler in 1985: "the original planners had a vision of what every Head Start family should receive [and] twenty years later this vision remains largely unfulfilled . . . ."[84]

Head Start has been one of the most popular public welfare programs, enjoying widespread bipartisan support in Congress. Its high approval rating stems in part from its ability to satisfy both liberals and conservatives.[85] By emphasizing the role of the family in the child's development and attempting to strengthen parental involvement with the child, Head Start has avoided being attacked as a federal anti-family program by conservatives. And by providing federal funds and services to poor people, Head Start has gathered support from liberals. In addition to its political attraction, Head Start has prospered because of strong support from the media, effective advocacy by Head Start participants and interest groups, such as the Children's Defense Fund, and a proven track record for positive results.[86] The high esteem in which Head Start has been held demonstrates that pleasing multiple political constituencies is crucial for the survival of a public welfare program.

Despite its political appeal, and in large part because Head Start, like WIC, never achieved the status of an entitlement program, delivery of its services has been constrained by lack of available funds. Like WIC, Head Start appears to have suffered from the predicament common to all children's poverty programs: inadequate funding.

Head Start Litigation

As with the WIC program, the federal courts were asked to resolve disputes over Head Start policies that arose out of differing interpretations of the federal law and regulations. The legal controversies over Head Start were essentially characterized by squabbles over authority among the agencies providing Head Start services. Thus, the court's role in Head Start policymaking was similar to its role in WIC policymaking, and quite different from its role in AFDC policymaking.

Intramural Disputes over Head Start

Like the WIC cases, most of the lawsuits involving the Head Start program were not brought by or on behalf of children; rather, most were filed by or against delegated Head Start agencies, seeking redress for a variety of grievances.[87] The typical suit involved Head Start as employer, with employees alleging discrimination, or more generally, an assortment of unfair labor practices. In these cases litigants asked the courts to determine the applicability of the Federal Torts Claims Act, the Fair Labor Standards Act, and the National Labor Relations Act to Head Start agencies. And, although these suits required adjudication of a Head Start policy or practice, these decisions did not relate to any issues implicating the interests of Head Start clientele or the distribution of Head Start Services.

Most of the remaining decisions involved contractual disputes among HHS, Head Start grantees, and delegate agencies.[88] Typical of such an action, the 1992 case of *Woodburn Child Care Clinic v. Migrant and Indian Coalition for Coordinated Child Care* arose when a grantee agency, the Migrant and Indian Coalition (MIC), discontinued funding of the Woodburn Child Care Clinic, the delegate agency. Alleging the existence of an implied contract between itself and MIC, Woodburn sought to force MIC to continue its funding for the rest of the year.[89] Woodburn charged MIC with statutory and constitutional violations for cutting off its funding in mid-year and depriving it of a pre-termination hearing. The court rejected MIC's motion to dismiss, finding that Woodburn was entitled to a hearing prior to termination.

Other cases involved HHS more directly. The 1989 decision of *Community Action of Laramie County v. Bowen* originated in an internal dispute between the community action agency and its policy council over the activities of the Head Start program director.[90] Following a hearing by an HHS administrative law judge, HHS terminated the agency's financial assistance, and the agency filed suit in federal court. The district court's order to restore the agency's status was reversed on appeal by the Tenth Circuit. Construing the applicable HHS regulations, the appellate court concluded that HHS has unlimited discretion to terminate grantee agencies, subject only to a due process hearing.

Health and Human Services was also directly involved in *New York v. Sullivan*, a 1992 case in which the city sued to retain funds disallowed by HHS following its charge that New York used improper financial and administrative procedures.[91] After reviewing the financial interactions of the city, HHS, and the delegate agencies, the court concluded that HHS had acted beyond the bounds of the Administrative Procedure Act and Head Start regulations. Although there is no indication in the decision, it is possible that this action arose out of a political dispute—between the Democratic-voting City of New York and the Republican-administered HHS.

In *Meriden Community Action Agency v. Shalala*, a 1993 opinion, the district court weighed the reciprocal rights and obligations of Head Start grantees and HHS.[92] In response to demands by the regional Head Start administrator, the City of Meriden attempted to cut off funds to the Meriden Community Action

Agency (MCAA). The MCAA sought a preliminary injunction to retain its status as Head Start grantee until HHS provided an opportunity for a hearing. Health and Human Services argued the city as the grantee had the authority to simply remove the MCAA and replace it with another agency, that HHS was only required to provide hearings when terminating the funds of Head Start grantees. The court held that MCAA was the grantee, and not the city. Indeed, it pointed out, under the statute, the city was incapable of grantee designation. Thus, HHS was enjoined from taking any action against the MCAA until it complied with the due process provisions of the statute.

   Salt Lake Community Action Program v. Shalala, another 1993 decision, also concerned HHS's authority over a grantee agency.[93] Following a hearing before the HHS Departmental Appeals Board (DAB), the Salt Lake Community Action Program (SLCAP) was ordered to reimburse HHS for money improperly spent. The issue in the case was confined to the narrow question of whether the lower court judge had properly decided that DAB lacked jurisdiction to determine the reimbursement question. The matter turned on whether the hearing involved a "disallowance" in which case the DAB had jurisdiction, or a "termination" in which case it did not and the SLCAP was entitled to a hearing before an administrative law judge. The court found that Congress entrusted HHS with the authority to distinguish between disallowances and terminations; because HHS termed it a disallowance, the court ruled that the DAB had proper jurisdiction.

   With the exception of the New York City case in which a great deal of money was involved, there is little indication that any of these rulings directly affected the delivery of Head Start services to children. The courts interpreted the federal statutes and regulations primarily to ensure that the grantees were adequately protected; rarely were the Head Start children even mentioned.

Head Start and Children's Nutrition Programs

   One case in which Head Start children appeared to have a stake in the outcome of the dispute between a Head Start grantee and the government was *Michigan Head Start Directors Association Tri-County Community Action v. Butz,* a class action suit decided in 1975. The community action group filed suit against the USDA to force the secretary to extend the benefits of the Special Food Service Program (SFSP) and the National School Lunch Act to non-school Head Start centers.[94]

   The issue arose when non-school Head Start programs, that is Head Start programs operating in centers other than schools, were barred from receiving the 80 percent reimbursement for food served to children under the SFSP. Although the non-school Head Start projects had originally been prohibited any reimbursement for children's meals, in 1973 the USDA began to permit reimbursement but only on a per-meal basis rather than the higher 80 percent level. This suit sought to allow the non-school Head Start centers to receive the higher level of reimbursement.

The question before the court was whether the secretary of agriculture had the authority to deny the SFSP 80 percent reimbursement rate to non-school Head Start programs. According to the National School Lunch Act, the higher form of reimbursement is required only in cases of "severe need," where the lower rate "is insufficient to carry on an effective feeding program." Citing "children in need" as the "ultimate beneficiaries of Congress' action," the plaintiffs argued that the secretary exceeded his statutory authority and acted arbitrarily by categorically excluding the non-school Head Start centers.[95] Allowing eligible non-school Head Start centers to receive the higher rate of reimbursement, they claimed, would enhance the quality of the Head Start program.

The court commented on the anomaly of dividing authority over Head Start food service programs between the Department of Agriculture and the Department of Health, Education, and Welfare, but after reviewing legislative history, found no conflict. The judge determined that the secretary of agriculture had no basis for concluding that no non-school Head Start programs were in "circumstances of severe need," and that he had exceeded his authority in barring all such programs from receiving the higher reimbursement rate. The court granted summary judgment to the plaintiffs and ordered the secretary to rescind the restrictive regulations.

Head Start Enrollment

In the thirty years of its existence, there has been only one reported decision involving a suit brought by a Head Start beneficiary. *Jimenez v. Garcia*, decided in 1981, arose as a suit filed by the parents of a three year old who sought to gain her admission to the local Head Start program. This case illustrates the gap between the promise offered by Head Start and the reality that limited funding imposes.[96]

Claiming it did not have the facilities to include three year olds, the school district, as the delegate Head Start agency, had restricted enrollment to four year olds. The parents of three-year-old Jessica sued the district in federal court for refusing to enroll her. They claimed it violated the federal regulations that confer Head Start eligibility on three year olds.

The case was complicated by the fact that the agreement between the Head Start grantee, the Community Action Council of South Texas, and the school district had expired at the end of the school year and had not been renewed. Rather than open the program to three year olds to comply with the regulations, the district decided to forgo federal funding. In the absence of a functioning Head Start program, the court ruled that the issue of Jessica's attendance was moot, that is, that it was no longer a viable legal controversy.

The judge dismissed the Garcia's complaint, saying he could not order the district to admit Jessica to its preschool program because the federal regulations no longer applied to it.

Although the court found that the district's conduct was not above reproach, it held that the decision to exclude Jessica was not a deliberate attempt to violate federal regulations but was simply a reflection of the reality of its inadequate facilities. Commenting on the unnecessary additional burden to local taxpayers caused by the district's decision to reject federal funds, the court urged it to apply directly for a Head Start grant that would permit it to limit enrollment to four year olds.

Conclusion

The cases show that the vast majority of legal disputes over the WIC and Head Start programs revolved around employment controversies within Head Start, government regulation of WIC vendors and suppliers, and internal conflicts among HHS and its Head Start grantee agencies. In thirty years there were only three legal controversies that involved program beneficiaries.

Although the *Dotson* and *Durham* litigants were able to persuade the District of Columbia court to order the executive branch to expend funds for WIC, these rulings had little long-term effect on the distribution of WIC benefits. Moreover, the cases were not decided on the basis of WIC program rules, but on principles of the separation of powers, specifically, the interaction of the executive and legislative branches over spending programs.

The *Alexander* litigation had enormous potential for the distribution of WIC benefits, but the courts declined to order the government to make WIC benefits available to all potential recipients who were statutorily eligible. The series of rulings in *Alexander* demonstrate the judiciary's commitment to upholding procedural guarantees for beneficiaries of public welfare programs as well as its reluctance to intervene in public welfare policymaking on substantive grounds.

Like *Alexander*, *Garcia* demonstrates the futility of turning to the federal courts to secure benefits when programs lack the resources to provide services to eligible beneficiaries. In *Garcia*, the only reported federal court decision brought by a potential Head Start beneficiary in almost thirty years, the court refused to order the child's admission to the program.

Although both Head Start and WIC are purported to be congressional favorites, they are forced to run the gauntlet of the budgetary process each year, and each has been underfunded since its inception. Consequently, these programs that combat educational and nutritional deficiencies in children are only able to serve about half of those meeting the eligibility guidelines.

The litigation over WIC and Head Start illustrates the limited reach of the federal courts in policies affecting the poor. In contrast to the entitlement status of the AFDC program—in which eligible participants have a legal right to benefits—participation in WIC and Head Start is governed by the availability of funding, not by rules of eligibility. Therefore, unlike in the AFDC program, for the most part the federal courts have been largely invisible in policymaking for WIC and Head Start, the courts being unable, or unwilling, to provide a remedy for excluded beneficiaries.

Together the cases examined here underscore the fact that when insufficient resources, rather than laws or regulations, are reasons for exclusion from federal programs, litigation is unlikely to be an effectual remedy.

Notes

1. Low-income families are defined as those with incomes below 185 percent of the poverty line. Because of legislation enacted in 1989, eligibility for AFDC, food stamps, or Medicaid benefits provides "adjunct eligibility" for WIC, that is, beneficiaries of these programs automatically meet the income requirements for WIC.

2. Some of WIC's earliest supporters were infant formula manufacturers who sought to create a market for formula among low-income women. In part, foods such as diary products, grains, and juice were selected for the program because they were high on the list of USDA excess commodities. *Congressional Quarterly Weekly* (June 27, 1992): 1879–1880.

3. "WIC Participant and Program Characteristics, 1988: Highlights from the Executive Summary," *Nutrition Today* (September-October 1990), p. 34.

4. Jay S. Buechner, et al., "WIC Program Participation—A Marketing Approach," *Public Health Reports* 106 (September-October 1991): 547–556.

5. S.Rep. No. 838, 96th Cong., 2d Sess. 37 (1980).

6. "WIC Participant and Program Characteristics, 1988," p. 34.

7. Food Research and Action Center, "Foodlines," *Social Policy* 20 (Winter 1990): 55.

8. *Congressional Quarterly Weekly* (June 27, 1992): 1876.

9. S.Rep. No. 884, 95th Cong., 2d Sess. 18 (1978). See Joseph S. Wholey, "WIC: Against the Tide," *The Bureaucrat* (Summer 1986): 26–30.

10. Leighton Ku, "Factors Influencing Early Prenatal Enrolment in the WIC Program," *Public Health Reports* 104 (May-June 1989): 302. See *Congressional Quarterly Weekly* (June 27, 1992): 1881 for summaries of studies since the 1970s.

11. *Congressional Quarterly Weekly* (June 27, 1992): 1876–1881.

12. Wholey, "WIC: Against the Tide," p. 29.

13. S.Rep. No. 259, 94th Cong., 1st Sess. 14 (1975).

14. "Section 32" funds, established by legislation in 1935, refer to an account maintained by yearly contributions of 30 percent of customs duties. Congress must specify the purpose for which the Section 32 funds may be spent.

15. S.Rep. No. 830, 93d Cong., 2d Sess. (1974).

16. *Congressional Quarterly Almanac*, 1975, p. 40A.

17. S.Rep. No. 259, 94th Cong., 1st Sess. 16 (1975).

18. At that time there were 753,000 approved WIC participants: 173,200 women, 210,800 infants, and 369,000 children. These figures refer to fiscal 1975. S. Rep. No. 259, 94th Cong., 1st Sess. 25 (1975).

19. *Congressional Quarterly Almanac*, 1975, p. 669.

20. *Congressional Quarterly Weekly* (November, 18, 1978): 3322.

21. S.Rep. No. 884, 95th Cong., 2d Sess. 17-18 (1978).

22. *Congressional Quarterly Almanac*, 1978, p. 628.

23. *Congressional Quarterly Almanac*, 1984, p. 468.

24. *Congressional Quarterly Weekly* (February 13, 1982): 242.

25. *Congressional Quarterly Weekly* (March 17, 1984): 624.

26. *Congressional Quarterly Almanac*, 1986, pp. 248–249.

27. 25 *Weekly Comp. Pres. Doc.* 1725 (November 13, 1989); *Congressional Quarterly Weekly* (November 4, 1989): 3010.

28. 29 *Weekly Comp. Pres. Doc.* 2142 (October 21, 1994).

29. George G. Graham, "WIC: A Food Program That Fails," *Public Interest* 103 (Spring 1991): 66–68.

30. *Dotson v. Butz*, C.A. No. 1210-73 (D.D.C. August 3, 1973); *Durham v. Butz*, C.A. No. 76-0358 (D.D.C. June 22, 1976).

31. The Clark County Welfare Rights Organization and the Maternity and Infant Care–Children and Youth Projects were also parties to the suit.

32. Several health clinics and the Commonwealth of Massachusetts and the Massachusetts commissioner of public health also appeared as plaintiffs.

33. S.Rep. No. 838, 96th Cong., 2d Sess. 34 (1980).

34. To ensure discovery of all reported opinions relating to the WIC program between 1972 and 1993, a Lexis search of the GENFED library, COURTS file, was

conducted, using "WIC or WIC Program" as the search terms. This search yielded fifty-seven reported appellate and district court decisions; there were no Supreme Court rulings related to the WIC program. Of these, there were twenty-four (twenty district court and four circuit court) *relevant* opinions, that is, opinions in which the courts resolved disputes over WIC policy by interpreting a state or federal law or regulation. Multiple opinions arising out of one underlying action were counted separately.

35. 830 F.2d 1078 (9th Cir. 1987).

36. 755 F.2d 1098 (4th Cir. 1985).

37. *Federal Trade Commission v. Abbott Laboratories*, 1992 U.S. Dist. Lexis 18030 (D.D.C. 1992). Other decisions related to this litigation involved interim discovery orders and pleading issues.

38. *Congressional Quarterly Weekly* (October 10, 1992): 3170.

39. *Alexander v. Polk*, 459 F.Supp. 883 (E.D. Pa. 1978).

40. *Alexander*, 459 F.Supp. at 895 n. 21 (emphasis added).

41. *Alexander v. Polk*, 572 F.Supp. 605 (E.D. Pa. 1983).

42. *Alexander v. Polk*, 750 F.2d 250 (3d Cir. 1984). The results of the remand hearing were not reported.

43. Plans for anti-poverty programs were begun during the Kennedy administration under the leadership of Walter Heller, chair of the Council of Economic Advisors, with support from Kennedy just before his death. Johnson showed immediate interest in the proposed programs and encouraged their development. Sar A. Levitan, *The Great Society's Poor Law: A New Approach to Poverty* (Baltimore: Johns Hopkins University Press, 1969), chapter 1.

44. S.Rep. No. 421, 101st Cong., 2d Sess. 47 (1990).

45. Judith A. Chafel, "Funding Head Start: What Are the Issues?" *American Journal of Orthopsychiatry* 62 (January 1992): 10.

46. *Congressional Quarterly Weekly* (March 5, 1994): 541–543.

47. See Julius B. Richmond, Deborah J. Stipek, and Edward Zigler, "A Decade of Head Start," in Edward Zigler and Jeanette Valentine, eds., *Project Head Start* (New York: Free Press, 1979), pp. 144–145 for further information on these programs; see also Valora Washington and Ura Jean Oyemade, *Project Head Start: Past, Present, Future Trends in the Context of Family Needs* (New York: Garland Publishing, 1987), chapter 2.

48. Laura Ariane Miller, "Head Start: A Moving Target," *Yale Law and Policy Review* 5 (Spring/Summer 1987): 322. This agency was formerly known as the Office of Child Development.

49. See Valerie Lee, Elizabeth Schnur, and J. Brooks-Gunn, "Does Head Start Work? A One-Year Follow-Up Comparison of Disadvantaged Children Attending Head

Start, No Preschool, and Other Preschool Programs," *Developmental Psychology* 24 (1988): 210–222; W. Steven Barnett, "Benefits of Compensatory Preschool Education," *Journal of Human Resources* 27 (1992): 279–312.

50. Chafel, "Funding Head Start," p. 10.

51. Douglas J. Besharov, "A New Start for Head Start," *The American Enterprise* 3 (March-April 1992): 55.

52. Valora Washington, "Head Start: How Appropriate for Minority Families in the 1980s?" *American Journal of Orthopsychiatry* 55 (October 1985): 578.

53. Frances Fox Piven and Richard A. Cloward, *Regulating the Poor: The Functions of Public Welfare*, 2d. ed. (New York: Vintage Books, 1993), chapter 9.

54. Edward Zigler and Karen Anderson, "An Idea Whose Time Has Come: The Intellectual and Political Climate for Head Start," in Zigler and Valentine, eds., *Project Head Start*, p. 12.

55. According to Shriver, the OEO was criticized by liberals who felt poor people should be empowered rather than simply be given services. It was also criticized by conservatives who felt OEO provided support to radical groups seeking to topple local power structures. "Head Start, A Retrospective View: The Founders," interview with The Honorable Sargent Shriver by Jeannette Valentine, in Zigler and Valentine, eds., *Project Head Start*, p. 59.

56. Lyndon Baines Johnson, "Remarks on Project Head Start, May, 18, 1965," in *Speeches by Lyndon B. Johnson*, cited in "Head Start, A Retrospective View: The Founders," in Zigler and Valentine, eds., *Project Head Start*, p. 69.

57. Quoted in Miller, "Head Start," p. 328.

58. Zigler and Anderson, "An Idea Whose Time Has Come," in Zigler and Valentine, eds., *Project Head Start*, pp. 15–16; see Edward Zigler, "Assessing Head Start at Twenty: An Invited Commentary," *American Journal of Orthopsychiatry* 55 (October 1985): 603–609.

59. David Zarefsky, *President Johnson's War on Poverty: Rhetoric and History* (University, Ala.: University of Alabama Press, 1986), chapter 3.

60. For the most part, Head Start has been favorably perceived, but views on its effectiveness have varied over time. Between 1965 and 1968, Head Start was typically positively evaluated; between 1969 and 1974, based to a large extent on the Westinghouse study, Head Start was criticized as having no immediate or long-lasting benefits. In 1975 there was a resurgence of support for the program. Zigler and Anderson, "An Idea Whose Time Has Come," in Zigler and Valentine, eds., *Project Head Start*, p. 13; see Lois-ellin Datta, "Another Spring and Other Hopes: Some Findings from National Evaluations of Project Head Start," in Zigler and Valentine, eds., *Project Head Start*, for reports of evaluations of Head Start.

61. Washington and Oyemade, *Project Head Start*, chapter 6.

62. H.Rep. No. 778, 91st Cong., 1st. Sess. (1969). In 1973 when the fee schedule had been implemented, there was much consternation among Head Start program administrators who argued the fee would force children in families living just above the poverty line (the near-poor) to drop out of the program. Some Head Start programs refused to collect fees and for those that did, the cost of collection was often greater than the amount collected. In 1973 Congress delayed fee collection until 1975. Eventually the fee requirement was dropped entirely. H.Rep. No. 671, 93d Cong., 1st Sess. (1973).

63. Piven and Cloward, *Regulating the Poor*, chapter 9.

64. Lawrence Mead, *The New Politics of Poverty* (New York: Basic Books, 1992), chapter 2.

65. *Congressional Quarterly Weekly* (August 28, 1970): 2153–2155.

66. Richmond, Stipek, and Zigler, "A Decade of Head Start," in Zigler and Valentine, eds., *Project Head Start*.

67. Miller, "Head Start: A Moving Target," p. 327.

68. S.Rep. No. 484, 98th Cong., 2d Sess. 11 (1984).

69. *Congressional Quarterly Weekly* (July 18, 1982): 1279–1280.

70. Per-pupil spending rose to $3,758 in fiscal 1993; adjusting for inflation, this represents about an 18 percent increase in spending between 1990 and 1993. *Congressional Quarterly Weekly* (March 5, 1994): 541–547.

71. *Congressional Quarterly Weekly* (March 25, 1989): 653.

72. The following discussion is drawn largely from *Congressional Quarterly Weekly* (April 21, 1990): 1191–1195.

73. *Congressional Quarterly Weekly* (April 21, 1990): 1191.

74. S.Rep. No. 421, 101st Cong., 2d Sess. 51 (1990).

75. Chafel, "Funding Head Start," p. 11.

76. In 1994, however, witnesses before the Senate Labor and Human Resources Committee were still debating the quality versus quantity issue. *New York Times* (January 14, 1994): A24.

77. Despite Head Start's popularity, however, the appropriations fell below these amounts. *Congressional Quarterly Almanac*, 1990, p. 552.

78. *Congressional Quarterly Weekly* (June 29, 1991): 1761.

79. *Education Week* (January 29, 1992): 1&26.

80. *Congressional Quarterly Weekly* (January 25, 1992): 171.

81. *Congressional Quarterly Weekly* (March 5, 1994): 546.

82. 30 *Weekly Comp. Pres. Doc.* 1112 (May 18, 1994); *Washington Post* (May 19, 1994): A1.

83. *Congressional Quarterly Weekly* (March 5, 1994): 541–547.

84. Zigler, "Assessing Head Start at Twenty," p. 608.

85. Peter Skerry, "The Charmed Life of Head Start," *The Public Interest* 73 (1983): 18–39.

86. Zigler, "Assessing Head Start at Twenty," believes Head Start survived the Reagan years for these reasons.

87. To ensure discovery of all reported opinions relating to the Head Start program between 1965 and 1993, a Lexis search of the GENFED library, COURTS file, was conducted, using "Head Start or Headstart and Child!" as the search terms. This search yielded 144 reported appellate and district court decisions; there were no Supreme Court rulings related to the Head Start program. Of these, there were 22 (16 district court and 6 circuit court) *relevant* opinions, that is, opinions in which the courts resolved disputes over Head Start policy by interpreting a state or federal law or regulation. Multiple opinions arising out of one underlying action were counted separately.

88. Cases in this category include: *Economic Opportunity Commission of Nassau County v. Weinberger*, 524 F.2d 393 (2d Cir. 1975); *Quiles v. Hernandez Colon*, 682 F.Supp. 127 (D.P.R. 1988).

89. 1988 U.S. Dist. Lexis 4540 (D.Ore. 1992).

90. 866 F.2d 347 (10th Cir. 1989).

91. 1992 U.S. Dist. Lexis 20054 (S.D.N.Y. 1992).

92. 1993 U.S. Lexis 9752 (D.D.C. 1993).

93. 11 F.3d 1084 (D.C. Cir. 1993).

94. 397 F.Supp. 1124 (W.D.Mich. 1975).

95. *Michigan Head Start Directors*, 397 F.Supp. at 1139.

96. 509 F.Supp. 973 (S.D. Tex. 1981).

4

THE CHILD WELFARE SYSTEM

The child welfare system, charged with protecting the interests—indeed the lives—of abused and neglected children, encompasses an interlocking network of state and local child welfare agencies, juvenile courts, and law enforcement authorities. The quality and quantity of services offered by child welfare agencies differ by state, county, and municipality; the variation in the delivery of services is attenuated by overarching federal constitutional and statutory requirements that help lend uniformity to the system.[1] As recently as 1988, child welfare advocate Marcia Lowry characterized state agencies, comprising the heart of the child welfare system, as "marked by totally unreliable information systems, inadequate training, high caseloads, Byzantine procedures, and administrative paralysis."[2]

The problems of the child welfare system are staggering. According to the American Humane Society, there were over two million incidences of child abuse and neglect reported in 1986. Between 1963 and 1986 abuse and neglect reports had increased by 1,233 percent.[3] And in 1991 it was estimated that over thirteen hundred children died from abusive treatment; about half the deaths occurred in children under one.[4]

Although reports of child abuse in the United States can be traced as far back as 1655, society did not focus much attention on the issue of abused and neglected children until 1874 when the story of the abused orphan Mary Ellen heightened its concern with children's well-being. The tragic saga of Mary Ellen caught the public's interest and led in part to the formation of the New York Society for the Prevention of Cruelty to Children in 1874, modeled after the Society for the Prevention of Cruelty to Animals.[5]

Child Abuse and Neglect

The issue of child abuse was brought to national attention again in an article entitled "The Battered-Child Syndrome," published in a 1962 issue of the *Journal of the American Medical Association*.[6] This article was the first to focus clinical attention on child abuse and to urge medical professionals to take responsibility for recognizing and reporting observed instances of child maltreatment.

Precise definitions of abuse and neglect vary among states but abuse is generally defined as non-accidental physical injury; neglect is more difficult to define and definitions range from tangible indicators, such as failure to provide food, clothing, or shelter, or to secure medical care, to intangible ones such as inadequate supervision or failure to supply emotional needs.[7]

The results of a twelve-month survey of child maltreatment in ten states showed that about 30 percent of maltreated children were physically abused (with about 10 percent of these receiving an injury serious enough to require professional attention), about 7 percent were sexually abused, and approximately 20 percent were emotionally abused. The remainder, almost 50 percent, were neglected, broadly defined to encompass educational and emotional neglect.[8]

The difficulty of confronting the issue of child abuse is exacerbated by the fact that it largely occurs within the bounds of family privacy, most frequently at the hands of the child's parent or another family member. Indeed, the incidence of physical violence perpetrated on children by their parents is overwhelming: a 1980 survey of child maltreatment in eighteen states by the American Humane Association found that of 173,247 perpetrators, 91.8 percent (158,935) were the child's parents, an additional 3.8 percent (6,570) were other family members.[9] One study of parental abuse estimates that 84 to 97 percent of parents subject their children to some type of physical punishment, and that 3 to 4 million children "have at some time been kicked, beaten, or hit with a fist by their parents."[10]

Child neglect was first identified in 1964 when a study by Leontine Young distinguished between neglectful and abusive behavior.[11] And although child abuse receives more attention, experts stress that neglect is more common and merits more public notice, including greater emphasis on prevention.[12] Data collected in a 1980 nationwide study showed that neglect tended to be more closely linked with socioeconomic status, while physical abuse was more closely associated with variables related to family structure, such as marital status.[13] Overall, the single most important factor associated with child maltreatment is poverty, with most studies documenting a higher rate of child maltreatment among poor families.[14] A number of scholars emphasize, however, that lower-socioeconomic-status families and/or single-parent families are more visible to social welfare agencies, and thus more likely to be reported to the authorities.

Assessing the difficulties of developing successful child neglect prevention programs, Michael Wald and Sophia Cohen argue that it is virtually impossible to identify "likely neglectors" and that the best strategy for preventing child neglect is to institute general social programs such as "income support, universal medical care, or school lunches."[15]

Foster Care

When abused or neglected children are removed from their homes by child welfare agencies, they commonly enter the foster care system.[16] Children in foster care have been characterized as a "tragic class of people."[17] Yet, despite the problems associated with it, the nation increasingly relies on foster care as a solution for its maltreated children: in 1963 about 75,000 abused and neglected children were placed in foster care; in 1980, according to one report, the number had risen to more than 300,000.[18]

Foster care, intended to provide a temporary safe haven for abused or neglected children removed from their homes, has generally not proven to be an effective long-term remedy for a number of reasons. Perhaps the most serious is that for too many children, it is not short-term, As early as the 1950s, studies identified the problem of "foster care drift," that is, children become lost in the foster care system, transferred from one foster care setting to another. Additionally, there was concern that children were being removed from their homes too readily, with too little attention paid to keeping the biological family together.[19]

The record of child welfare agencies in returning children to their homes is not good: a 1993 American Bar Association report entitled *America's Children at Risk* documented the dimensions of foster care drift in 1988: in that year 48 percent of foster care children were shifted around to as many as five new foster homes; 7 percent were assigned to six or more placements.[20]

Douglas Besharov argues that children are placed in foster care too readily—even when they are not in immediate danger at home—and urges the child protection system to provide more effective family services on an in-home basis.[21] Recognizing its necessity at times, Benjamin Wolf, director of the Chicago-based Children's Rights Project of the ACLU believes that the "most common bad decision is removing children from their homes."[22]

Child Welfare Policymaking

The responsibility for spending and decisionmaking in the child welfare area is dispersed, with authority divided between the state and federal governments, and within states, among local governmental units. But although federal funding is available, ultimate responsibility for child welfare lies in the hands of state and local agencies that provide the front-line services such as substance abuse treatment, parental support groups, homemaker support, parenting classes, job training, and child care.[23]

The multi-faceted problems of the child welfare system have led to a variety of measures to prevent and/or react to child maltreatment.[24] Most agree, however, that there is a need for a more effective government response. As late as 1990, the U.S. Advisory Board on Child Abuse and Neglect characterized the federal government's role in child protection as "one of an absence of a coherent Federal policy." It accused Congress and the White House of "foster[ing] a national child protection system that is fragmented, inadequate, and often misdirected."[25]

CAPTA

Following society's re-awakening to the existence of child abuse with the publication of the Kempe article, a 1963 conference on child abuse sponsored by the Children's Bureau recommended that states adopt laws requiring designated professionals, initially physicians, to report cases of abuse to child welfare authorities.[26] Such laws were considered fairly controversial for they were instrumental in "breach[ing] the wall protecting the family from outside intervention."[27] Within four years of the conference, all states had laws requiring professionals such as physicians, teachers, and social workers to report suspected cases of abuse or face the possibility of criminal charges as well as civil damages.[28]

In 1974 Congress enacted the Child Abuse Prevention and Treatment Act (CAPTA), sponsored by Democrats Walter Mondale of Minnesota in the Senate and Patricia Schroeder of Colorado in the House. The act was intended "to provide [federal] financial assistance for [state] demonstration programs for the prevention, identification, and treatment of child abuse and neglect and to establish a National Center on Child Abuse." Mondale had chaired the Subcommittee on Children and Youth of the Senate Committee on Labor and Public Welfare which held a series of subcommittee hearings on child abuse during the previous year.

The 1974 act broadly defined child abuse and neglect as

the physical or mental injury, sexual abuse, negligent treatment, or maltreatment of any child under the age of eighteen by a person who is responsible for the child's welfare under circumstances which would indicate the child's health or welfare is harmed or threatened thereby.[29]

The statute also provided for relatively small amounts of grant money to states. To be eligible for these funds, states were required to have laws defining and prohibiting abuse and neglect, mandating reports of suspected abuse or neglect with immunity for those reporting, and specifying procedures for investigating reports; states also had to provide a range of protection services to children, including the appointment of a legal advocate, typically a guardian *ad litem*, to represent the interests of the child during the abuse or neglect proceeding.

Finally, CAPTA established a National Center for Child Abuse and Neglect (NCCAN) to act as a clearinghouse for the development and distribution of information on child protection activities. The center's funding was primarily used to sponsor a variety of research and demonstration projects to improve child protection programs. Between 1974 and 1977 NCCAN funded twenty-one such projects, at a cost of $40 million.[30]

In 1978 CAPTA was reauthorized and renamed the Child Abuse Prevention and Treatment and Adoption Reform Act (CAPTARA); most of the debate over its reauthorization was over the proposed, but ultimately deleted, section of the law restricting child pornography. The 1978 act demonstrated a concern about other forms of child sexual abuse as well as use of children in pornographic films. Passed rather uneventfully, it increased the percentage of funds to be allocated to state programs through fiscal 1981.[31]

When CAPTARA was reauthorized in 1981, it barely survived the Reagan budget cuts. Its funding for fiscal 1982 and 1983 was authorized in the 1981 OBRA, partially as a result of an agreement over coal consumption between northern liberals and southerners. The prevailing sentiment among its opponents was that child abuse was a state concern, and that federal funding for it should be woven into the existing social service block grants. Additionally, conservatives were disturbed about the specter of federal intervention into the family, especially the potential for interfering with family autonomy over child discipline. Although the statute was reauthorized, the federal government's financial commitment to preventing child abuse sharply declined. Funds for research dropped to $2 million in 1982 (from $17 million in 1980) and staffing cuts among child abuse experts in the Children's Bureau and other federal agencies were also dramatic.[32] Overall federal funding for CAPTA was reduced in 1982 from about $23 million to about $16.2 million.[33]

The issue of child abuse again achieved national prominence in 1982 when the parents of Baby Doe, a Bloomington, Indiana infant born with Down's Syndrome and a blocked esophagus, refused to allow doctors to perform corrective surgery. A state court upheld his parents' right to refuse consent, and the baby soon died.

Taking a leading role, President Reagan issued orders to HHS to prevent future Baby Doe situations. Health and Human Services responded by promulgating rules under § 504 of the 1973 Rehabilitation Act, the act barring discrimination in federally funded programs against handicapped individuals. The rules, issued in 1983 and known as the "Baby Doe" regulations, prohibited health care providers from denying treatment and nourishment solely on the basis of handicap to infants who could benefit from such treatment. Despite these rules and the administration's concern with the issue, the courts were unwilling to second-guess medical judgments, and enforcement was limited. Finally, in 1986 the Supreme Court ruled that the regulations exceeded the agency's statutory authority under § 504; the Court pointed out that the act only reached the activities of hospitals, and with no evidence that hospitals had been guilty of discrimination, there was no foundation for the regulations.[34]

When renewing CAPTA in 1984, Congress attempted to influence the ongoing debate over withholding medical treatment from handicapped infants. The 1984 Child Abuse Amendments, extending CAPTA through fiscal 1987, required states as a condition of receiving federal funds to establish reporting and investigating procedures for complaints of handicapped infants with life-threatening conditions receiving inadequate medical care. Although there were some exceptions in the act, parents and physicians were statutorily required to provide appropriate nutrition, water, and medication to handicapped newborns as they would to non-handicapped infants. To implement this, the amendments also expanded liability for abuse or neglect to persons outside the child's family or home, to include foster parents and hospital employees, among others. But because there was no federal standard of neglect, the statute had limited consequences for Baby Doe situations.[35]

Congress renewed CAPTA in successive years: in 1986 the Children's Justice and Assistance Act encouraged states to enact reforms designed to improve legal and administrative proceedings in the investigation and prosecution of child abuse cases, particularly sexual abuse cases. The goal of the law was to "reduce trauma" to the child victim and safeguard "procedural fairness for the accused." It also aimed at fostering state demonstration projects for temporary child care for children with special needs and crisis nurseries for abused and neglected children.

In 1988 Congress passed the Child Abuse Prevention, Adoption, and Family Services Act, extending CAPTA for three more years and creating an Inter-Agency Task Force on Child Abuse and Neglect to coordinate federal programs. Two members of the task force became members of the newly authorized U.S. Advisory Board on Child Abuse and Neglect, which was instructed to prepare annual reports on the nation's efforts to achieve the goals set forth in CAPTA.[36]

The 1988 amendments also established a National Clearinghouse for Information on programs designed to deal with abuse and neglect in the general population, as well as for "special risk" children, those with disabilities and children of drug and alcohol abusers. Funds were also provided for programs designed to facilitate adoption, especially of minority children.

Congress again amended CAPTA in 1992 in an attempt to strengthen state child protection services. The Child Abuse, Domestic Violence, Adoption, and Family Services Act required the advisory board to propose a strategy for all levels of government to reduce children's deaths due to maltreatment. Other provisions pertained to federal grants to fund state child protection research and demonstration projects. With this bill Congress reauthorized CAPTA through the end of fiscal 1995; funding for fiscal 1992 was authorized at $321.7 million; funding levels through fiscal 1995 were unspecified. However, for 1992, at least, Congress appropriated far less than the amount authorized.[37]

P.L. 96-272

Federal involvement in the child abuse issue had risen dramatically in 1980 with the enactment of the Adoption Assistance and Child Welfare Act, commonly known as Public Law (P.L.) 96-272.[38] Reflecting the influence of child welfare reformers who advocated permanency in child placement, P.L. 96-272 aimed at "lessen[ing] the emphasis on foster care placement and encourag[ing] greater efforts to find permanent homes . . . either by making it possible to return [children] to their families or by placing them in adoptive homes."

Passage of P.L. 96-272 was secured by the efforts of congressional staffers, executive agency officials (largely from the Children's Bureau), and interest groups, with the CDF and the Child Welfare League of America playing leading roles.[39] They were motivated by their concern for children trapped in the foster care system for too long with little effort by states either to reunify them with their families or to terminate parental rights and expedite adoption.

During hearings on P.L. 96-272, supporters of the bill testified that states were failing to provide effective alternatives to foster care placement.[40] Believing that children's interests are usually best served if they can be cared for at home, they sought to prod states to reduce reliance on foster care and prevent the unnecessary removal of children from their homes.[41]

Senator Alan Cranston, Democrat of California, explained that the purpose of the act was to counteract the pattern of "far too many children and families . . . [being] broken apart when they could have been preserved with a little effort." In his view, P.L. 96-272 emphasized the principle that "foster care ought to be a last resort rather than the first."[42]

The bill was signed into law on June 17, 1980, at a time when it was reported that nearly half of the five hundred thousand children in foster care had been in the system for over two years and almost one hundred thousand had been in foster homes for over six years.[43] Senator Daniel Patrick Moynihan, Democrat from New York, hailed P.L. 96-272 as "the most significant piece of social welfare legislation to pass the Congress since the inauguration of President Carter."[44]

Based on the principle of family preservation, the law had two primary goals: to protect children from abuse and neglect by placing them in temporary foster care and to reunify families as rapidly as possible so that children would suffer a minimum of disruption in their lives and maintain their bonds with their families.[45]

Public Law 96-272 attempted to refocus the energies of the child welfare system with the lure of federal funds. Under previous law, states had a financial incentive to prolong the child's foster care experience; under the new law, the incentives were intended to be reversed.[46] The act contained a set of interrelated substantive requirements and financial incentives to provide a national framework for foster care and adoption policymaking. Although for the most part it reimbursed states for the child welfare expenses of children in poverty, its funds were not solely limited to poor children.

Title IV-B

Public Law 96-272 amended the existing Child Welfare Services Program, Title IV-B of the Social Security Act, authorizing funds for a range of child welfare services—including foster care prevention and family reunification services. Title IV-B, found in 42 U.S.C. §§ 620–628, applies to *all* children in state-supervised foster care, not just to poor children.

In an effort to restrict spending on foster care and curtail its use, the act required that any money made available to states under the IV-B program— above the state's share of $56.5 million, which was the amount appropriated in fiscal 1979—be directed to family support services rather than to foster care.

The actual amount of a state's IV-B funding was contingent on several factors. States were *eligible* to receive additional funds (in excess of their share of the $56.5 million) if Congress raised IV-B appropriations to over $141 million. Prior to 1980 the largest amount of money appropriated for Title IV-B had been $56.5 million, despite authorizations of up to $266 million from 1977 to 1989.[47]

States would be allotted an increased share of federal dollars under certain conditions: they must institute a case plan and review system, as specified in Title IV-E of the act, for *all* children in state-supervised foster care, regardless of their eligibility for federal reimbursement. The idea of case plans was not new: plans for case management had been required under prior federal law but were seldom produced. Indeed, during hearings on P.L. 96-272 Congress learned that states rarely conducted reviews of the status of children in foster care, and in some states, officials were even unaware of the number of children in the system.[48]

Additionally, to receive Title IV-B funds states were required to compile an inventory of all children in foster care, create statewide information systems, and establish preventive and reunification services programs. The law specified that when IV-B appropriations reached $266 million for two consecutive years, states without case plans for all their children in care would be limited to only their share of the $56.5 million of IV-B funding.[49]

Title IV-E

Public Law 96-272 created a new Foster Care and Adoption Assistance Program as Title IV-E of the Social Security Act, found in 42 U.S.C. §§ 670-679.

Title IV-E replaced the existing Title IV-A Foster Care Program in which the federal government provided unlimited matching funds to states for the foster care expenses of AFDC children. With no funding for programs aimed at keeping families together, and no check on the length of time children stayed in the system, Title IV-A created a disincentive for states to reduce long-term foster care. In contrast, the new Title IV-E created a presumption in favor of keeping families together, or failing that, to preparing children for adoption.

Title IV-E reimburses states for their foster care expenses for AFDC children; as an open-ended entitlement, it covers an unlimited number of children who are eligible for AFDC before the foster care placement. To receive Title IV-E funds, states must have approved IV-E plans.[50] The secretary of HHS is authorized to reduce or eliminate payments if the plan fails to comply with the act or if the state fails to comply with its plan. State plans must specify that "in each case, reasonable efforts will be made (A) prior to the placement of a child in foster care, to prevent or eliminate the need for removal of the child from his [or her] home, and (B) to make it possible for the child to return to his [or her] home." The statute does not define reasonable efforts, leaving it up to the juvenile court judge to decide whether the agency has complied. If a judge determines that "reasonable efforts" have not been made, the state is denied federal matching funds for the child's foster care placement.[51]

Elaborating on the case plan and review requirements for children covered by Title IV-B, Title IV-E requires the child welfare agency to file a written case plan, indicating the type and appropriateness of the placement, for each child in federally reimbursed foster care. Furthermore, to prevent "foster care drift," there must be a review of the status of each child in foster care at least once every six months to ensure that each child has a case plan "designed to achieve placement in the least restrictive (most family-like) setting available and in close proximity to the parents' home, consistent with the best interest and special needs of the child . . . ." Either a court or court-approved body external to the child welfare agency is required to hold a "dispositional hearing" within eighteen months of the foster care placement ("and periodically thereafter during the continuation of foster care") to determine the child's status in the system.

Congress intended Titles IV-E and IV-B to reinforce each other: fulfilling the reasonable efforts requirement for the individual child depends on the existence of statewide preventive and reunification service programs. As a further disincentive to foster care, P.L. 96-272 allows states to cap expenditures under their Title IV-E foster care programs and shift unused IV-E funds to preventive and reunification service programs. Under this scheme states may draw on Title IV-E foster care funds for Title IV-B family service programs, but not the reverse.[52]

Recognizing that sometimes children must be removed from their homes and the parents' rights terminated, Title IV-E also created an entitlement program to encourage the adoption of hard to place children. It provided payment to families adopting SSI or AFDC-eligible children with special needs and made such children automatically eligible for medical benefits.[53]

Funding for Child Welfare Services

Funding levels for Title IV-B and Title IV-E varied greatly. Yearly appropriations for Title IV-B services were by no means secure, having to compete with a vast array of domestic programs, including other child welfare programs. In fiscal 1981 Title IV-B was funded at $164 million; in fiscal 1991 funding rose to $273 million. In comparison, as an entitlement program, Title IV-E's expenditures for foster care (excluding adoption assistance expenses) rose from $309 million in fiscal 1981 to almost $1.8 billion in fiscal 1991. Adoption assistance expenses received $189.8 million in fiscal 1991.[54]

Thus, despite the intent of the act, states often committed fewer resources to family preservation services because there was less federal money available for such programs. With many children individually entitled to federal foster care funds under Title IV-E, states implicitly received greater encouragement to continue children in foster care rather than provide family preservation services and return them to their homes.

As part of its efforts to reduce federal spending for social programs, within a year after its enactment the Reagan administration proposed to "block grant" all P.L. 96-272 programs. It was widely believed that such a plan would have led to "the Act's effective repeal."[55] When this attempt failed, the administration reduced funding for P.L. 96-272 programs. Especially hard hit were demonstration programs that aimed at facilitating family reunification and reducing the incidence of foster care. And not surprisingly, although the number of children in foster care had diminished after the passage of P.L. 96-272, it now began to climb.[56]

By the early 1990s children's advocates became increasingly critical of the child welfare system. Gregory Coler, chair of the American Public Welfare Association's project on child welfare and family preservation, and former head of Florida's welfare agency under Republican Governor Bob Martinez, proclaimed that it was "underresourced and outgunned." David Liederman, executive director of the Child Welfare League of America, endorsed the need for increased resources, saying that "we need billions, not millions"; and Eileen Pasztor, of the Child Welfare League, declared: "we are serving 1990s children in an 1860s model."[57]

With costs continually rising, there was a growing sense that the child welfare system was unable to cope with the pressures on it. There was also frustration at the contradictory policy of unlimited funding for expensive foster care and limited funding for less expensive preventive and reunification services.

In 1990 Congress began to consider an overhaul of the child welfare system, with greater emphasis on prevention efforts.[58]

The House Ways and Means Subcommittee on Human Resources approved a bill (H.R. 5020) that would have added approximately $5 billion to the child welfare system. Although the bill died at the end of the session, new bills were later introduced in the Senate Finance and House Ways and Means Committees.

In 1991 Senate bill S. 4 called for spending about $2 billion for child welfare services, while House bill H.R. 2571 proposed spending about $7 billion. As a capped entitlement, H.R. 2571 spending for Title IV-B would have begun at $600 million in fiscal 1993, and risen to a ceiling of $1.3 billion in fiscal 1996; after that, it would have risen annually with inflation.[59] Although there was initial bipartisan support for child welfare reform, soon partisan differences and the reality of budgetary restrictions on money for new entitlement programs hampered the efforts of reformers to create new spending programs or increase funds for existing programs. The Bush administration objected to the idea of establishing Title IV-B as an entitlement, the key element of the House bill, claiming it would violate the 1990 budget agreement between Congress and the White House. It urged instead that new spending for Title IV-B child welfare services come out of Title IV-E funds.

No hearings were held on the Senate bill, and despite the approval of the Human Resources Subcommittee, chaired by Democrat Tom Downey of New York, H.R. 2571 was never considered by the full committee or the House.

The next year the House Ways and Means Committee approved H.R. 3603, a new version of H.R. 2571, and proposed to finance it with a 10 percent surtax on families with incomes over $1 million. H.R. 3603, entitled the Family Preservation bill, was approved by the full House on August 6, 1992.[60] Although there was bipartisan support for the concept of family preservation, and the Family Preservation bill in particular, partisan differences erupted over its cost and funding provisions. Additionally, the administration threatened a veto because the bill included the millionaire surtax which the president had been denouncing for several years.[61]

On the same day that H.R. 3603 passed through Ways and Means, the full House approved a $17 billion urban aid tax bill (H.R. 11) in response to the 1992 Los Angeles riots. On the Senate side, the Senate Finance Committee added language to the urban aid bill that created an entitlement for Title IV-B, borrowed from H.R. 3603.

The attempt to reform the child welfare system soon became entwined with the politics of the presidential election campaign. Begun as a focused urban aid measure, H.R. 11 grew into a massive revenue bill, with a $27 billion price tag. Passed by both chambers in late 1992 (just before the election), it became the subject of intense conference negotiations. When H.R. 11 passed out of conference, the child welfare provisions included major portions of the Family

Preservation bill from S. 4 and H.R. 3603 and were estimated to cost $2.8 billion over five years.

Although Bush had originally endorsed the enterprise zone tax benefits of H.R. 11, fearing that he would be attacked for agreeing to another tax increase, he vetoed the bill on November 4, 1992.[62]

Efforts to increase funding for P.L. 96-272 continued in the new Clinton administration with greater success. Early in March 1993 Clinton announced proposals to strengthen state family services programs. He proposed a $60 million capped entitlement for fiscal 1994, to increase to $600 million by fiscal 1998. On March 16, 1993, Senators John D. Rockefeller IV, Democrat from West Virginia, and Christopher Bond, Republican from Missouri, introduced the Family Preservation and Child Protection Reform Act (S. 596), with a $2.2 billion price tag. A House bill, costing about $1.5 billion, was introduced a month later. Both Senate and House versions contained child welfare provisions that were similar to those in the version of H.R. 11 that was reported out of conference.[63] Ultimately, the Family Preservation and Support Act emerged from the conference committee as part of the Omnibus Budget Reconciliation Act of 1993 which was approved by Congress on August 4 and signed by Clinton on August 10.[64]

Thus after three years of unsuccessful efforts to reform the child welfare system, Congress amended Title IV-B of the Social Security Act—the Child Welfare Services Program—by adding a new Subpart 2, entitled Family Preservation and Support Services, effective October 1, 1993. The new law provided funding for family preservation and community-based family support services by creating a capped entitlement totalling $930 million over a five-year period. Specifically, Congress authorized $60 million for fiscal 1994, $150 million for fiscal 1995, $225 million for fiscal 1996, $240 million for fiscal 1997, and at least $255 million for fiscal 1998, depending on inflation. The act authorized the secretary to set aside $26 million (over five years) within the entitlement for HHS expenditures on research, training, assistance, and evaluation of state programs. It also reserved $35 million (over four years), beginning in fiscal 1995, to fund grants to allow states to assess and improve state procedures in foster care, adoption, and termination of parental rights.

New funds were allocated for use *only* in family preservation and community-based family support services. As defined in the statute, "family preservation services" are "services for children and families designed to help families (including adoptive and extended families) at risk or in crisis." Examples include preplacement preventive services, training in parenting skills, respite care for parents or foster parents, and follow-up services for adoptive or reunified families.

The law defined "family support services" as

> community-based services to promote the well-being of children and families designed to increase the strength and stability of families (including

adoptive, foster, and extended families), to increase parents' confidence and competence in their parenting abilities, to afford children a stable and supportive family environment, and otherwise to enhance child development.

For unknown reasons, specific mention of these services, contained in the House bill, were deleted by the conference committee; the conferees noted, however, that they intended the term "family support services" to include community-based services such as respite care for parents or caregivers, early developmental screening for children, center-based activities, such as parent support groups, and home visitations.

The law intended states to undertake a comprehensive planning process to coordinate and integrate family-oriented service programs. States were authorized to spend up to $1 million, with no state match required, for the first year (fiscal 1994) for planning and developing new five-year state plans. Fiscal 1995 funds would only be available to states with approved five-year plans. At a minimum, the plans must state the goals to be accomplished by the end of the fifth fiscal year and provide for coordinated services with other state or federal programs serving the same population.[65]

Thus by 1993 the child welfare system had come closest to achieving the funding status envisioned by its advocates almost fifteen years before when P.L. 96-272 was enacted to provide a nationwide solution to the problem of child abuse and neglect. But despite the federal government's commitment to increased funding of family preservation programs, future spending for child welfare services remains uncertain. Under the terms of the House Republican's Contract with America, modeling itself after the Reagan administration proposal, Titles IV-B and IV-E would be repealed and replaced by a block grant to the states for child welfare and foster care expenses. Additionally, federal supervision of state child welfare programs would be eliminated, replaced by state citizen review panels.

Increased funding alone, although vital, will not solve all the problems of the child welfare system.[66] But almost certainly undoing the effects of the 1993 reforms and reducing the level of federal involvement by decreasing funding and supervision is antithetical to the goal of caring for abused and neglected children. Contrary to the rhetoric in the Contract with America, this is not a debate about improving the efficiency of the system; curtailing the role of the federal government in the child welfare system will not lower the costs of combatting child abuse and neglect. Moreover, experience suggests that allowing states virtual autonomy over the child welfare system will lead to an uneven and erratic distribution of services to troubled families throughout the nation, dependent on varying degrees of commitment and financial resources among the states.

Child Welfare Litigation

Because authority over child welfare policy, ranging from child abuse to child custody and adoption, was traditionally left to the state, the federal government's involvement was relatively limited. Over the last two decades as the federal government has assumed a greater financial and supervisory role in child welfare activities, following the passage of CAPTA and P.L. 96-272, the role of the federal courts in child welfare policy has concomitantly grown. Such laws helped create an environment in which child welfare advocates could seek federal court intervention to reform child welfare agencies. Thus, in the 1980s, children's advocacy groups increasingly turned to the federal courts to support their efforts to protect children from abuse and neglect.

Federal Court Jurisdiction over Family Policy

Litigation over the child welfare system raises questions about the proper boundaries of the state and federal government over family policy and, in particular, about the jurisdictional limits of state and federal courts.[67] In three opinions, spanning almost fifteen years, the Court explicated the proper jurisdiction of the federal courts in certain issues related to family policy.[68]

In *Moore v. Sims*, decided in 1979, the Court barred the lower federal courts from ruling on a constitutional challenge to a Texas child abuse law. Without reaching the merits, the Court stressed that this case was about "family relations," a "traditional area of state concern," over which the state courts must have primary responsibility.[69] Because it held that the lower federal court should have dismissed the case, the high court never addressed the validity of the child protection law nor did it discuss the proper balance between the rights of the parents and the safety of the children.

In 1982, in *Lehman v. Lycoming County Children's Services Agency*, the Court again confronted the issue of federal court intervention into child welfare law by defining the reach of the writ of habeas corpus over children in foster care.[70] Again, the Court emphasized that the adjudication of family issues was primarily reserved for state courts. Ruling that children in foster care were not within the state's custody within the meaning of habeas corpus, the Court denied a mother's attempt to regain custody of her children. It held that she was merely seeking federal court intervention to relitigate the issue of her parental rights. Citing concerns for federalism and finality in child custody disputes, the Court concluded that federal habeas relief is unavailable to challenge child custody decisions.

Ten years later, in *Ankenbrandt v. Richards*, the Court again clarified the limits of federal court jurisdiction in family matters by determining the extent to which the "domestic relations" exception barred federal courts from adjudicating issues of alimony, divorce, and child custody in cases brought under diversity of citizenship jurisdiction.[71] The Court justified retaining the exception on policy grounds, namely, that federal court judges lacked the expertise of state court judges in these areas and were less suitable for monitoring compliance with judicial decrees.[72]

Overall, these three decisions had little effect on the practices of state child welfare systems. Because the Supreme Court never reached the merits of the litigants' arguments, the opinions revealed little of the Court's views on the actions of the child welfare agencies. Of course, in the circumstances of these cases, the states appeared to be fulfilling their declared purpose of promoting the best interests of the children; in the first two cases at least, it was the parents who complained that their rights were being denied by overzealous child protection efforts.

Parental Rights and Due Process

The Supreme Court rendered six opinions related to child welfare matters between 1977 and 1993; in each the Court was required to assess whether states were fulfilling their responsibilities to children within the guidelines set by the Constitution and federal law. The first three cases involve appeals brought by parents and/or foster parents challenging state child welfare policies.

In *Smith v. Organization of Foster Families for Equality and Reform*, decided in 1977, the Court examined New York's procedure for removing children from foster homes.[73] *Smith* embodies the complex rules and regulations governing the relationships among children, foster parents, biological parents, and the state. It illustrates the myriad of legal problems arising from the foster care relationship, especially when the foster care parents, intended to be temporary caretakers, seek to establish more permanent ties with their foster children over the objections of the biological parents.

Under New York State law, foster parents received ten days' notice before the state removed a child from their home and were permitted to appear with counsel for a "conference" with the Social Services Department to object to the removal. The department's final determination to remove the child could be appealed in an administrative "fair hearing" held before other department officials; that decision was subject to judicial review. A child in care for less than eighteen months was removed prior to the hearing and judicial review. Under rules applicable to New York City alone, foster parents could request a hearing before the child was taken out of their home if she or he were to be sent to another foster home, rather than returned to the biological parents.

The plaintiffs in this case were Madelaine Smith and other New York foster parents whose foster children had been reunited with their biological parents. The foster parents argued that they were entitled to an automatic pre-removal hearing before children living in their homes for at least a year were removed. A group of biological mothers of children in foster care intervened in the case, defending the current procedure and arguing that more formal hearings would undercut the department's stated preference for returning children home as quickly as possible and would also violate their right of privacy. Appointed independent counsel representing the children also advocated retaining the current policy.

The foster parents asserted that the children developed psychological ties with them, giving rise to a "liberty" interest that was entitled to constitutional protection. Avoiding the novel issue of the rights of foster parents, the lower court held the procedure constitutionally inadequate because it denied foster children an opportunity to be heard before suffering a "grievous loss," that is, removal from their foster families.

Children's advocacy groups were divided on the matter: the National Juvenile Law Center submitted a friend of the court brief urging the Court to reverse the lower court; A Group for Concerned Persons for Children sought to persuade the high court to affirm. Amici briefs were also filed by the Community Service Society of New York, the Juvenile Rights Division of the Legal Aid Society, and the Puerto Rican Family Institute.[74]

Speaking for the Court, Justice Brennan reversed the court below. In a lengthy prologue, he pointed to numerous ways in which the reality of the foster care system differed from its idyllic picture as a temporary solution for children whose parents were temporarily unable to care for them. He noted how the system seemed to be failing everybody: biological parents, foster parents, and the children themselves. But, said Brennan, the courts are not equipped to reform the system. Their task is merely to assess the constitutionality of the state's procedures in removing children from foster homes. Concerns about foster care, he insisted, must be addressed to the legislature.

In determining the legal parameters of the relationship between children and foster parents, the Court assessed the potency of the liberty interests involved. The foster parents renewed their argument that their liberty interest, acquired through the foster relationship, required a pre-removal hearing. Counsel for the children argued that foster parents have no liberty interest apart from the interests of the children who are best served by the current procedure.

Although persuaded that a foster family's emotional ties could match, or even exceed, a biological family's, the Court held that the legal attributes differed significantly. Whatever the emotional bonds, the foster relationship arises from state law and is entitled to only a narrowly defined liberty interest. Thus, when the foster family's interest conflicts with the biological family's, it must yield to the latter's superior claim over the child. Thus, given the limited constitutional protection due a foster relationship, the challenged procedures were sufficient.

In 1981, in *Lassiter v. Department of Social Services of Durham County, North Carolina*, the Court considered a mother's claim that she was entitled to appointed counsel in a hearing to determine the termination of her parental rights.[75] The state appointed counsel only in abuse, neglect, and dependency hearings.

In 1975 the state declared Abby Lassiter's infant son William a neglected child and transferred custody to the Department of Social Services. A year later Lassiter was convicted of second-degree murder and sentenced to twenty-five to forty years in prison. In 1978 the department petitioned to terminate her parental rights on the grounds that she expressed virtually no interest in her son's welfare, having made no attempt to contact his social worker.

Lassiter was brought to court in prison clothes, and after concluding that she had "ample opportunity" to secure the help of an attorney, the judge proceeded with the hearing; she never claimed she was unable to afford an attorney but merely argued that she wanted the child raised by his grandmother, her mother. After a formal hearing in which the grandmother and the child's social worker appeared as witnesses, the court terminated her parental status.

On appeal, Lassiter claimed she was denied due process because she lacked counsel during the hearing. After losing in the state courts, her appeal to the U.S. Supreme Court was supported by amici curiae briefs from the National Center on Women and Family Law, the National Legal Aid and Defender Association, and the North Carolina Civil Liberties Union. The American Bar Association also filed an amicus curiae brief.[76]

Conceding that parental terminations must be governed by the due process clause, the Court sought to determine what process was due. It balanced the parties' interest in fairness against the state's interest in avoiding costs and complexity in the termination procedure. Acknowledging that most jurisdictions (thirty-three states plus the District of Columbia) appoint counsel in dependency and termination proceedings, the Court nevertheless declined to require states to appoint counsel in all circumstances, holding that trial courts must be able to decide whether to appoint counsel on a case-by-case basis. Assessing the facts of her case, the Court believed that although she might have been marginally helped by having an attorney present, the evidence of her indifference to her child was so overwhelming that the absence of counsel did not make the proceedings "fundamentally unfair."

Santosky v. Kramer, decided a year later, also challenged the procedure for terminating parental rights.[77] Under New York law there must be an initial finding, supported by a preponderance of the evidence, that a child is "permanently neglected." At a subsequent dispositional hearing, the judge determines whether the best interest of the child is served by terminating the parent's rights.

In 1973 two of the Santosky children were taken from their home; ten months later three-day-old Jed was also removed. The children were declared "permanently neglected" at a hearing initiated by the Ulster County Department of Social Services. At the dispositional hearing that followed, the New York

Family Court judge terminated the Santosky's parental rights in the three children. The state high court affirmed.

The Santosky's appeal was supported by amici curiae briefs from the Children's Rights Project of the ACLU and Community Action for Legal Services, urging the Court to reverse the court below. The Supreme Court vacated the judgment and remanded the case to the lower court.

Speaking for the majority, Justice Blackmun reiterated the familiar position that the parents' interest in the family is protected by the liberty clause of the Fourteenth Amendment and is not nullified when they neglect their children or lose temporary custody over them. Consequently, all parents are entitled to "fundamentally fair procedures" when facing the abolition of their parental rights.

The Court stressed that the dispute here is between the parent and the state: that neither the children nor the foster parents play a role. The purpose of the neglect hearing, it said, is to determine whether the parents are fit to raise their children, not whether the children would be better off with foster parents. Indeed, the high court noted, until the parents are declared unfit, they share a common interest with the children in preserving the family.

Because the state's interest in the family is furthered by determining parental unfitness as accurately as possible, the termination of parental rights requires a clear and convincing evidence standard, customarily used when significant interests, "more substantial than mere loss of money," are involved.[78] Distinguishing *Lassiter*, the Court held that the need to meet a specified standard of proof must be known in advance by both parties and cannot be adjudicated on appeal.

Throughout these cases the Court only gave a cursory examination to the interests of the children, devoting its attention to the conflict between the state and the parent over the meaning of the due process clause. The next three decisions, however, arose out of cases in which children's interests were squarely at odds with those of the state and had the potential for producing significant reform of the child welfare system.

A State's Duty to Protect

DeShaney v. Winnebago County Department of Social Services, a 1989 opinion, concerned a four-year-old boy so severely beaten by his father that he became permanently paralyzed and severely disabled.[79] The Supreme Court was asked to decide whether the Fourteenth Amendment imposed an affirmative obligation on the state to protect Joshua from the parental violence of which it was aware. However, despite the fact that the child's well-being was at issue, the Court refused to address the adequacy of the state child protection system or to consider whether the state's own child protection laws impose a special obligation on it for children known to be at risk.

Joshua DeShaney's parents obtained a Wyoming divorce in 1980 when he was one year old; his father, Randy, was awarded custody and moved to Wisconsin with Joshua. Later remarried, the father was again divorced in 1982. During the second divorce proceedings, DeShaney's wife (not Joshua's mother about whom not much is known) told police that he hit the boy who was, in her view, a "prime case for child abuse." A Winnebago County Wisconsin Social Services Department (DSS) investigated the charges, which were denied by the father, and took no official action. The agency never interviewed Joshua.

A year later, in January 1983, Joshua was hospitalized with multiple bruises and abrasions. Under the state's mandatory reporting law, required by CAPTA as a condition of federal aid, DSS was called in; the agency, solely responsible for investigating child abuse reports, obtained an emergency order placing him in the hospital's temporary custody. An ad hoc child protection team, consisting of a lawyer, psychologist, pediatrician, police detective, and several DDS caseworkers and hospital officials, met, and although they suspected abuse, they concluded there was insufficient evidence for the state to act. The team advocated several methods for protecting Joshua from harm: enrolling him in Head Start, providing counseling for his father, and removing the father's girlfriend from the home. DeShaney agreed to all the terms. On the team's recommendation, the juvenile court dismissed the case and Joshua was returned home.

In March 1983 Joshua was back in the hospital, and although his caseworker was called, she took no immediate action. For a period of about six months, she made monthly visits to Joshua's home, made detailed notes of signs of abuse, and carefully recorded her concern for him. During one visit she saw evidence of a mark on his chin that looked like a cigarette burn.

Randy DeShaney ignored the agreement with DSS from the start, yet the agency took no action against him.[80] The caseworker failed to protect Joshua, and during 1983 he was seen in the hospital for bumps, a scratched cornea, a bloody nose and bruised shoulders, and a swollen ear.[81]

On March 8, 1984, two weeks shy of his fifth birthday—a day after the caseworker's last visit to the home—Joshua was so severely beaten by his father that he fell into a deep coma. In notifying Joshua's mother of his injury, the caseworker said, "I just knew the phone would ring some day and Joshua would be dead."

Emergency surgery revealed that his injuries, including extensive brain damage, were the result of a series of assaults over many months. He survived the operation, but the irreversible brain damage he suffered requires him to be institutionalized for the rest of his life. Randy DeShaney was convicted of child abuse, and sentenced to two to four years in prison; he was paroled after serving less than two years.[82]

Claiming that the state deprived him of liberty without due process of law, Joshua's mother and guardian *ad litem* sued the state on Joshua's behalf for failing to protect him from his father's violence; the liberty interest at stake was his right to bodily integrity. In an unpublished opinion, the lower court dismissed the lawsuit, and the Seventh Circuit affirmed.[83]

The appeal to the Supreme Court was widely supported by amici curiae briefs from the Children's Rights Project of the ACLU and the Massachusetts Committee for Children and Youth. The amici's purpose was to focus the Court's attention on the issue of substantive rights arising from the state's commitment to protect children.[84]

The Supreme Court affirmed the lower court in a six to three vote. Refusing to venture into the territory of substantive due process analysis (the basis of Joshua's claim against the state), the Court denied the state's responsibility to Joshua. Speaking for the majority, Chief Justice Rehnquist held that the state's failure to ensure Joshua's safety did not rise to a constitutional violation. The Constitution, he explained, was intended to protect people from oppression by the state; the framers left the task of defining the government's obligation to protect members of society from each other "to the democratic political processes."

Based on a literal reading of the Constitution, Rehnquist asserted that there is no constitutional "entitlement" to positive liberties. The due process clause limits state action; on its face, it does not impose affirmative obligations on the state to ensure life, liberty, or property.[85] Because the state does not have a duty to act on Joshua's behalf, it is not constitutionally liable for failing to act.

Even if there is no duty to protect the public as a whole, Joshua's attorneys argued, the state had a "special relationship" with him, deriving from the social service agency's knowledge of his father's abuse and its attempts to prevent it.[86] Additionally, they claimed, Wisconsin law charged the state with responsibility for protecting children from abuse. Thus, the state's inaction created its liability.

Not true, said the Court, its analysis turning on the nature of Joshua's relationship to the state. Unlike prisoners or involuntarily committed mental patients, to whom it owed a duty of adequate care, the state had no special relationship to Joshua. Despite its supervision over him, he was in his father's custody, not the state's. Nor had the state limited his actions in any way. In the majority's view, the state's duty to protect an individual arises from restraining the actions of an individual; it is the restraint that constitutes the "deprivation of liberty" that triggers the due process requirement.[87]

In a footnote, the Court explained that had the state removed Joshua from "free society and placed him in a foster home operated by its agents," the outcome of the case *might* have been different. It acknowledged that in such situations, some lower courts, analogizing foster care to institutionalization or imprisonment, held states liable for injuries to children in foster care.[88] The Court stressed that because *DeShaney* was based on a different set of facts, that is, Joshua was not in foster care, it was "express[ing] no view on" the soundness of the analogy.

In sum, despite the child welfare agency's awareness of the danger he was in, in the Court's view, state actors had played no role in creating or increasing it; the majority maintained that returning Joshua to his home made him no worse off than if he had not been removed at all. Thus, the state was not constitutionally liable for the ultimate tragic result.

Rehnquist warned against letting "natural sympathy" for Joshua lead to blaming the state for the little boy's plight. Randy DeShaney caused the boy's injuries, he stressed, not the state. The worst that state officials could be charged with, he said, is passivity, that they "stood by" and let it happen. But, he pointed out, had they moved too quickly to take custody of Joshua, they would have been criticized for intruding into the parent-child relationship and been subject to charges of interfering with the family's right to privacy.

Rehnquist's fear that the state could have been liable to the DeShaney family for violating its right of privacy was likely misplaced. A "state-of-mind" requirement would insulate the state from liability for mistaken intervention while protecting the child from harm in the case of extreme misconduct by a state official. But because it found there was no duty, the Court never addressed the question of the standard for mounting a colorable claim against the state for a due process violation.[89]

Although Rehnquist's statement might appear on its face as an argument for family preservation, no advocate of family preservation would recommend that the state ignore evidence of Joshua's abuse in order to keep him at home. The purpose behind passage of P.L. 96-272 was to prevent harm to the child by providing services to the family to allow it to stay together. Here, the state did neither: while there appeared to be a service plan, DSS made no real attempt to implement it and made little or no effort to confront Joshua's father with evidence of the boy's abuse. Whatever the deficiencies of the foster care system, under circumstances such as these there is no question that Joshua should have been placed in care while attempts were made to re-educate his father; ultimately, a decision would be made about whether Joshua should be returned to his parent or placed for adoption.

Rehnquist emphasized that although the state's voluntary efforts to protect Joshua might have created liability under state tort law, the due process clause does not convert every state tort claim into a constitutional violation. Stressing the importance of state autonomy, he declared that the people of Wisconsin may wish to hold state officials responsible for situations such as Joshua's. But he would not "thrust it upon them by this Court's expansion of the Due Process Clause of the Fourteenth Amendment."

In refusing to apportion any responsibility to the state, *DeShaney* advanced the Rehnquist Court's preference for diminishing federal court interference with state autonomy, based in part on a fear that conceding its potential liability for Joshua's injuries would open a floodgate of litigation against the state. The Court was concerned that federal courts would be required to adjudicate cases in which people complained of inadequate police protection if they were robbed, inadequate fire protection if their homes burned, or an inadequate food supply if they were hungry.[90]

Seeking to avoid an undue display of sympathy for him, the majority characterized Joshua's situation in adult terms: as an "individual" seeking aid in a "free society" against violence from "private actors."[91] By depicting Joshua as a grown-up, capable of taking care of himself, the Court avoided the necessity of distinguishing children from other types of recipients of government services. But consigning the Joshuas in the nation to the "democratic political processes" seems tragically ironic when children are not represented in the political process.

In contrast, the dissenting justices, Marshall, Blackmun, and Brennan, rejected the majority's formalistic approach of basing the decision on the distinction between action and inaction, custody and non-custody.[92] Justice Brennan focused instead on the results of the state's inaction after taking responsibility for protecting children such as Joshua and failing to do so. He challenged the majority's "stingy" reading of the cases involving the state's duty to act in prisons and mental hospitals, arguing that in those cases the state's responsibility arose because having cut off sources of private aid, it was obliged to replace them.[93]

Brennan examined the role of the state in establishing a child protection system, especially for children like Joshua. By conferring sole responsibility on the local department of social services to protect Joshua from abuse, the state effectively cut him off from other sources of aid and consequently worsened his situation. In Brennan's view, because the state knew the danger Joshua was in and removed any other sources of assistance, it was obliged to prevent the harm that ultimately befell the little boy.

Brennan was less concerned than the majority with preserving the state's autonomy and more than willing to impose constitutional liability on the state for Joshua's injuries. Perhaps there was a legitimate reason for the caseworker's decision not to remove Joshua, he said, but because his claim was dismissed, Joshua was unable to require an explanation from the state agency.

The majority's rejection of the state's responsibility for child protection in *DeShaney* raises several disturbing questions about the state's long-standing role as *parens patriae*. *DeShaney* appears to contradict the Court's statement in *Santosky v. Kramer* that the state has a "*parens patriae* interest in preserving and promoting the welfare of the child."[94] Similarly, in *Schall v. Martin*, a juvenile court case decided a few years earlier, the Court had asserted that children "are assumed to be subject to the control of their parents, and if parental control falters, the State must play its part as *parens patriae*."[95] Clearly, the Court could have held the state responsible for failing to serve as *parens patriae* and averting the disaster in the DeShaney house. Such a result would have been well within the Court's traditional view of the state's relationship to the child.

Justice Blackmun began his impassioned dissent with the words, "Poor Joshua." Rising to an emotional pitch, Blackmun pointed out that the Court had an opportunity to strengthen the state's commitment to abused children. But, he charged, the Court instead allowed the state to abdicate its responsibility to all the "Poor Joshuas" in the nation.

Enforcing P.L. 96-272

Passage of P.L. 96-272 had raised hopes that states would improve their child protection and foster care systems. In the 1980s child welfare advocates began to file a series of class action suits against social service agencies for failing to conform to the mandates of the statute. The litigation was characterized by charges that a combination of rising caseloads, underfunding, and inadequate staffing resulted in the agencies' systematic failure to care for abused and neglected children. In each case, however, before proceeding to the merits of the case, the courts had to decide whether the plaintiffs were entitled to judicial relief. The defendants argued that under the statute the Department of Health and Human Services had sole authority to enforce P.L. 96-272. In legal terms, the courts had to determine whether Congress intended to allow plaintiffs to enforce the act through a private right of action or through a § 1983 cause of action.[96]

The post–Civil War statute, 42 U.S.C. § 1983, provides a federal remedy for deprivation of federal rights by persons acting under color of state law.[97] By itself, § 1983, as it is commonly known, does not confer a substantive right; it is merely a vehicle to seek federal court relief for violation of a federally protected right.

According to case law, a § 1983 remedy is available if the federal law creates an enforceable right, absent evidence of congressional intent to foreclose such a remedy. The Court has created an exception to this principle for statutes enacted under the congressional spending power. Such statutes must "unambig-uously" guarantee rights to individuals; one that simply indicates a congressional preference for a certain mode of conduct rather than creates a binding obligation on the state is not enforceable under § 1983.[98]

Alternatively, under guidelines developed by the Supreme Court in *Cort v. Ash* in 1975, a private remedy to enforce provisions of a federal statute that does not expressly allow it may be judicially implied in the following circumstances: the plaintiff must be a member of the class for whose "especial benefit" the statute was enacted; there must be evidence of legislative intent, either explicit or implicit, to create such a remedy; the implication of the remedy must be consistent with the statutory scheme; and the cause of action must not be one traditionally relegated to state law.[99]

Reflecting the Supreme Court's philosophy of limiting federal court jurisdiction over traditional areas of state court authority, in the years since *Cort* was decided the Court has become increasingly reluctant to imply private causes of action in federal statutes.[100]

An extensive body of P.L. 96-272 case law began to develop in the lower courts during the 1980s. In the 1983 case of *Lynch v. Dukakis* the First Circuit held that the secretary's power to withhold federal funds notwithstanding, P.L. 96-272 could be enforced in a § 1983 action. The appellate court let stand a lower court order requiring the state agency to assign a caseworker to each child within twenty-four hours, to restrict caseworker workloads, and to follow the case plan and case review requirements of Title IV-E.[101] In 1988 the Fourth Circuit ruled in *L. J. ex rel. Darr v. Massinga* that violations of P.L. 96-272 were enforceable under § 1983; it upheld a lower court injunction requiring the state to implement the case plan and case review provisions of the act.[102]

Shortly thereafter three 1989 Illinois district court cases created some uncertainty over the enforceability of P.L. 96-272 in federal court. In the first, *B. H. v. Johnson*, the court ruled that P.L. 96-272 created enforceable rights (either through § 1983 or a private right of action) to a case plan and case review system, but found the "reasonable efforts" and the "least restrictive setting" clauses too vague to enforce.[103] In the second case, *Aristotle P. v. Johnson*, the district court agreed that the class of foster children could bring a § 1983 suit for violation of certain rights under P.L. 96-272, but not the "reasonable efforts" provision.[104] Then, in *Artist M. v. Johnson*, another Illinois district court found the "reasonable efforts" clause enforceable under § 1983 or a private right of action.[105]

With a slightly different twist, a 1990 case, *Norman v. Johnson*, held that indigent parents who had been separated from their children because they could not provide for them had standing to sue under § 1983 to enforce parts of P.L. 96-272 including the "reasonable efforts" provision.[106] And ruling on a wide-ranging challenge to the Department of Human Services (DHS) of Washington, D.C., in 1991, the District Court for the District of Columbia ruled in favor of a class of present and potential foster care children. In *LaShawn v. Dixon* the court found that DHS had committed systematic violations of P.L. 96-272 and CAPTA by failing to investigate reports of abuse and neglect in a timely fashion, to provide services for children and families, to make appropriate foster care placements, to develop case plans, and to assure permanent homes for the children in its care.[107]

Thus, most lower federal courts found that P.L. 96-272 conferred at least some enforceable rights on children in the child welfare system. The crucial test came in 1992 when the Supreme Court was asked to rule on the extent to which children had federally enforceable rights under P.L. 96-272.

Suter v. Artist M., known as *Artist M. v. Johnson* in the lower courts, began as a class action suit against the Illinois Department of Children and Family Services (DCFS) in December 1988 by a class of present and potential children in foster or state-supervised care.[108] The plaintiffs charged that DCFS violated the act by routinely failing to assign caseworkers in a timely fashion (or failing to reassign replacement caseworkers as necessary).

The district court held that P.L. 96-272, including the "reasonable efforts" provision, was enforceable in federal court. After finding that DCFS made no effort to prevent foster care placement, the district court ordered the agency to assign (or reassign) a caseworker to each child placed in its custody within three working days. The Seventh Circuit affirmed, holding that despite the state's discretionary authority to fulfil the "reasonable efforts" requirement, the court is "capable of" judging whether the state's efforts are "reasonable."[109]

In reaching this decision, the appellate court principally relied on the Supreme Court's opinion in *Wilder v. Virginia Hospital Association*.[110] The *Wilder* Court had ruled that the Boren Amendment to the Medicaid Act, requiring states to reimburse health care providers treating Medicaid patients at "reasonable and adequate" rates, was enforceable under § 1983. Despite the state's discretionary authority to determine how to calculate the rates, the Court found that the act met the test for the availability of a § 1983 remedy: it was intended to benefit the "putative" plaintiff; it created a "binding obligation" on the state; and it was not "too vague and amorphous" to be "beyond the competence of the judiciary to enforce."[111] Applying the *Cort v. Ash* factors, the appellate court ruled that the statute created an implied private right of action in the plaintiffs.

The state appealed. The likely nationwide effect of this decision was indicated by the parties attempting to influence the Court. The U.S. solicitor general, thirty-eight states and the District of Columbia, as well as the National Governors Association, the National League of Cities, the National Association of Counties, and the National Conference of State Legislators filed amici briefs on behalf of Illinois urging the Supreme Court to reverse. On the side of plaintiff Artist M., thirteen Illinois state and local bar associations, child welfare and advocacy groups, eleven national child welfare organizations, as well as groups such as the American Bar Association, the National Association of Counsel for Children, the ACLU, the Youth Law Center, and the National Council of Juvenile and Family Court Judges submitted amici briefs urging the Court to affirm.

In a seven to two opinion the Supreme Court held that congressional intent was the key to whether P.L. 96-272 allowed a § 1983 remedy and the burden was on the plaintiffs to prove it. Acknowledging that the act speaks in mandatory language, the Court held that it merely directs the state to submit a plan to HHS for approval. It interpreted the phrase, "the plan shall be in effect in all political subdivisions of the State," to simply require the plan to apply to the entire state, not to require it to be "in effect." Moreover, unlike the Boren Amendment and its accompanying regulations that contained detailed methods for determining reasonable reimbursement rates, P.L. 96-272 did not indicate how to measure the reasonableness of the state's prevention and reunification efforts. It was self-evident, said the Court, that the meaning of this phrase will "vary" according to the facts of each case.

Because the act confers no enforceable rights on the children it purports to benefit, the Court concluded that they cannot sue state officials for deficiencies in the child welfare system. But the statute is far from being "a dead letter," the Court stressed as the secretary is empowered to withhold federal funds from non-compliant states.

Despite the Court's assurances, the remedy it cites is questionable, for as Justice Scalia observed during oral argument in *Suter*, the secretary has never terminated a state's funding under the act.[112] Moreover, it is difficult to see how the beneficiaries of the act—the abused and neglected children of Illinois—would be aided by a remedy that withheld federal funds from the state child welfare agency. Indeed, in the past the Court had rejected the argument that a federal agency's ability to withhold funds is evidence of congressional intent to preclude enforcement under § 1983.

Finally, the Court briefly "disposed of" the appellate court's ruling that a private right of action could be implied under the statute. As with § 1983, the *Cort v. Ash* analysis turns on the question of congressional intent. Having demonstrated that Congress did not intend to confer a federally enforceable right to "reasonable efforts" in P.L. 96-272, the Court reasoned that the private right of action is also unavailable.

Dissenting on behalf of himself and Justice Stevens, Justice Blackmun accused the majority of ignoring the precedent it had created less than two years before in *Wilder*. Comparing the Medicaid Act with P.L. 96-272, he argued that both statutes imposed binding obligations on the states. And he reminded the Court that in *Wilder* it had rejected the state's argument that the Medicaid Act only required it to file a plan, not to actually carry out the plan and provide reasonable rates. Disdaining the majority's assertion that P.L. 96-272 was "too vague and amorphous" to be enforced, he declared that there was no greater specificity in the "reasonable rates" requirement of the Boren Amendment than in the "reasonable efforts" requirement of P.L. 96-272; in both cases, he said, courts were competent to assess the results of the state's efforts. Blackmun criticized the Court for ignoring precedent and changing "the rules of the game" without justification. He charged the majority with reversing traditional § 1983 case law by now requiring plaintiffs to bear the burden of showing that Congress intended to create enforceable rights in them. He ended by sadly noting that "after all, we are dealing here with children," indicating his belief that the Court's narrow interpretation of P.L. 96-272 will severely harm this vulnerable group of litigants.

Congress Reacts to *Suter*

There was little interaction between Congress and the federal courts over child welfare policymaking, as for the most part, Congress appeared to pay little attention to judicial decisions in child welfare law. The *Suter* decision, roundly criticized by most observers, was an exception to this principle. The Supreme Court's refusal to allow private enforcement of P.L. 96-272 raised questions about the enforceability of other provisions of the Social Security Act, especially those relating to children such as AFDC, child welfare, child support enforcement, and the JOBS program, all containing state plan requirements. For although there was a solid line of cases allowing judicial enforcement of Title IV-A through § 1983, for example, it was possible that courts would interpret *Suter* to reverse this trend.[113] Moreover, while some courts had recognized § 1983 causes of action in mothers seeking to compel states to provide child support enforcement under Title IV-D, it appeared likely that *Suter* would call a halt to this practice.[114]

Congress initially attempted to limit *Suter* in H.R. 11, the urban aid bill vetoed by President Bush. In 1993, while deliberating on the Family Preservation and Support Bill (enacted as part of the Omnibus Budget Reconciliation Act of 1993), Congress again considered measures to contain *Suter*.

A House-proposed bill attempted to reinstate the *status quo ante* with respect to allowing individuals to sue states for their failure to comply with state plan requirements. But this so-called "*Suter* Fix" was dropped in conference, despite some fairly strong support for it. In any event, its passage would not have disturbed the Court's ban on private enforcement of the "reasonable efforts" clause. The House version would merely have required the secretary to conduct a study of the way in which the states implemented the reasonable efforts requirement of P.L. 96-272. This language was dropped in the final bill as well, the conferees instead "strongly urg[ing]" the secretary to conduct such a study and to convene an advisory group to make recommendations.[115]

In October 1994, Congress included a version of the "*Suter* Fix" as part of the Elementary and Secondary Education Reauthorization Act. Following its earlier approach, this legislation reversed the Supreme Court's ban on private rights of action to force compliance with state plans under Title IV, but let stand the Court's prohibition on judicial enforcement of the "reasonable efforts" requirement in P.L. 96-272. On October 20, 1994, Clinton signed the Elementary and Secondary School Act into law, thus partially reversing the *Suter* decision.

Due Process for Immigrant Children

Reno v. Flores, decided in 1993, involved a due process challenge to an Immigration and Naturalization Service (INS) regulation requiring juveniles arrested by the INS on suspicion of entering the country illegally to be released only to "parents, close relatives, or legal guardians."[116] The litigation initially arose in the early 1980s, and led to a consent decree in which the INS had agreed to place juveniles awaiting their deportation hearing in a care facility meeting "acceptable child welfare standards."

The issue before the Supreme Court was whether the Constitution and United States immigration laws required the INS to release children under eighteen to *any* "responsible adults" and provide an individualized hearing to determine "their best interests."

Speaking for a seven to two majority, Justice Scalia noted that Congress grants the attorney general broad discretionary authority to determine the conditions of release of suspected illegal immigrants. Placing the government on the moral highground, Scalia stated that unlike adults, who are for the most part routinely released pending their deportation hearing, the INS has a responsibility to children that prevents it from "simply send[ing] them off into the night."

The juveniles claimed that the due process clauses of the Fifth and Fourteenth Amendments barred the government from infringing on their liberty without a compelling reason. Without denying that the juveniles had a right to due process, Scalia narrowly characterized the legal issue as whether a child without available guardians or relatives, and for whom the government is responsible, has the right to be placed in the custody of a private individual rather than in a government-approved child care institution.

Recognizing this right as fundamental, he asserted, would cast doubt on the legitimacy of all forms of state custody over children, including those orphaned and abandoned. Additionally, it would give the federal courts authority over the day-to-day operations of state orphanages and other child care facilities, and, to his knowledge, no court below had recognized such a right. Because of its "novelty," it clearly could not be described as a deeply rooted fundamental right. Whatever right the juveniles did possess was easily outweighed by the government's interest in their welfare as well as by the agency's administrative needs.

Finally, Scalia concluded, because the government's custody over them is not unconstitutional, there is no need for a hearing to determine whether their current placement is more or less desirable than any other. He denied that the "best interests" standard plays a useful or even legitimate role in these circumstances. Speaking more broadly, he stated that the government is not constitutionally bound by the "best interests" standard. Barred only from denying fundamental rights, states have no constitutional obligation to place the interests of children over competing concerns, such as fiscal responsibility or administrative efficiency.

Justice Stevens, dissenting, pointed out the contradiction between the Court's refusal to apply the "best interests" standard to the INS detention policy and the agency's own claim that it was holding the juveniles in custody for their "best interests." He noted the irony of the Court justifying the regulation on the basis of administrative convenience and cost, while the INS insisted that its policy was motivated by concern for the children's welfare. More specifically, Stevens revealed some facts omitted in the majority opinion: that these children, who were rarely deported, were subject to indeterminate detention—in some cases as long as a year; that detention was a form of imprisonment; and that the INS definition of "close relatives" excluded even cousins.

Conclusion

Beginning in the mid-1970s the federal government attempted to create a more cohesive child welfare policy in the United States, hoping that state child welfare systems would reduce their reliance on foster care and exert greater efforts to preserve the children's family bonds. Not surprisingly, because of the goals they sought to achieve, these policies received a good deal of support from Congress, the executive branch, and child welfare advocates. By providing financial incentives to the states, and assuming a supervisory role, the federal government attempted to exercise some degree of control over child welfare policies in the nation. But with most of child welfare policymaking still traditionally committed to the jurisdiction of the states, most of the legal actions related to child welfare policy involve challenges to state laws and practices. And in deciding these cases, the Court was greatly concerned about the federal courts unduly intruding into state prerogatives in the area of child welfare law.

Through its use of the abstention doctrine, the domestic relations exception, limits on habeas corpus, constraints on private rights of action, and narrow interpretations of federal constitutional principles, the Supreme Court has thus limited the federal judiciary's role in child welfare policy. The Court was motivated in large part by its concern that the federal courts would become responsible for the daily management of state child welfare agencies.[117]

Of the child welfare cases decided on the merits, those brought by parents on their own behalf required the Court to ascertain the degree to which state procedures in matters involving custody, foster care, and the termination of parental rights conformed to the due process clause of the Fourteenth Amendment. In these cases, the children often appeared merely as bystanders in the battle between the parents and the state and their interests were rarely addressed by the Court. The group of cases brought by or on behalf of children raised fundamental questions about society's responsibility to protect children from harm. These cases, arguably adjudicating the interests of society's most disadvantaged children, dramatically illustrated the outer limits of the Court's willingness to interfere with the state's autonomy in policymaking for children.

By emphasizing the distinction between public and private in *DeShaney*, the Supreme Court helped remove the biological family from the state's reach in safeguarding the child. And although the Court surely did not mean to suggest that laws against child abuse and neglect should be abolished, its ruling in this case undermines the nation's child protection systems. Moreover, by insulating social service agencies from claims against a grossly negligent caseworker (seemingly an accurate description of Joshua's caseworker), the Court may have unwittingly contributed to a replay of Joshua's story.[118]

The Supreme Court's dismissal of the needs of abused and neglected children in *DeShaney* and *Suter* suggests that federal court litigation is problematic for improving the child welfare system; as a result of these two cases, children in state-supervised care are discouraged from bringing constitutional or P.L. 96-272 claims in the federal courts. The constitutional status of children in foster care is still unsettled, and although some lower courts have extended protection to foster care children on substantive due process grounds, the Supreme Court has consistently refused to resolve inconsistencies in the law.[119]

In *Suter* the Court's refusal to allow private suits for violation of P.L. 96-272 barred beneficiaries of the act from seeking relief in the federal courts and consigned them to remedies specified in the statute—administrative enforcement by an agency that lacked the resources to ensure compliance with the act—with loss of funding as the only available sanction. And if the House-passed bill is enacted, and child welfare services are funded through block grants, there will be even less accountability by the states as well as fewer resources for funding child welfare services. In diminishing the federal government's role in encouraging states to improve their child welfare systems, the new legislation—if enacted—will jeopardize the advances made by the child welfare system since passage of P.L. 96-272.

Notes

1. See Susan Robison, *Putting the Pieces Together: Survey of State Systems for Children in Crisis* (Denver: National Conference of State Legislatures, 1990).

2. Marcia Lowry, "Derring-Do in the 1980s: Child Welfare Impact Litigation after the Warren Years," in Douglas J. Besharov, ed., *Protecting Children from Abuse and Neglect: Policy and Practice* (Springfield, Ill.: Charles C. Thomas, 1988), p. 288.

3. The American Humane Association figures are cited in Patricia G. Tjaden and Nancy Thoennes, "Predictors of Legal Intervention in Child MalTreatment Cases," *Child Abuse and Neglect* 16 (1992): 807; the percentage increase statistic is calculated by Tjaden and Thoennes, p. 807.

4. American Bar Association, *America's Children at Risk: A National Agenda for Legal Action* (Washington, D.C.: American Bar Association, 1993), p. 45. George E. Fryer, Jr., *Child Abuse and the Social Environment* (Boulder: Westview, 1993), p. 31, notes that infancy is the likeliest time for children to be mistreated.

5. The extent to which the Mary Ellen "legend" was the catalyst that stirred society's interest in protecting children has been questioned. See Sallie A. Watkins, "The Mary Ellen Myth: Correcting Child Welfare History," *Social Work* 35 (November 1990): 500–503; Lela B. Costin, "Unraveling the Mary Ellen Legend: Origins of the Cruelty Movement," *Social Service Review* (1991): 203–223.

6. C. Henry Kempe et al., "The Battered Child Syndrome," *The Journal of the American Medical Association* 181 (1962): 17–24.

7. See Jeanne M. Giovannoni and Rosina M. Becerra, *Defining Child Abuse* (New York: Free Press, 1979); and Douglas J. Besharov, *Recognizing Child Abuse* (New York: Free Press, 1990) for discussion of the problems caused by the lack of an acceptable definition of abuse and neglect.

8. Douglas J. Besharov, "The Misuse of Foster Care: When the Desire to Help Children Outruns the Ability to Improve Parental Functioning," in Besharov, ed., *Protecting Children from Abuse and Neglect*, p. 194.

9. Fryer, *Child Abuse and the Social Environment*, p. 33.

10. Vincent J. Fontana, "Child Abuse, Past, Present, and Future," *Human Ecology Forum* 15 (1984): 6.

11. Leontine Young, *Wednesday's Children: A Study of Child Neglect and Abuse* (New York: McGraw-Hill, 1964).

12. Joan DiLeonardi, "Families in Poverty and Chronic Neglect of Children," *Families in Society* 74 (November 1993): 557–562; see Kristine E. Nelson, Edward J. Saunders, and Miriam J. Landsman, "Chronic Child Neglect in Perspective," *Social Work* 38 (November 1993): 661–671; Susan J. Rose and William Meezan, "Defining Child Neglect: Evolution, Influences, and Issues," *Social Service Review* (June 1993): 279–293; Howard Dubowitz, et al., "A Conceptual Definition of Child Neglect," *Criminal Justice and Behavior* 20 (March 1993): 8–26.

13. Fryer, *Child Abuse and the Social Environment*, chapter 4. See chapter 3 for research on factors associated with child maltreatment, including studies that focus on the parents' psychological disorders. See also Robert Caldwell, G. Anne Bogat, and William S. Davidson II, "The Assessment of Child Abuse Potential," *American Journal of Community Psychology* 16 (1988): 609–624 who discuss research associated with explanations of child maltreatment.

14. See Joan I. Vondra, "Childhood Poverty and Child Maltreatment," in Judith A. Chafel, ed., *Child Poverty and Public Policy* (Washington, D.C.: Urban Institute, 1993), for summaries of such studies.

15. Michael Wald and Sophia Cohen, "Preventing Child Abuse—What Will It Take?" in Besharov, ed., *Protecting Children from Abuse and Neglect*, p. 298 n. 7. See also Judith Areen, "Intervention Between Parent and Child: A Reappraisal of the State's Role in Child Neglect and Abuse Cases," *Georgetown Law Journal* 63 (1975): 887–937.

16. See Joseph Goldstein, Anna Freud, and Albert Solnit, *Beyond the Best Interests of the Child* (New York: Free Press, 1973); Michael Wald, "State Intervention on Behalf of 'Neglected' Children: Standards for Removal of Children from Their Homes, Monitoring the Status of Children in Foster Care, and Termination of Parental Rights," *Stanford Law Review* 28 (1976): 623–699; Michael Wald, "State Intervention on Behalf of 'Neglected' Children: A Search for Realistic Standards," *Stanford Law Review* 27 (1975): 985–1040 for views on intervention in the family in cases of abuse and neglect.

17. *Artist M. v. Johnson*, 917 F.2d 980, 996 (7th Cir. 1990) (Manion, J., dissenting).

18. Besharov, "The Misuse of Foster Care," in Besharov, ed., *Protecting Children from Abuse and Neglect*, p. 190.

19. See Duncan Lindsey, *The Welfare of Children* (New York: Oxford University Press, 1994), chapter 3 for a discussion of studies of, and demonstration projects on, the foster care system.

20. American Bar Association, *America's Children at Risk*, p. 50. The report states that 3 percent of children in foster care are abused by their foster care parents.

21. Besharov, "The Misuse of Foster Care," in Besharov, ed., *Protecting Children from Abuse and Neglect*; Margaret Beyer and Wallace J. Mlyniec, "Lifelines to Biological Parents: Their Effect on Termination of Parental Rights and Permanence," in Besharov, ed., *Protecting Children from Abuse and Neglect*.

22. Benjamin Wolf, personal interview.

23. DiLeonardi, "Families in Poverty."

24. See Robison, *Putting the Pieces Together*, for an overview of the delivery of state child welfare services for abused, neglected, and dependent children, juvenile offenders, non-criminal (status) offenders, and emotionally disturbed children.

25. U.S. Advisory Board on Child Abuse and Neglect, *The Continuing Child Protection Emergency: A Challenge to the Nation* (Washington, D.C.: Department of Health and Human Services, Administration for Children and Families, 1993), p. 4.

26. See Linda Gordon, *Pitied but Not Entitled: Single Mothers and the History of Welfare* (New York: Free Press, 1994), chapter 3.

27. Joseph M. Hawes, *The Children's Rights Movement: A History of Advocacy and Protection* (Boston: Twayne Publishers, 1991), p. 100.

28. John E. B. Myers, *Legal Issues in Child Abuse and Neglect* (Newbury Park, Calif.: Sage Publications, 1992), chapters 4, 7.

29. See Barbara Nelson, *Making an Issue of Child Abuse* (Chicago: University of Chicago Press, 1984), chapter 6.

30. Theodore Stein, "The Child Abuse Prevention and Treatment Act," *Social Service Review* 58 (June 1984): 306–307. Stein raises questions about inadequate evaluation techniques in most of these research projects and questions CAPTA's effectiveness, particularly its requirement of mandatory reporting, in making children safer.

31. H. Rep. No. 159, 98th Cong., 1st Sess. 15 (1983).

32. Nelson, *Making an Issue of Child Abuse*, p. 129.

33. Stein, "The Child Abuse Prevention and Treatment Act," p. 305.

34. *Bowen v. American Hospital Association*, 476 U.S. 610 (1986). This case is omitted from the discussion on child welfare litigation below because it was decided on the basis of the secretary's rulemaking authority under § 504. See Timothy G. Kelly, "Protecting the Handicapped Newborn: Where the Courts Failed and the Legislature Succeeded—The Child Abuse Amendments of 1984," *John Marshall Law Review* 19 (1986): 397–429 for a discussion of related state and lower federal court cases.

35. Jessica Dunsay Silver, "Baby Doe: The Incomplete Federal Response," in Besharov, ed., *Protecting Children from Abuse and Neglect*. See Kelly, "Protecting the Handicapped Newborn," for a comparison of the § 504 rules and rules promulgated under the Child Abuse Amendments.

36. U.S. Advisory Board on Child Abuse and Neglect, *The Continuing Child Protection Emergency*

37. *Congressional Quarterly Weekly* (April 11, 1992): 959.

38. Another source of funding for programs serving abused and neglected children is the Social Services Block Grant, Title XX of the Social Security Act, established in 1975. Overall, states spend about half their Title XX allocations on child welfare services. Theodore Stein, *Child Welfare and the Law* (New York: Longman Publishing, 1991), p. 45.

39. Barbara Pine, "Child Welfare Reform and the Political Process," *Social Service Review* 60 (1986): 339–359, discusses the groups that formed an "issue network" to achieve passage of the bill, as well as the forerunners of the 1980 bill.

40. MaryLee Allen, Carol Golubock, and Lynn Olson, "Guide to the Adoption Assistance and Child Welfare Act of 1980," in Mark Hardin, ed., *Foster Children in the Courts* (Boston: Butterworth Legal Publishers, 1983).

41. See Theodore J. Stein and Gary David Comstock, *Reasonable Efforts: A Report on Implementation by Child Welfare Agencies in Five States* (Washington, D.C.: American Bar Association, 1987), chapter 3 for examples of services available to families in distress.

42. 126 Cong. Rec. S6942 (daily ed. June 13, 1980) (statement of Sen. Cranston).

43. *Congressional Quarterly Weekly* (June 21, 1980): 1731–1732.

44. *Congressional Quarterly Weekly* (June 21, 1980): 1731.

45. Unfortunately, family preservation is often misunderstood, in large part because of excessive media attention on its failures and infrequent mention of its successes. Most experts agree that the importance of bonding and family ties cannot be overestimated in a child's life; yet, because the media typically ignores such issues, the public usually clamors to remove children from their homes too readily and does not support their return home. This perception is reinforced when highly publicized tragedies, such as the 1993 case of Joseph Wallace in Chicago, occur. See Richard Wexler, "The Children's Crusade," *Chicago Reader* (March 24, 1995), for a discussion of the family preservation principle and how the media's attention on the Wallace case helped convince the public that the system endangers children in all cases by returning them to their parents' custody.

46. Because of its concern that too many Native American children were being placed in foster care, Congress enacted the Indian Child Welfare Act in 1978, requiring state welfare agencies to make "active efforts" to provide services to prevent the removal of Native American children from their homes. See Michele K. Bennett, "Native American Children Caught in the Web of the Indian Child Welfare Act," *Hamline Law Review* 16 (1993): 953–973.

47. In 1989 Congress increased the authorization to $325 million for fiscal 1991. Barbara Atwell, " 'A Lost Generation': The Battle for Private Enforcement of the Adoption Assistance and Child Welfare Act of 1980," *University of Cincinnati Law Review* 60 (1992): 606 n. 81.

48. Stein, *Child Welfare and the Law*, chapter 3.

49. Allen, Golubock, and Olson, "Guide to the Adoption Assistance and Child Welfare Act of 1980," in Hardin, ed., *Foster Children in the Courts*.

50. The plans were required to be in place by October 1, 1982.

51. See Alice C. Shotton, "Making Reasonable Efforts in Child Abuse and Neglect Cases: Ten Years Later," *California Western Law Review* 26 (1989–1990): 223–256, for examples of situations in which juvenile court judges found a lack of reasonable efforts.

52. Although Title IV-B does not contain a "reasonable efforts" clause, the case plan and case review requirements apply to all children in state-supervised foster care. And because all case plans must be reviewed periodically to ensure that the child is in the least restrictive environment and returned to the family as soon as possible, states must provide reunification services to all children. Allen, Golubock, and Olson, "Guide to the Adoption Assistance and Child Welfare Act of 1980," in Hardin, ed., *Foster Children in the Courts*.

53. See Alice Bussiere, "Federal Adoption Assistance for Children with Special Needs," *Clearinghouse Review* 19 (October 1985): 587–599.

54. *Congressional Quarterly Weekly* (March 30, 1991): 796–801.

55. Abigail English, "Litigating under the Adoption Assistance and Child Welfare Act of 1980," in Hardin, ed., *Foster Children in the Courts*, p. 613.

56. Lindsey, *The Welfare of Children*, p. 66.

57. *Congressional Quarterly Weekly* (March 30, 1991): 796–801.

58. Efforts to amend the Adoption Assistance and Child Welfare Act were spurred after the Supreme Court ruled in *Suter v. Artist M.*, 112 S.Ct. 1360 (1992), that P.L. 96-272 does not confer on individuals a right to enforce the act's "reasonable efforts" requirement. The decision, discussed in detail below, was uniformly denounced by child welfare advocates and prompted efforts to reverse the Court through congressional legislation. Although that effort was partially successful when legislation aimed at reversing *Suter* was passed, the Court's holding on the "reasonable efforts" provision was not reversed.

59. *Congressional Quarterly Weekly* (August 10, 1991): 2241; *Congressional Quarterly Weekly* (September 28, 1991): 2791. H.R. 2571 would have also raised the capped entitlement of Title XX from $2.8 billion to $3.4 billion by 1996.

60. 138 Cong. Rec. H7537–7546 (daily ed. August 6, 1992).

61. See, e.g., 138 Cong. Rec. H7543 (daily ed. August 6, 1992) (statement of Rep. Grandy) in which Representative Fred Grandy, Republican of Iowa, warns that President Bush will veto the bill, H.R. 3603. As early as November, 1990, President Bush had been campaigning against imposing a surtax "on the rich." 26 Weekly Comp. Pres. Doc. 1758 (November 5, 1990); 26 Weekly Comp. Pres. Doc. 1750 (November 3, 1994).

62. "Memorandum of Disapproval for the Revenue Act of 1992, 28 Weekly Comp. Pres. Doc. 2283 (November 4, 1993); *Congressional Quarterly Weekly* (October 10, 1992): 3132–3135.

63. 29 Weekly Comp. Pres. Doc. 395 (March 11, 1993); *Congressional Quarterly Weekly* (April 24, 1993): 1029.

64. *Congressional Quarterly Weekly* (September 18, 1993): 2482. The conference committee deleted the part of the House version calling for a study of "reasonable efforts" and providing for a state's failure to carry out a state plan. This aspect of the bill is discussed below.

65. Pub. L. No. 103-66, H. Rep. No. 213, 103d Cong., 1st. Sess. (1993); *Congressional Quarterly Weekly* (September 18, 1993): 2494–2495.

66. Children's advocates believe that a total overhaul of the child welfare system from training to technology—that is, a "cultural change"—is essential to produce meaningful results. Carole Shauffer, personal interview.

67. To ensure discovery of all Supreme Court opinions relating to child welfare policy through 1993, a Lexis search of the GENFED library, US file, was conducted.

Because child welfare policy encompasses a number of distinct areas, three separate searches were conducted using the following search terms: "Child Abuse or Child Neglect or Title IV-B or Title IV-E"; "Foster Care or Foster Child! or Foster Parent"; and "Child Welfare." These searches yielded 125 decisions—39, 37, and 49 respectively, with a good deal of overlap among the searches. Of these, there were 11 *relevant* opinions, that is, opinions in which the Court resolved disputes over state or federal child welfare policy by interpreting a state or federal law or regulation. Cases related to a biological parent's right to a child born out of wedlock are excluded unless they involve allegations of abuse or neglect; similarly, cases involving claims brought by persons facing prosecution for child abuse are excluded because they do not adjudicate the child's rights.

68. In *Mississippi Band of Choctaw Indians v. Holyfield*, 490 U.S. 30 (1989), the Court narrowly interpreted the Indian Child Welfare Act (ICWA) of 1978 to hold that it gave exclusive jurisdiction to determine the domicile of Native American children to tribal courts. Although this case concerns state court jurisdiction of a child welfare dispute, it is not included here because it does not revolve around jurisdictional boundaries of the state and federal courts.

69. 442 U.S. 415 (1979). Such cases arise because litigants contend that state courts are less committed to protecting federal constitutional rights and look to the federal courts for relief. In an effort to discourage this practice and preserve the autonomy of state courts, the Supreme Court has increasingly relied on the abstention doctrine, first articulated in *Younger v. Harris*, 401 U.S. 37 (1971), to restrict the lower federal courts from interfering with state authority. See Susan Gluck Mezey, "The Burger Court and *Younger* Abstention: Enhancing the Role of State Courts in Constitutional Adjudication," *Publius* 19 (1989): 25–40, for discussion of *Younger* and its progeny.

70. 458 U.S. 502 (1982). Habeas corpus is a civil remedy authorized by federal statute; a petition for habeas relief challenges the validity of a state court judgment by claiming that a person is being held "in custody" in violation of the laws, treaties, or Constitution of the United States

71. 112 S.Ct. 2206 (1992). The "domestic relations" exception for alimony and divorce issues stemmed from *Barber v. Barber*, 21 How. 582 (1859); it was later expanded in *In re Burrus*, 136 U.S. 586 (1890), to include child custody issues.

72. See Thomas Dobbs, "The Domestic Relations Exception Is Narrowed after *Ankenbrandt v. Richards*, 112 S.Ct. 2206 (1992)," *Wake Forest Law Review* 28 (1993): 1137–1166; Maryellen Murphy, "Domestic Relations Exception to Diversity Jurisdiction: *Ankenbrandt v. Richards*, 112 S.Ct. 2206 (1992)," *New England Law Review* 28 (1993): 577–601.

73. 431 U.S. 816 (1977).

74. The opinion does not indicate the positions taken by these groups, but it is likely they supported the biological parents.

75. 452 U.S. 18 (1981).

76. The opinion does not indicate the position taken by this group.

77. 455 U.S. 745 (1982).

78. Civil commitment, deportation, and denaturalization hearings require a higher standard of proof.

79. 489 U.S. 189 (1989).

80. Brief for Petitioners, cited in Laura Oren, "The State's Failure to Protect Children and Substantive Due Process: *DeShaney* in Context," *North Carolina Law Review* 68 (1990): 661 n. 17.

81. There is no explanation for why, despite her obvious concern for him, Joshua's social worker failed to protect him, confining herself merely to documenting his injuries. See Oren, "The State's Failure to Protect Children and Substantive Due Process."

82. Paul Reidinger, "Why Did No One Protect This Child?" *American Bar Association Journal* (December 1, 1988): 48–51.

83. Joshua's § 1983 suit was dismissed in a summary judgment, with no decision on the merits.

84. Oren, "The State's Failure to Protect Children and Substantive Due Process."

85. Akhil Reed Amar and Daniel Widawsky, "Child Abuse As Slavery: A Thirteenth Amendment Response to DeShaney," *Harvard Law Review* 105 (1992): 1359–1385, assert that the Thirteenth Amendment's ban on involuntary servitude could apply to child abuse and could have been more successful than a substantive due process claim. Acknowledging that all children are in some form of custody, they distinguish parental custody from slavery when the parent acts in the best interests of the child. But, they argue, a parent who mistreats a child and does not act in his or her best interests is guilty of violating the Thirteenth Amendment. A key point of their argument is that unlike the Fourteenth which is limited to state action, the Thirteenth applies to private action as well. Moreover, they claim the language of the Thirteenth commands the state to take affirmative steps to abolish servitude, or, in this case, to protect the abused child when it knows of the abuse.

86. See Curry First, " 'Poor Joshua!': The States' Responsibility to Protect Children from Abuse," *Clearinghouse Review* 23 (August-September 1989): 525–534, for discussion of cases involving the special relationship theory. First, litigation director of the Legal Aid Society of Milwaukee, was Joshua's guardian *ad litem*. In *Estate of Bailey ex rel. Oare v. County of York*, 768 F.2d 503 (3d Cir. 1985), for example, the Third Circuit held that a special relationship, arising between the child and the state once the state becomes aware of the threat of child abuse, creates a constitutional duty to protect the child from abuse; the court held the state liable for the five-year-old child's death.

87. The Court is somewhat vague as to what triggers the state's responsibility to protect. The opinion suggests that a duty would arise if the state creates the danger or worsens it.

After *DeShaney* the lower courts have been divided on whether a compulsory attendance law gives rise to an affirmative duty to protect a child from violence by other students. See Aileen M. Bigelow, "In the Ghetto: The State's Duty to Protect Inner-City Children from Violence," *Notre Dame Journal of Law, Ethics and Public Policy* 7 (1993): 551–552 nn. 94–95.

88. In *Taylor ex rel. Walker v. Ledbetter*, 818 F.2d 791 (11th Cir. 1987), the Eleventh Circuit held that the state had a special relationship to a child in foster care and a duty to protect her. Refusing to rule on the issue left open in *DeShaney*, the Supreme Court denied certiorari. More recently, the Supreme Court also denied certiorari in *Milburn ex rel. Milburn v. Anne Arundel County Department of Social Services*, 871 F.2d 474 (4th Cir. 1989), in which the Fourth Circuit denied the state's liability because the child was "voluntarily" placed in foster care by her parents, and because the child was in the custody of the foster parents, not the state. Thus, just like with Joshua, the state was not responsible for the violent acts of a private individual. This decision, if followed by other courts, would nullify the state's obligations to the vast number of children whose parents voluntarily place them in foster care.

89. Oren, "The State's Failure to Protect Children and Substantive Due Process," argues that the state was liable on these facts even if the courts had applied a "deliberate indifference" standard.

90. Seventh Circuit Judge Richard Posner wanted to limit state responsibility in these areas and believed that allowing DeShaney's claim would lead to more litigation against the state in federal court. *DeShaney v. Winnebago Country Department of Social Services*, 812 F.2d 298 (7th Cir. 1987).

91. Oren, "The State's Failure to Protect Children and Substantive Due Process."

92. Legal and physical custody over an abused or neglected child are often parceled out among private individuals and state and private agencies. States have argued that custody does not include children placed in foster care voluntarily by their biological parents or children in state-supervised care in their own homes.

93. The dispute between the majority and the dissent stemmed in large part from their differing interpretations of *Youngberg v. Romeo*, 457 U.S. 307 (1982), a mental hospital case, and *Estelle v. Gamble*, 429 U.S. 97 (1976), a prison case. In these cases, the Court held that substantive due process rights require the state to provide basic human needs and protect the individual from injury.

94. *Santosky*, 455 U.S. at 766.

95. 467 U.S. 253, 265 (1984). The state relies on the *parens patriae* doctrine to justify child protection laws in cases of parental abuse or neglect as well as delinquency. Bigelow, "In the Ghetto," argues that this doctrine should be extended to require state responsibility for protecting children from violence in the inner-city.

96. Section 1983 was intended to protect individuals when states were unwilling or unable to do so. For use of § 1983 and private rights of action in federal courts,

see Susan Gluck Mezey, "Judicial Interpretation of Legislative Intent: The Role of the Supreme Court in the Implication of Private Rights of Action," *Rutgers Law Review* 36 (1983): 53–89.

97. In *Maine v. Thiboutot*, 448 U.S. 1 (1980), the Supreme Court held that § 1983, whose terms specify "rights, privileges, or immunities," provides a cause of action for violation of a federal law as well as the Constitution.

98. There is a long line of cases discussing the availability of a § 1983 remedy; see, for example, *Pennhurst State School and Hospital v. Halderman*, 451 U.S. 1 (1981); *Middlesex County Sewerage Authority v. National Sea Clammers Association*, 453 U.S. 1 (1981); *Wright v. Roanoke Redevelopment and Housing Authority*, 479 U.S. 418 (1987); *Wilder v. Virginia Hospital Association*, 496 U.S. 498 (1990).

99. 422 U.S. 66 (1975).

100. Leo Smith, "Reducing State Accountability to the Federal Government: The *Suter v. Artist M.* Decision to Dismiss Section 1983 Claims for Violating Federal Fund Mandates," *Wisconsin Law Review* (1992): 1267–1297.

101. 719 F.2d 504 (1st Cir. 1983).

102. 838 F.2d 118 (4th Cir. 1988).

103. 715 F.Supp. 1387 (N.D. Ill. 1989). Following the Seventh Circuit decision in *Artist M.*, 917 F.2d at 980 in which the appellate court affirmed and agreed that the "reasonable efforts" provision was enforceable in court, at the court's urging the parties agreed to settle the case. On December 20, 1991, they entered into a consent decree in which they agreed that the Supreme Court's awaited decisions in *Suter v. Artist M.* would not cause them to seek modification of the decree.

104. 721 F.Supp. 1002 (N.D. Ill. 1989).

105. 726 F.Supp. 690 (N.D. Ill. 1989). The decision was affirmed by the Seventh Circuit in *Artist M.*, 917 F.2d at 980.

106. 739 F.Supp. 1182 (N.D. Ill. 1990).

107. 762 F.Supp. 959 (D.D.C. 1991).

108. *Suter*, 112 S.Ct. at 1360.

109. *Artist M.*, 917 F.2d at 980.

110. *Wilder*, 496 U.S. at 498.

111. The *Wilder* Court cited *Wright*, 479 U.S. at 418, in which it found that the Brooke Amendment to the Housing Act of 1937, requiring public housing authorities to include a "reasonable" amount for the use of utilities in the rent, can be enforced by public housing tenants.

112. Arlene Fried, "The Foster Child's Avenues of Redress: Questions Left Unanswered," *Columbia Journal of Law and Social Problems* 26 (1993): 475.

113. In *Clifton v. Schafer*, 969 F.2d 278 (7th Cir. 1992), for example, the court held that § 1983 is not available to enforce a provision of the Social Security Act requiring the state to hold hearings before reducing AFDC benefits. The law merely required the state to adopt a plan, said the court. Lisa Frye, "*Suter v. Artist M.* and Statutory Remedies under Section 1983: Alteration without Justification," *North Carolina Law Review* 71 (1993): 1203 n. 219.

114. Ashish Prasad, "Rights without Remedies: Section 1983 Enforcement of Title IV-D of the Social Security Act," *University of Chicago Law Review* 60 (1993): 197–222.

115. H.Rep. 213, 103d Cong., 1st Sess. 1993.

116. 113 S.Ct. 1439 (1993).

117. Smith, "Reducing State Accountability to the Federal Government."

118. The amicus brief submitted by the Massachusetts Committee for Children and Youth detailed the extent of the agency's culpability in Joshua's case; there were numerous examples of the caseworker's failure to follow proper procedure. Oren, "The State's Failure to Protect Children and Substantive Due Process."

119. Fried, "The Foster Child's Avenues of Redress."

5

CHILD SUPPORT ENFORCEMENT

Child support enforcement is an issue that affects families across racial and economic lines. In 1989 only 58 percent of single women with children had legally enforceable child support orders. Of this group only 51 percent received the entire amount awarded them; slightly less than 25 percent obtained partial payment, and 25 percent received no payment at all.[1]

According to a report issued by the Clinton administration's Working Group on Welfare Reform, Family Support, and Independence, based on data reported in a 1994 Urban Institute study, there is a discrepancy of $33.7 billion between the amount of child support actually collected ($13.9 billion) and the amount that could be collected ($47.6 billion). This disparity results from factors such as the failure to secure an award, the lack of enforcement of existing awards, and the failure to revise awards upward when the parent's ability to pay rises.[2]

Almost all children experience a downward shift in their lifestyles when their parents divorce or separate.[3] Beyond that, however, when an absent parent fails to honor a child support obligation, or the amount awarded is insufficient, the child is more likely to live in poverty. In 1991 almost half of the 15.7 million children living with only one parent were poor.[4]

These statistics reveal a system badly out of control. The most troubling aspect of its failure is that with a 146 percent increase in women-headed families with children under eighteen between 1970 and 1990, reflecting higher rates of divorce and nonmarital births, the need for support from non-custodial fathers is rapidly growing. Studies show that about 90 percent of custodial parents are women, and the overwhelming majority of unpaid child support obligors are male. Not surprisingly, therefore, studies of child support enforcement almost universally refer to the father as the absent parent.[5]

A national survey of single mothers conducted by the Child Support Assurance Consortium in 1992 found that despite strong legal efforts, a majority of their children were being deprived of regular support payments.[6] The investigation also showed that the lack of support led to homelessness, hunger, and inadequate medical care for their children—conditions typically associated with poverty.

Recent studies have concluded that inability to pay is not the primary reason for the failure to pay child support. One study found that over 70 percent of absent fathers had incomes at twice the poverty line.[7] Put simply, many fathers do not provide for their children because they can avoid doing so; some studies found that strong efforts by government agencies, including imprisonment of non-compliant parents, enhanced the rate of payment.[8]

The government has devoted considerable resources to resolving the problem of children whose parents are either unable, or unwilling, to support them. Yet, despite increasing government involvement in establishing paternity, locating absent parents, and obtaining and enforcing child support orders, it is readily apparent that collections have remained discouragingly low over the years, and more vigorous action needs to be taken.

Child Support Policymaking

Under English common law, the fathers of children born out of wedlock were not responsible for supporting them; most of the colonial governments abandoned this common law approach and mandated paternal obligations. Although laws differed, mothers were able to bring actions for support, called bastardy proceedings, against their child's father.

During the Progressive Era, most states strengthened their laws against non-supporting fathers, including the imposition of possible criminal penalties. For the most part, however, mothers were required to initiate legal proceedings against the fathers and enforcement was sporadic.[9]

Child support policy remained largely outside of the purview of the federal government until concern over rising AFDC costs prompted it to play a supervisory role in child support enforcement. The first federal legislation was enacted in 1950 when Congress required public welfare agencies to inform local law enforcement authorities when the father of a welfare family abandoned his family. Entitled the NOLEO (Notice to Law Enforcement Officials) Amendment, it was enacted as part of the 1950 Amendments to the Public Assistance and Maternal Child Welfare Provisions of the Social Security Act. Although this provision did not explicitly make the mother's cooperation a condition of eligibility for AFDC benefits, a number of states interpreted NOLEO to require a woman to file a criminal non-support complaint against the putative father or lose her family's benefits.

Congress enacted a number of laws in the mid-1960s to encourage states to seek out absent parents and demand overdue support payments. The laws had little effect, however, because states considered the federal government's contribution of 50 percent of their operating costs insufficient.[10]

Title IV-D

According to Harry Krause, an expert in child support policy, by 1974 "child support enforcement lay in shambles."[11] State officials, including judges, displayed a marked lack of enthusiasm for enforcing child support obligations for several reasons. First, they were reluctant to intrude in family matters after the initial support order was established. Second, the legal procedures for pursuing absent fathers, especially across state or even county lines, were cumbersome and ineffective. And finally, they assumed, often incorrectly, that non-compliant parents were unable to fulfil their duties to their children.

Congress took the first serious step toward child support enforcement in 1974 by amending Title IV of the Social Services Amendments of 1974 to add the Child Support and Establishment of Paternity provisions as Part D. The federal government's growing involvement in this issue was largely precipitated by its concern over the rising costs of public assistance and its belief that the states were not sufficiently committed to enforcing child support obligations to reduce AFDC expenditures.[12]

Congress was reacting in part to an increasing number of AFDC children with "absent parents," including a growing number of unmarried fathers. The Senate Finance Committee report accompanying the legislation noted that four out of every five children on the AFDC rolls are deprived of support because of an absent father.[13] Although there was some attention paid to children not in the AFDC system, legislators displayed less concern about child support enforcement for this group, viewing the law primarily as a means to prevent their future reliance on AFDC.

A coalition of feminists, child welfare advocates, and fiscal conservatives rallied to support Title IV-D. Feminist organizations such as the National Organization for Women were especially concerned about the treatment of non-poor women in the child support system and sought to ensure that the law would also provide for children who were not receiving public welfare assistance benefits.[14]

Proponents of the legislation submitted evidence showing that most child support orders were low enough ($50 a month) that obligors should be capable of paying; they showed that non-compliant men often remained in their communities and that government attempts at enforcement affected the rate of compliance with the child support order. Additionally, they presented a study conducted by the Rand Corporation in 1974 that demonstrated that children of financially well-off fathers were often forced to become dependent on public assistance when their fathers did not fulfil their child support obligations.[15]

Opposition to the child support enforcement legislation arose from liberals who argued that the bill would detract from the state's responsibility for poor children and conservatives who protested the increased federal intrusion into the family. President Ford, for example, expressed concern about the intrusive role that federal agencies, such as Health, Education, and Welfare (HEW) and the Internal Revenue Service (IRS), and the federal courts would play in domestic relations, an area traditionally under state control. Despite these reservations, he signed the bill into law on January 4, 1975, indicating his hope that Congress would soon remedy the intrusive aspects of the law.[16]

Thus, although the testimony that promised savings in the AFDC program "was *not* well documented," Congress became convinced of the cost effectiveness of a federal program to aid states in increasing child support enforcement.[17] Enthusiastically supported by Russell Long, Democrat of Louisiana and chair of the Senate Finance Committee, the 1974 legislation required states to create or identify agencies (termed IV-D agencies) to develop programs to shift the child support burden from the public sector through the AFDC program to individual parents. Long, an intense foe of the expanding AFDC program, stated that he wanted to "take the financial reward out of desertions" by forcing the fathers of children receiving AFDC benefits to support them.[18]

By providing a set of rewards and penalties for state and local governments, the 1974 act delineated the respective obligations of the states and federal government in their child support enforcement efforts. The law specified that state IV-D agencies, with technical assistance from HEW, must prove the paternity of children born to unmarried mothers and establish and enforce child support obligations. Each state was required to submit a "IV-D plan" to HEW, outlining its procedures for compliance with the statute and regulations. Among other things, the plan had to demonstrate the state's financial participation, be in effect throughout the state, and create or designate a state agency to administer it.

With states assigned the responsibility for enforcement, the federal government aided in establishing and organizing the IV-D agencies and provided matching funds for enforcement efforts.[19] States were faced with the prospect of losing AFDC funds for failing to meet federal performance standards, a provision that would ultimately harm AFDC recipients by reducing money for the program. To oversee the work of the IV-D agencies, as well as to provide assistance and assess results, the act created an Office of Child Support Enforcement (OCSE) within HEW to compile statistics on program costs and report back to Congress.

States were required to maintain intrastate parent locator services, and HEW was charged with establishing a federal Parent Locator Service (PLS) to allow states access to federal social security and internal revenue records for information on the absent parent's address and place of employment.[20] While states had been permitted access to IRS records prior to 1975, the new PLS was intended to streamline the process and improve its efficiency.[21] The law also allowed states to garnishee the wages of federal employees, a provision especially relevant for military parents, and prohibited absent parents from declaring bankruptcy to avoid meeting their child support obligations.

As part of its effort to recoup AFDC expenses, Title IV-D required AFDC mothers to assign their child support to the state. As a result, the father pays the child support award directly to the state, with the child receiving AFDC benefits in place of the child support award. The assignment ends when the welfare grant is terminated, but states may collect unpaid child support obligations that have accrued while the family is receiving public assistance.

Although the services of the IV-D agencies were intended to be available to non-AFDC families (for a fee), the lure of reduced AFDC expenditures led states to direct the bulk of their IV-D enforcement activities at AFDC cases. Child support enforcement for non-AFDC families was left to largely indifferent state agency employees and private attorneys. In either case, the results were generally worth neither the cost nor the effort.

The Good Cause Requirement

To fulfil the congressional aim of using Title IV-D to trim the welfare rolls, the statute compelled an AFDC mother to identify and help locate the father of her child as a condition of AFDC eligibility; an unmarried mother was also required to assist in establishing paternity.[22] A woman who did not cooperate risked losing her portion of the family's AFDC award (the caretaker benefit), with the child's portion paid to a third party, called a "protective payee."[23] There was an exception to the cooperation requirement, exempting a woman from cooperating with state welfare authorities for "good cause."

Some members of Congress were concerned, however, that the "good cause" exception would create a loophole that would allow a mother to evade her duty to reveal the father's identity too easily. During a brief colloquy on the floor of the House of Representatives, Robert Bauman, Republican of Maryland, complained that the exception would become a "wide-open loophole" for a welfare mother who chose not to name the father of her child. Fellow Republican Guy Vander Jagt from Michigan disagreed, stating that he would term it "an-eye-of-the-needle loophole rather than a wide-open loophole." Bauman responded by saying that "it was a camel that was alleged to pass through the eye of the needle," and predicted that if passed, "whole herds of camels [would go] galloping through this one."[24]

After much delay, HEW promulgated final regulations in 1978, defining "good cause" very narrowly by limiting it to circumstances in which "cooperation would not be in the best interest of the child," such as when it would lead to "serious" physical or emotional harm, or when the child was conceived as a result of "forcible rape or incest," or when adoption was a realistic possibility. A successful showing of emotional harm required "a demonstration of an emotional impairment that substantially affects the individual's functioning."[25]

Because of concern over the potential for fraud, the regulations emphasized the child's safety only; the mother's physical or emotional harm was
relevant merely to the extent that it interfered with her ability to care for the
child. The narrow circumstances in which "good cause" could be found, and
the extensive proof required to show it, indicated that it was to be granted
infrequently.[26] And, indeed, few "good cause" claims are made, and, of these,
few are granted.[27] Thus, the fear of "galloping camels" proved largely groundless.

By providing financial incentives and a framework for state action, the
federal government had hoped that Title IV-D would increase state efforts to
obtain child support awards. But while some states devised relatively effective
enforcement procedures, most did not.[28] In response to inadequate and uneven
levels of child support enforcement in the nation, Congress amended Title IV-
D in 1984 to require states to establish and execute child support orders more
vigorously.

The 1984 Amendments

The Child Support Enforcement Amendments of 1984 sought to improve
the collection of support dollars for children in non-AFDC families by
establishing a new incentive structure for states. Unanimously passed by both
houses of Congress, and signed into law by President Reagan in August, the
1984 amendments were immensely popular, combining two winning themes:
reduced welfare dependency and increased parental responsibility. The legislation was especially attractive because it permitted its supporters, including
the White House, to take a stand on a social issue at little cost of federal dollars.
The bill, as one member of Congress put it, "had a 'halo around it.' "[29]

The 1984 act required states to adopt laws, applicable to all support orders
issued or modified after October 1, 1985, to automatically withhold the absent
parent's income when the equivalent of one month's payment was past due.[30]
States were also required to enact laws allowing property liens to be placed
on the delinquent parent, to report defaults to consumer credit reporting
agencies, and, building on existing law, to expand tax intercept mechanisms.
In 1981 states had been given authority to request the IRS to intercept any federal
tax refund due to fathers of AFDC children who owed at least $150 and were
three months behind in their payments; the 1984 amendments extended this
provision to non-AFDC children in the IV-D system who were owed past due
support of $500 or more.[31]

States were also charged with devising numerical statewide standards for
determining child support awards. Advisory until 1988, the standards were
intended to make the system more consistent and equitable by combatting the
problems of inadequate payment levels and regressive awards that placed a
proportionately heavier burden on low-income fathers. Supporters argued the

guidelines would raise award levels and bring greater uniformity and predictability to the system.

As a result of the 1984 legislation, most states adopted an approach that combines cost-sharing and income-sharing by allocating a percentage of the parents' joint income to the child and then dividing that amount according to the income of each parent.[32]

The 1984 amendments also required IV-D agencies to petition to include medical support as part of the child support order whenever health care insurance is available to the non-custodial parent at "reasonable cost." Despite this, in 1989, 75 percent of custodial mothers in interstate child support cases reported that their children did not receive health insurance; the comparable figure for intrastate custodial mothers was 63 percent.[33]

Representative Marge Roukema, Republican of New Jersey, had optimistically stated during passage of the 1984 law that it would create "a national network to force scofflaws to honor their legal and moral obligations . . . [and] will prevent parents from simply skipping from state to state to avoid payment."[34] Despite the optimism that accompanied the legislation and federal government expenditures of almost $1.5 billion from 1980 to 1987 to enhance state child support collections, in part because of a rising caseload, there was no increase in the *percentage* of cases in which a collection was made.[35]

The Family Support Act

Congress next attempted to solve the problem of ineffective child support enforcement by enacting Title I of the Family Support Act (FSA) of 1988. Proclaiming the lack of child support from absent parents as one of the leading causes of poverty among female-headed households, Title I created federal standards for establishing paternity and provided up to 90 percent of the cost of the tests involved.[36] It encouraged paternity actions by specifying that any suits dismissed since 1984 because of a statute of limitations of less than eighteen years could be re-filed. It further required states to expedite paternity actions by mandating that all parties in a contested case submit to genetic tests upon the demand of one of the parties. States were encouraged to facilitate voluntary acknowledgment of paternity and, absent good cause, to place the social security numbers of both parents on the child's birth certificate.

The FSA attempted to improve access to the non-custodial parent's income by requiring that, as of November 1, 1990, states must provide for immediate wage withholding from an *absent* parent, without regard to delinquency, for all new or modified orders in the IV-D system; existing cases in the IV-D system, for the most part, were still subject to the one-month arrearage rule. In non–IV-D cases, all child support orders issued after January 1, 1994 must provide for immediate wage withholding.

The law aimed at coordinating the child support enforcement system with the AFDC system. The 1984 Deficit Reduction Act had allowed AFDC recipients to retain the first $50 of a child support payment from an absent parent, but most states failed to process this sum in a timely manner. The FSA required states to improve collection procedures and forward the $50 to the AFDC family in a more timely fashion.

Although the 1984 act had attempted to impose greater uniformity on the child support enforcement system by encouraging states to adopt uniform standards for awards, state judges retained a great deal of discretion over the amounts awarded. Only half the states had adopted the guidelines as rebuttable presumptions, and in the remaining half, the guidelines had been advisory. Thus, there remained a great deal of variation in child support awards within and among states. Attempting to lessen these disparities, the FSA required states to treat the child support guidelines as rebuttable presumptions and to review the individual awards and guidelines periodically.[37]

The Problems of Interstate Enforcement

Addressing one of the major obstacles to effective child support enforcement, the FSA also turned its attention to the complex problem of interstate award orders.[38] Such orders are particularly resistant to efforts at collection. According to a 1992 study about 30 percent of child support cases involve parents living in different states, yet these cases account for only $1 of every $10 collected.[39]

The difficulties of collecting child support across state lines are enhanced by concerns for federalism and the constitutional prohibitions against adjudicating the rights of an absent parent living in another state.[40] Additionally, because half to two-thirds of all child support cases are not within the IV-D system, interstate enforcement is even more problematic.[41]

A support order entered in one state is enforceable in any other state under the "full faith and credit" clause of the U.S. Constitution (Article IV), but the difficulties created by interstate enforcement often undermine the mandate of "full faith and credit." Even though states are constitutionally required to enforce the final judgments of other states as they would their own, in part, because custody and support decrees are rarely considered final, child support awards are seldom accorded "full faith and credit."

There have been a number of attempts to counter the problem of states failing to enforce child support orders issued in their sister states. The Uniform Reciprocal Enforcement of Support Act (URESA), originally drafted in 1950 and revised in 1968, created a mechanism for enforcing child support orders across state lines.[42] Under URESA, adopted by all states in differing versions by the mid-1970s, the state agency or private attorney in the custodial parent's state (the initiating jurisdiction) files a petition with the state agency or court of the state in which the non-custodial parent lives (the responding jurisdiction). In ideal circumstances, after receiving notice of the unpaid child support obligation, the responding state holds a hearing to determine whether the claim against the non-custodial parent is valid, and if so, issues an identical order binding the non-custodial parent as though the order were entered in the responding state. Again in ideal circumstances, the responding court collects the payment and forwards the money to the initiating state's IV-D office.

While collections may be somewhat enhanced by URESA, responding states are typically not anxious to commit time and funds to enforcing child support orders of citizens of other states, and requests from outside the state often receive little attention from the responding IV-D agency.[43] Finally, even if states are willing to commit resources to collecting awards originating from another state, the laws and procedures of each state must be followed, adding to the complexity and uncertainty of interstate enforcement.

In 1986 Congress attempted to deal with the difficulties caused by interstate child support enforcement by passing the Bradley Amendment, requiring states to enact laws prohibiting courts from retroactively reducing child support awards, that is, from failing to give "full faith and credit" to support judgments entered in other states on the grounds that they are not final judgments.[44]

In its attempts to counter the problems of interstate child support enforcement, the FSA established a fifteen-member Commission on Interstate Child Support, with members jointly appointed by the congressional leadership and the secretary of HHS. The commission was charged with reporting to Congress on "improving the interstate establishment and enforcement of child support awards, and revising the Uniform Reciprocal Enforcement of Support Act." In August 1992 the commission released a 446-page report to Congress entitled *Supporting Our Children: A Blueprint for Reform*. It recommended that states establish a Registry of Child Support Orders for all IV-D cases, including a computerized database of orders to be linked to those in other states and to the federal PLS. It suggested a national reporting system of new hires on modified W-4 tax forms and a revision of state laws to allow a custodial parent to send income withholding requests directly to the out-of-state employer rather than having to route them through the two state IV-D agencies. It sought increased training and funding of state child support agency staffs and immediate simultaneous adoption by all states of the proposed Uniform Interstate Family Support Act.[45]

A number of children's advocates hoped the commission would recommend that the federal government's authority over interstate child support enforcement be expanded by giving responsibility for collection to the IRS and establishing federal court jurisdiction over interstate enforcement. With one dissenting view, the commission opted to maintain the current state-based system, indicating that it feared a federalized system would add to the complexity of the enforcement process and further depersonalize the services available to custodial parents seeking to enforce child support orders. Despite the problems associated with the current system, it believed state and local agencies were in the best position to locate parents and collect child support obligations.[46]

In one of its most recent efforts to overcome the obstacles presented by the enforcement of interstate child support orders, Congress enacted the Child Support Recovery Act of 1992, barring the willful failure to pay a known past due support obligation (owing for more than one year or for an amount greater than $5,000) for a child living in another state. The penalty is a fine and/or six-month prison sentence for the first offense, and a two-year prison term for a subsequent offense. With numerous defenses included in the act, including inability to pay, interference by the custodial parent with visitation, or contributing payment in kind such as clothing or food, it seems unlikely that this will effectively deter child support delinquency. Moreover, as with all child support enforcement, the law left implementation to local government units.[47]

Child Support Assurance

The federal government's attempt to reform the child support system was initially begun because of its concern for AFDC expenditures. Yet despite its belief that it could save federal dollars by diminishing the welfare rolls, the evidence indicates that child support enforcement has not been cost effective for the federal government, especially with respect to AFDC families, largely because of the increase in state administrative costs and incentive payments to the states.[48]

Despite the numerous improvements in the child support enforcement system over the last twenty years, data from the 1982 Current Population Survey shows that the low amounts awarded are unlikely to greatly diminish childhood poverty. More recently, other studies suggest that increasing efforts to collect existing child support awards would have little overall effect on reducing either AFDC participation or childhood poverty, in part because of the low income of the fathers of AFDC children, and because of the large number of children without child support awards.[49]

Notwithstanding more stringent enforcement mechanisms instituted by the federal government, Irwin Garfinkel concluded that:

> the U.S. child support system is still failing many of the nation's children. Some of them are living in poverty because child support was never awarded them; some are living in poverty because the payments are not collected. Many are living lives of insecurity because of irregular payments; still others, although not in poverty, are living insecurely because of drastic drops in income.[50]

To counteract the inadequate and inconsistent support offered in the current system, scholars such as Garfinkel, David Ellwood, and Paula Roberts have suggested it should be replaced by a child support assurance system (CSAS), arguing that the costs associated with a CSAS would be offset by decreased AFDC expenses. A CSAS builds on some of the measures put in place by the FSA: registering both parents' social security numbers on the child's birth certificate, developing uniform standards of payment based on income, and automatic wage withholding.

Patterned after systems in nations such as Norway, Sweden, Israel, and Austria, under a CSAS, the government would establish a minimum benefit for each child (perhaps $2,000 to $2,500 a year for the first child and a smaller amount for each child thereafter) to be paid to the custodial parent, and collect, to the extent possible, the sum from the non-custodial parent.[51] If the child support obligation, established as a percentage of the absent parent's income, is less than the minimum benefit or the parent does not meet the obligation, the government supplies the difference. If the child support award exceeds the minimum monthly benefit, the government passes the entire sum onto the family without subsidy.[52]

Ellwood has proposed a payment consisting of a minimum of 25 to 30 percent of the non-custodial parent's gross income; in most cases, he noted, the government would not need to subsidize the payment.[53] A study of the incomes of non-custodial fathers by Garfinkel and Donald Oellerich concluded that they could afford to pay about two and a half times the amount of their current child support obligations and more than three times as much as they were actually paying. At most they believed that only 25 percent of the non-custodial fathers would be unable to pay child support.[54]

The principle advantage of a CSAS is that unlike AFDC the benefits would supplement, not replace, the custodial parent's earnings. Indeed, because the child support payment would be too low to ensure survival, mothers would need employment earnings to supplement the payment.[55] Moreover, while poor fathers may not be able to support their children unassisted, with the child support obligation based on a percentage of income, all fathers who earn income would provide some support for their children. By combining the guaranteed benefits with wages, and adding refundable earned income tax credits, food stamps, and child care tax credits, the family could even raise itself above the poverty line. Such a system would thus serve the dual purpose of fighting poverty and reducing welfare dependency.[56]

Unlike welfare, its advocates claim, a CSAS would be designed as a universal program, more like social security survivors' insurance, than public welfare assistance.[57] As a benefit available to all income classes, it would avoid the stigma of a means-tested program. Moreover, as Ellwood argued, the child support assurance system has the added benefit of deflecting attention away from welfare mothers to the absent parent, most often the father. If complaints arise about public expenditures on child support, "they will say," he predicted, " 'those darn *fathers* are not pulling their weight; we are paying their child support for them.' "[58]

Under a CSAS, the focus on the absent parent would encourage states to intensify their efforts to establish child support awards at the outset. Studies have shown that states devoting greater resources to identifying the fathers of children born out of wedlock are more successful in enforcing child support obligations. Michigan, for example, expending greater effort, establishes paternity in about two-thirds of such births, while Texas succeeds in doing so in only 2 percent of its cases.[59] But under the present system, many states invest little energy in identifying unwed fathers because they believe it unlikely that major welfare savings will result from the search.[60]

Although advocated by many in the scholarly community, the CSAS has not received support from the nation's political leaders; it is frequently attacked as an expensive entitlement that would encourage more out of wedlock births and desertion by absent fathers. And in the current climate of public assistance policymaking, there is little hope for implementing a version of a CSAS, despite its many attractive features.

Thus, the government's role in child support policymaking has been largely limited to attempts to strengthen the enforcement efforts of state and local governments through a series of incentives and penalties. Notwithstanding passage of three major pieces of legislation in fourteen years, some child support experts argue that the federal government has not fully carried out its responsibility to the children of absent parents. They maintain that the federal government must make greater efforts to get involved, through more aggressive action by the IRS or the federal courts, in collecting awards for all children, whether on public assistance or not.[61] Again, judging from the current political climate that seeks to reduce the federal role in policymaking, these results are unlikely.

Child Support Litigation

As federal policymakers began to pay increasing attention to the issue of parents who evade their duty to support their children, the role of the federal courts in settling child support disputes concomitantly grew. Beginning in the 1970s, the Supreme Court was asked to rule on a variety of state and federal laws related to child support enforcement policy. In attempting to resolve the myriad legal controversies arising out of child support enforcement, the judiciary became embroiled in debates over government intervention in the family, differing interpretations of the principles of federalism, and disputes over the reach of constitutional guarantees of privacy and due process.

The Court's rulings in the child support cases can be divided into two broad categories. Not surprisingly, because mothers comprise the vast majority of custodial parents, both categories of cases revolve around fathers' responsibilities for child support.[62] The first set of decisions arises from suits brought by a mother seeking to impose a child support obligation on a putative father. A number of these are prompted by the woman's obligation to cooperate with the state in pursuing the father of her child as a condition of AFDC eligibility.[63] The second set stems from legal controversies arising over a woman's attempt to collect a past due child support payment from an absent father, often her ex-husband.

Establishing Child Support Obligations

One of the first cases brought to test a state child support law was *Linda R.S. v. Richard D.*[64] In this 1973 decision the Court dismissed a class action challenge to a Texas law that threatened prosecution of any "parent" who failed to support his child but limited enforcement to married parents only. Linda R.S., an unmarried mother, claimed that the state's restrictive interpretation of the statute violated the Fourteenth Amendment's equal protection clause. She sought an injunction against the district attorney for refusing to prosecute the father of her child for not paying child support. A three-judge court dismissed her case, holding that she lacked the requisite standing to bring the action.

The Supreme Court affirmed, holding that one private citizen does not have a legal interest in the prosecution of another citizen. Ironically, the Court acknowledged that the mother has a valid interest in seeking support for her child, but declared that applying the statute to the child's father could only lead to his incarceration without benefiting the child.

The *Linda R.S.* case illustrates the state's limited enforcement efforts in collecting child support for children who are not on the AFDC rolls. In contrast, when children are AFDC beneficiaries, states frequently display great energy in seeking out their fathers. Before 1974, enforced by the threat of termination of welfare benefits or, in some cases imprisonment, many states required an unmarried woman on public assistance to identify and help locate the father of her child. When challenged by welfare recipients on the grounds that these provisions violated constitutional guarantees of equal protection, privacy, and the privilege against self-incrimination, the lower courts uniformly upheld the state laws. Litigants were more successful in attacking the laws as violations of the Social Security Act; for the most part, the lower courts struck the state regulations, reasoning that they constituted criteria for AFDC eligibility that had not been authorized by Congress.[65]

Following passage of Title IV-D, litigants began to challenge these state laws on the ground that they were pre-empted by the "good cause" exemption of the *federal* statute. *Roe v. Norton*, decided in 1975, involved a Connecticut law requiring an unwed mother to cooperate in a paternity action against the father of her child or face imprisonment of up to one year.[66]

A three-judge district court upheld the statute, and a group of AFDC mothers appealed to the Supreme Court. Their claim was supported by an amicus curiae brief from the American Academy of Child Psychiatry. Noting the passage of the 1974 act, the Supreme Court simply vacated the lower court judgment and remanded the case for further consideration in light of Title IV-D.[67]

Lascaris v. Shirley, also decided in 1975, involved a similar New York law requiring an AFDC recipient to cooperate with the state in securing child support payments from her child's father.[68] A three-judge district court struck the state statute, ruling that it conflicted with federal AFDC law by adding additional eligibility criteria. After the Supreme Court noted probable jurisdiction in the state's appeal, the cooperation requirement was incorporated in Title IV-D. In light of this development, the Supreme Court briefly affirmed the ruling of the lower court.

In deciding these cases, the Court confined itself to the narrow question of the conflict between state and federal law, without considering the larger question of the effect of the cooperation requirement on the AFDC mother or the child.

Although *Roe* and *Lascaris* were decided on statutory grounds, most of the cases in this first group required the Supreme Court to determine whether state paternity laws comported with the requirements of the Fourteenth Amendment, specifically, whether the attempt to impose a child support obligation on a man violated his right of due process.

Little v. Streater, decided in 1981, began as a paternity suit brought by Gloria Streater against Walter Little.[69] Because Streater was an AFDC mother, the state welfare department prompted her suit and provided an attorney for her. Little, a state prisoner, denied fatherhood and asked the court to order blood tests to exculpate him. Under state law the moving party was required to pay for the testing procedure. Little claimed he could not afford the tests, and, because the state refused to pay, no tests were performed.

The court ruled that Little was the father of Streater's child and ordered him to remit the child support award to the state. Despite his weekly $5 income as a prisoner, with no assets and a weekly $5 expenditure, the court entered a judgment of $6,974.48 against him for past due support, in addition to costs of the pregnancy and attorney fees. He was ordered to pay the state $2 a week: $1 to pay off the judgment and $1 toward his child support obligation of $163.58. He appealed, supported by an amicus curiae brief by the ACLU, arguing that by refusing to pay for the blood test, the state had violated his due process rights.

Citing the 1976 case of *Mathews v. Eldridge*, the Supreme Court identified the three factors to be assessed: the private interests at stake, the risk that the challenged procedure will produce erroneous results, and the government interests affected.[70] The Court held that the state's legitimate interests in accurately determining paternity and in obtaining support for children on public assistance were outweighed by the importance of avoiding an incorrect finding of paternity, especially when considering the reliability and low cost of the blood test (the federal government paying for 75 percent of the cost of the test). The Court ruled that the state must pay for the test; any other policy, it said, denied a man accused of paternity a "meaningful opportunity to be heard."

In *Rivera v. Minnich*, a 1987 case, the Court ruled on the level of proof necessary to establish paternity.[71] Jean Marie Minnich named Gregory Rivera as her son's father and sought child support. Applying a "preponderance of evidence" standard, customary for civil proceedings, the jury found him to be the father. On appeal to the Pennsylvania Supreme Court, Rivera claimed that due process required paternity to be established by the more exacting "clear and convincing evidence" standard. He cited *Santosky v. Kramer*, the 1982 decision in which the Court ruled that courts must use a higher standard of proof in cases involving the termination of parental rights.[72] Over the dissent of its chief justice, the Pennsylvania high court denied his appeal and upheld the preponderance of evidence standard.

Affirming the state high court decision, the U.S. Supreme Court agreed that the lower "preponderance of evidence" standard satisfied due process. Rejecting Rivera's argument that *Santosky* required paternity proceedings to have a higher level of proof, the Court differentiated between extinguishing a parental-child relationship and creating one.

With the state's superior resources arrayed against the parent in termination cases, said the Court, due process required a higher level of proof of unfitness. In a paternity proceeding, however, the state was neutral, and the parties were relatively evenly matched. And with all parties, including the child, sharing equally in the consequences of an adverse ruling, it was only fair that all share equally in the risk of an inaccurate determination. Thus, concluded the Court, like most states, Pennsylvania could establish paternity by a preponderance of the evidence that a man was the father of the child.

The paternity actions in *Rivera* and *Little* were brought shortly after the child's birth. However, an unmarried woman may be reluctant to bring immediate action against the man she believes fathered her child. When she delays, her paternity suit is often dismissed for exceeding the statute of limitations, a limitation that usually applies only to claims of paternity against unwed fathers. The Supreme Court addressed the question of procedural limitations on paternity actions in four cases, including two that followed passage of the 1984 Child Support Amendments.

In the first case, *Mills v. Habluetzel*, a 1982 decision, the Court ruled on the constitutionality of a Texas statute imposing a one-year limit on paternity suits brought by children of unmarried parents.[73]

The suit was filed by the child's mother and the Texas Department of Human Resources, charging that the distinction between marital and nonmarital children violated the Fourteenth Amendment's equal protection clause. Applying the heightened scrutiny used in equal protection cases involving illegitimacy classifications, the Court stressed that time limits in paternity actions must be "substantially related" to the state's interest "in avoiding the litigation of stale or fraudulent claims." Because the one-year limit served neither interest, it violated the equal protection clause. Just as with "legitimate" children, the state must allow "sufficient" time for nonmarital children to bring claims for support.

A year later, in *Pickett v. Brown*, the Court once again determined the constitutionality of limitations on paternity suits brought on behalf of nonmarital children.[74] Tennessee imposed a two-year limit on filing a paternity suit unless the father had provided support or a written acknowledgment of paternity or "unless the child is, or is liable to become a public charge." In the latter circumstance, reflecting the state's interest in avoiding liability for public welfare assistance, the statute of limitations was extended to the child's eighteenth birthday.

The mother's claim on behalf of her ten-year-old child was dismissed by the state courts. She appealed to the U.S. Supreme Court, claiming a violation of the equal protection clause; the CDF filed an amicus curiae brief supporting her appeal.

Applying heightened scrutiny, the Court ruled that the two-year limit was not substantially related to the state's interest in preventing stale and fraudulent claims—especially in light of the exception made for children likely to "become public charges." A woman might delay a paternity action for longer than two years for any number of reasons, said the Court: to prevent publicity over the child's birth, to reduce the emotional stress accompanying it, and to avoid alienating the child's father. The Court questioned the state's motives in adopting this particular statute of limitations when it tolled (excused) limits in most suits brought by or on behalf of children.

The 1984 amendments attempted to resolve any lingering uncertainty about appropriate time limits by requiring states to permit paternity actions until the child's eighteenth birthday. Two years after the amendments were enacted, in *Paulussen v. Herion*, the Court considered the question of whether they affected existing state statutes of limitations.[75]

Barbara Paulussen had brought a paternity suit against George Herion on behalf of her seven-year-old child in 1980. Her claim was dismissed because the state law limited such actions to six years after the child's birth. When her equal protection challenge lost in the state courts, she sought review by the U.S. Supreme Court. Her appeal was supported by amici curiae briefs from the CDF and the Neighborhood Legal Services Association.

Two weeks after the Supreme Court noted probable jurisdiction of her appeal, the state legislature amended the law to conform to the congressional mandate. Although Herion admitted the new law applied to him, he insisted that he was only liable for support from the time he admitted paternity, not back to 1980 when Paulussen filed the original petition. The Court vacated the state court ruling and remanded the case to allow the state court to rule on his claim in light of the statute.

Two years later in *Clark v. Jeter*, the Court was again forced to deal with the issue of the retroactivity of the eighteen-year statute of limitations.[76] The facts were similar to those in *Herion*. In 1983 Cherlyn Clark filed a complaint for support against Gene Jeter on behalf of her ten-year-old daughter; she produced a blood test showing a 99.3 percent probability that he was the father. Her action was barred by the six-year statute of limitations on paternity suits brought by a nonmarital child.

The lower court dismissed her case, and she appealed to the Pennsylvania high court. While her appeal was pending, the state extended the statute of limitations to eighteen years as required by federal law. The state supreme court held that the new statute of limitations was not retroactive and upheld the six-year limit on constitutional grounds.

Clark's appeal to the Supreme Court, accompanied by amici curiae briefs by the ACLU and the CDF, raised both statutory and constitutional issues. Applying the approach adopted in *Mills*, the Court assessed the reasonableness of the time limit and its relationship to the state's interest in preventing stale and fraudulent claims. On the first question, the Court found that the six-year limit "does not necessarily provide a reasonable opportunity" to present a claim for child support. There were too many reasons, suggested the Court, why an unmarried woman would hesitate to bring a paternity action within the requisite six years. On the second question, the Court found that the statute was not substantially related to the state's interest in avoiding fraudulent claims. By extending the limit to eighteen years, both federal and state governments had evidenced little concern about the difficulty of proving a paternity action after that length of time.

The decisions show that the cases in this first category chiefly required the court to balance the interests of a man seeking to avoid the responsibilities of fatherhood against the interests of the child, and to some extent the state, trying to enforce those responsibilities. Reflecting in part its desire to remove the legal disabilities of nonmarital children, the Court tilted the balance in the direction of the state and the child. Not surprisingly the Court provided little succor to fathers believed guilty of attempting to escape their child support obligations. In *Streater*, the only decision with an unambiguous ruling in favor of the father, the Court merely acted to increase the accuracy of a finding of paternity by requiring the state to pay for a blood test.

Enforcing Child Support Obligations

The second category of cases involved existing child support obligations, with mothers applying to the courts for help in collecting delinquent awards. For the most part, these cases revolved around conflicts between divorced middle- or working-class parents, with the state playing only a minor part.

In *Stanton v. Stanton*, a case which came before the Supreme Court twice, a divorced Utah father ceased supporting his daughter when she became eighteen, citing a state law establishing eighteen as the age of majority for women.[77] Because men reached majority at twenty-one in Utah, he continued to support his son.

The daughter filed suit, arguing that the differential age limit violated the equal protection clause. In its first ruling in this case, in 1975, the Court agreed and struck the statute on equal protection grounds. The Court said that the law, based on the assumption that men mature later than women and require more support to acquire education and training, was irrational. The Court remanded the case to the Utah high court, with instructions to construe the law to avoid the inequality based on sex.

Two years later the Supreme Court revisited this issue.[78] Following the 1975 decision, the Utah legislature established eighteen as the age of majority for both women and men, but allowed divorce courts to order children to be supported by their parents until they reached twenty-one. When the lower state court decided the Stanton case on remand, it held that children attain majority at the age of twenty-one for child support purposes and ordered the father to pay the daughter past due support. Oddly, the state supreme court reversed. Referring to "biological facts of life," the state high court upheld the statute establishing eighteen as the age of majority for women. And declining to "legislate" on an issue not before it, it made no ruling on whether the state was permitted to establish a different age of majority for men.

The U.S. Supreme Court firmly reminded the Utah Supreme Court that the essence of its 1975 decision was that males and females must be treated alike for child support purposes, with support for children of both sexes ceasing at either eighteen or twenty-one. The Court once again remanded the case to the state court.

Not surprisingly, the federal courts also became involved in the myriad of problems created by interstate child support enforcement. In such cases federal jurisdiction arises when fathers appeal state court decisions in the U.S. Supreme Court on the basis of the Fourteenth Amendment's due process clause. The situations emanate from suits in which women seek to enforce child support obligations in their own state courts, rather than taking the matter to the state court where their ex-husbands reside, usually a much more costly and difficult procedure. Such an action often raises issues of the limits of state court jurisdiction over the delinquent out-of-state parent. The Supreme Court's 1978 opinion in *Kulko v. Superior Court of California*, based on these facts, had far-reaching implications for interstate child support enforcement.[79]

Following a marriage ceremony in California, the Kulkos resided in New York where their children were born. After a thirteen-year marriage, they divorced, with Sharon Kulko moving to California. The parents agreed that the children would live with their father during the year and spend summers and vacations with their mother; he would pay her $3000 during the time the children were with her. Both children decided, apparently on their own but with their parents' consent, to alter these arrangements and reside almost exclusively with their mother. She filed suit in a California court, seeking full custody and increased support payments.

Her ex-husband appeared specially in the state court, challenging her demand for higher child support and arguing that as a nonresident, the California court lacked personal jurisdiction over him.[80] The state supreme court upheld the lower court ruling that California had proper jurisdiction in the matter; he appealed to the U.S. Supreme Court, arguing that the state violated his due process rights by summoning him to appear there to defend himself in the suit.

The Supreme Court agreed. Applying a due process analysis, the high court reversed the state high court. The due process clause governs the extent to which states may exercise personal jurisdiction over nonresidents, said the Court, and precludes a California court from adjudicating a New York child support dispute. Because the father was a New York resident and the separation agreement was negotiated in New York, the Court ruled that the mother's claim properly belonged in the New York courts.

The Court acknowledged that California had a legitimate interest in the support of its resident children but added that both California and New York had enacted versions of URESA. The mother could have filed a URESA petition in a California court. Ignoring URESA's many shortcomings, the Court stated that the issue could have been resolved in the New York courts without either parent having to leave his or her home state.

Most observers would reject the Court's estimation of the ease with which the mother could have resolved the issue under the provisions of URESA. And in this case by refusing to lessen the burden on women trying to litigate child support obligations in distant states, and making it easier for men in such situations to evade their child support responsibilities, the Court did not avail itself of the opportunity to increase the effectiveness of interstate child support enforcement.

The case of *United States v. Morton*, decided in 1984, further illustrates the difficulty of collecting child support from an out-of-state parent; in this case, the parent happened to be in the military.[81]

While stationed with the Air Force in Alaska, Colonel Morton received notice that the Air Force Finance Office would withhold $4,100 from his salary to satisfy an Alabama judgment for alimony and child support. He informed the finance officer that the Alabama court order was void because the Alabama court lacked personal jurisdiction over him. Over his objections, the money was deducted from his salary and forwarded to the Alabama court.

Morton filed suit in the U.S. Court of Claims, seeking to force the government to return his money. The government argued that a provision of the 1974 Child Support Act that subjected federal employees to "legal processes" to enforce child support obligations and granted immunity to the government for compliance with a writ "regular on its face," immunized it from liability. The Court of Claims, however, held the government liable, ruling that the writ was wrongly applied because the Alabama court did not have jurisdiction over him. The court of appeals affirmed the ruling.

On appeal, the Supreme Court reviewed the legislative history of the 1974 act and noted that Congress demonstrated its concern for swift dispatch of child support obligations by making federal employees subject to legal process to aid their enforcement. The Court assumed, as did the lower court, that the Alabama court lacked jurisdiction over Morton. But it nevertheless found that the state court was a "competent court" within the meaning of the statute. Thus, because the court had proper subject matter jurisdiction over the divorce, it had the authority to issue a writ of garnishment. The Court held that it would contravene congressional intent to force the federal government to demand investigation into a court's jurisdiction *over an individual* before complying with a writ of garnishment properly presented. Moreover, said the Court, Congress intended to treat the federal government the same as private employers with respect to honoring such writs. The Court cited the well-established state law principle that employers are immune from suit when they comply with properly issued writs of garnishment.

In *Sorenson v. Secretary of the Treasury*, a 1986 decision, the Court was asked to determine whether the earned income tax credit was subject to the federal income tax intercept process, an issue dividing the appellate circuits.[82]

Prior to 1984, the majority view of the lower federal courts was that the tax intercept procedures did not conform to constitutional due process requirements. The courts held that the obligated parent was entitled to notice indicating any available defenses and must be given a hearing prior to the intercept. The hearing must allow the obligated parent to appear, present evidence on his own behalf, and review the information submitted by the IV-D agency. There must be a written finding and an opportunity for judicial review of the decision. Any individual who filed a joint income tax return with the obligated parent was also entitled to pre-intercept notice. The 1984 legislation, extending the tax intercept procedure to non-AFDC parents in the IV-D system, subsequently incorporated many of these due process requirements.[83]

In February 1982 the Sorensons filed a joint tax return for 1981 for which they expected to receive a refund of $1,408. Mrs. Sorenson provided the family income; the refund was based on withholdings from her wages as well as the EITC. Because Mr. Sorenson owed child support to his children from a previous marriage, they became eligible for AFDC benefits. And as required by law, their mother assigned their child support award to the state, which invoked the intercept procedure to recover the amount of the AFDC benefits from the Sorensons' tax refund. The Sorensons received notice that the bulk of their refund was being intercepted by the IRS and turned over to the state.

Mrs. Sorenson filed a class action suit, arguing that the tax intercept provisions did not pertain to refunds attributable to the EITC. She urged the Court to recognize that the purpose of the tax credit was to provide benefits to the poor, and that if Congress had intended to apply the tax intercept process to the EITC, it would have stated so explicitly.

Based on the language and legislative history of the law, the Supreme Court rejected both arguments. First, the Court ruled, the 1981 Omnibus Budget Reconciliation Act provided that "any amount payable through the federal tax-refund process" could be intercepted. And since earned income tax credits were distributed through the income tax refund process, there was no reason to think Congress intended to preclude these funds from recovery through the tax intercept process. Second, the Court held that the EITC was not a welfare program but was designed to reduce disincentives to work, to funnel more money into the economy, and to lessen the hardship to persons hurt by the rising energy and food prices of the mid-1970s. In the face of congressional silence, the Court did not feel these goals outweighed the competing interests of the state in securing child support from absent parents and diminishing the welfare rolls.[84] Justice John Paul Stevens noted in dissent that this was really a conflict between a low-income family—which the EITC was designed to help—and the state. He pointed out that the state government was the prime beneficiary of the tax intercept process because the money compensated it for its AFDC expenses; he questioned whether Congress had sought to enrich state treasuries with EITC funds. Although he conceded that the language of the statute supported the Court's interpretation, Stevens said he doubted that Congress had intended such a result.

Rose v. Rose, a 1987 opinion, similarly dealt with the issue of whether federal benefits were beyond the reach of state-ordered child support obliga-tions.[85] Here, the Court was asked to decide whether a father whose income consisted entirely of veteran's disability benefits could be ordered to pay child support.

Charlie Wayne Rose was a totally disabled Vietnam veteran with two sons; he received approximately $3,400 a month in social security and veteran's disability benefits. As part of the divorce settlement ending his ten-year marriage, the Tennessee state court ordered him to pay $800 a month in child support. He refused and was jailed for contempt. He was released ten days later when he agreed to pay $400 in child support and $400 to a trust fund.[86]

Rose appealed the contempt order, arguing that it was invalid because his federal disability pensions were immune from the reach of the state. He lost in the state appellate court, and appealed to the U.S. Supreme Court. Arrayed against him were a large number of amici curiae briefs submitted by state attorneys general as well as attorneys for the Women's Legal Defense Fund.

Rose argued that the contempt order conflicted with the 1984 Child Support Enforcement Amendments and a provision of the U.S. Code governing disability benefits and was therefore pre-empted by the Supremacy Clause of the Constitution. Noting that state, and not federal, law largely governs family relations, the Court ruled that there must be clear evidence of congressional intent to pre-empt a state domestic relations statute. After reviewing the language and legislative history of the relevant federal statutes, the Court concluded that Congress did not intend to pre-empt the state's authority to order Rose to use his veteran's benefits to fulfil his child support obligation. On the contrary, the Court was persuaded that Congress intended veterans to use their benefits to support their dependents and did not intend to preclude states from enforcing support orders.[87] Despite its sympathy for Rose's "physical sacrifice" on behalf of his country, the Court declined to allow him to evade his child support obligations.

Justice Sandra Day O'Connor concurred in the result but argued that, in her view, the Court should have simply declared that public policy requires family support obligations to be treated differently from other debts. "Our Anglo-American tradition accords a special sanctity to the support obligation," she said, and federal law should not bar a state from enforcing it.[88]

Ten years after the Supreme Court's ruling in *Kulko*, another case illustrated the difficulties of interstate child support enforcement and the problems of relying on URESA to collect a child support debt.

Hicks v. Feiock, a 1988 decision, revolved around the controversy created by Phillip Feiock's failure to fulfil his child support obligation to his three children living in Ohio.[89] In January 1976, after his ex-wife filed a URESA petition in Ohio, a California state court ordered him to begin to make regular monthly payments. The California trial judge held that under California law, a parent is presumed able to pay a court-ordered child support award unless he demonstrates an inability to do so.

Feiock's record of payments in response to the court order was erratic until December 1982 when he stopped paying entirely. Two years later, his ex-wife sought judicial enforcement of the original order, and the trial judge ordered him to pay $150 a month. After two months of compliance, the payments again ceased. Nine months passed and he was ordered back into court to show cause why he should not be held in contempt for nine counts of failure to pay. Despite his plea that he had no money, the court found him guilty of contempt on five counts and sentenced him to twenty-five days in jail. The sentence was suspended, and he was placed on probation for three years, on condition that he resume the monthly payments, including payments on the arrearage he had accumulated. Rather than pay, Feiock appealed the contempt order, claiming that the presumption of an ability to pay involved a shifting burden of proof that violated due process when it was part of a criminal contempt proceeding.

The key to the validity of the contempt order was whether he had been found guilty of civil or criminal contempt. Although civil and criminal contempt share a number of characteristics, the latter carries with it a higher level of due process protection. Thus, shifting the burden of proof from the state to the defendant is permissible in a civil contempt proceeding but not in a criminal contempt proceeding.

The state appellate court, characterizing the contempt hearing as "quasi-criminal" in nature, held that the contempt order violated his right of due process and annulled it. The state supreme court denied review, and the U.S. Supreme Court agreed to hear the case. Among amici curiae briefs from the U.S. solicitor general and the California attorney general, was a brief from the Women's Legal Defense Fund, all urging reversal.

The Supreme Court's task in this case was to decide, based on principles of federal law, whether the contempt proceeding should be classified as criminal or civil.[90] After carefully constructing the tenets of federal law with respect to contempt, the Court determined that the record was unclear as to whether Feiock had been jailed in an effort to force him to comply with the court order (civil contempt) or to punish him for disobeying the court order (criminal contempt). The Court remanded the case to allow the lower court to resolve this issue.

In dissent, O'Connor strove to focus the Court's attention on the fact that the action arose because of the father's unfulfilled child support obligation. She stressed that the case demonstrated the difficulty of "obtaining even modest amounts of child support from a noncustodial parent."[91] Calling the child support enforcement system a "national scandal," O'Connor cited statistics from the brief submitted by the Women's Legal Defense Fund. She highlighted Feiock's delinquency in meeting his child support obligations and emphasized that his wife viewed her original child support order as a "worthless scrap of paper." O'Connor disagreed with the majority's decision to remand, believing that the Court had sufficient information to characterize the punishment as civil contempt and therefore not a due process violation.

Conclusion

Most of the cases involving child support enforcement policy required the Supreme Court to balance the competing interests of the father's constitutional due process rights, the state's authority over domestic policymaking, specifically, its role in the dominion of family law, and the father's fulfillment of his duty to his child. Overall, most of the cases involved adjudication of the rights of fathers seeking to elude their obligations to their children. For the most part, in these cases the interests of the state and the child converged, and the decisions were based on the rights and duties of the absent parent. The Court's rulings reflected its belief that, as a matter of public policy, society gains when parents are made to assume financial responsibility for their children—over their protests of unfairness or inability to pay.

In part these decisions were merely another manifestation of the Court's view that children should be protected from the consequences of their parent's failings, the view that was largely responsible for the Court's use of a higher level of review in deciding on the constitutionality of laws based on the child's birth status. Applying heightened scrutiny to statutes of limitation in paternity suits brought by unmarried mothers and their children was an important factor leading to the Court's decisions to strike these laws.[92]

Clearly, the Court's decisionmaking resulted in increased societal protection of children. But the Court's effort to hold fathers accountable for supporting their children did not arise solely from its sympathy for the plight of abandoned and vulnerable children. The Court's belief in principles of federalism also played a role in its decisionmaking; the rulings served to uphold child support orders issued by state courts as well as to allow states the opportunity to recoup child support expenses for AFDC children from their putative fathers.

Concern for the father's due process rights only predominated in two areas: in *Kulko*, a decision that very likely would hinder the interstate enforcement process, the Court refused to allow California to adjudicate the child support obligation of the nonresident father—a citizen of another state—even though the children lived there. The Court justified its decision in part by pointing out that both states had enacted versions of URESA. In urging the disputing parents to resolve their conflicts through the mechanisms provided by URESA, the Court was also preserving the independence of each state's domestic policymaking process.

Less significantly, due process also prevailed when, in *Streater*, the Court ordered states to pay the costs of blood tests to resolve questions of contested paternity. This ruling, however, likely caused states little difficulty: the tests would help eliminate the risk of an erroneous determination of paternity, even strengthening the state's case against the father when the test result proved positive, and were, in any event, largely funded by the federal government.

The increased role of the federal government in child support enforcement, an area of traditional state responsibility, was prompted in large part by the desire to contain the rising costs of welfare payments as well as to avoid the pitfalls of piecemeal and uneven state enforcement. Notwithstanding the rising interest of national policymakers, child support enforcement in the United States continues to be decentralized and indeterminate, with the bulk of enforcement still entrusted to state and local authorities and, in too many cases, to private attorneys outside the IV-D system.

Despite the fact that Supreme Court decisionmaking usually leads to greater uniformity in national policymaking, the rulings in the child support enforcement cases had few policy implications at the national level. Although in the main the children won their cases as the Supreme Court validated state laws requiring absent parents to fulfil their child support obligations, these rulings seemed to have little effect in bringing consistency and uniformity to the fragmented child support enforcement system. While the Court's rulings usually enhanced the collection process, it is unlikely that the system can be brought under control without greater centralization of the enforcement process, likely necessitating greater involvement by the federal government, especially in dealing with the intricacies of the interstate enforcement system.

Notes

1. American Bar Association, *America's Children at Risk: A National Agenda for Legal Action* (Washington, D.C.: American Bar Association, 1993), pp. 69–70.

2. The $47 billion figure is based on the non-custodial father's current ability to pay. Working Group on Welfare Reform, Family Support, and Independence, *Background Papers on Welfare Reform: Child Support Enforcement* (Washington, D.C.: Administration for Children and Families, Department of Health and Human Services, 1994), pp. 1–2.

3. Mary Jo Bane, "Household Composition and Poverty," in Sheldon H. Danziger and Daniel Weinberg, eds., *Fighting Poverty: What Works and What Doesn't* (Cambridge: Harvard University Press, 1986).

4. American Bar Association, *America's Children at Risk*, p. 69.

5. Committee on Ways and Means, U.S. House of Representatives, *Overview of Entitlement Programs, 1993 Green Book: Background Material and Data on Programs within the Jurisdiction of the Committee on Ways and Means* (Washington, D.C.: Government Printing Office, 1993), p. 741; Sally F. Goldfarb, "Child Support Guidelines: A Model for Fair Allocation of Child Care, Medical, and Educational Expenses," *Family Law Quarterly* 21 (1987): 325.

6. National Child Support Assurance Consortium, *Childhood's End: What Happens to Children When Child Support Obligations Are Not Enforced* (Uniondale, N.Y.: National Child Support Assurance Consortium, February 1993). The study was based on interviews with three hundred custodial mothers from Ohio, New York, Georgia, and Oregon.

7. Center for Law and Social Policy, *Family Matters* (Washington, D.C.: April, 1991).

8. See Raymond I. Parnas and Sherry Cermak, "Rethinking Child Support," *University of California, Davis Law Review* 22 (1989): 759–800; they also report findings of other studies relating to personal and psychological attributes of the custodial and non-custodial parents.

A study of the Michigan child support enforcement system notes that "jailing seems to work." David L. Chambers, *Making Fathers Pay* (Chicago: University of Chicago Press, 1979), p. 9.

9. Mary Ann Mason, *From Father's Property to Children's Rights: The History of Child Custody in the United States* (New York: Columbia University Press, 1994), chapter 3.

10. Lori K. Serratelli and Alvora Varin-Hommen, "The 1974 Child Support Provisions: Constitutional Ramifications," *Capital University Law Review* 6 (1976): 277. See Irwin Garfinkel and Sara S. McLanahan, *Single Mothers and Their Children: A New American Dilemma* (Washington, D.C.: Urban Institute Press, 1986), chapter 4.

11. Harry D. Krause, *Child Support in America: The Legal Perspective* (Charlottesville, Va.: The Michie Co., 1981), p. 281.

12. Steven M. Fleece, "A Review of the Child Support Enforcement Program," *Journal of Family Law* 20 (1981–1982): 490–491; see Diann Dawson, "The Evolution of a Federal Family Law Policy under Title IV-A of the Social Security Act—The Aid to Families with Dependent Children Program," *Catholic University Law Review* 36 (1986): 197–218.

13. S.Rep. No. 1356, 93d Cong., 2d Sess. (1974).

14. Judith Cassetty, *Child Support and Public Policy* (Lexington, Mass.: Lexington Books, 1978).

15. S.Rep. No. 1356, 93d Cong., 2d Sess. (1974).

16. Harry D. Krause, "Reflections on Child Support," *University of Illinois Law Review* (1983): 99–119.

17. Cassetty, *Child Support and Public Policy*, p. 14 (emphasis in the original).

18. Judith Stouder, "Child Support Enforcement and Establishment of Paternity as Tools of Welfare Reform—Social Services Amendments of 1974, pt. B, 42 U.S.C. §§ 651–60 (Supp. V, 1975)," *Washington Law Review* 52 (1976): 170–171, n. 20.

19. In 1992 almost $2 billion ($1,995 million) was spent on administrative expenses in child support collections, $1,343 million by the federal government and $652 million by the state. Additionally the federal government provided $299 million in incentives to state and local governments. Committee on Ways and Means, U.S. House of Representatives, *Overview of Entitlement Programs, 1993 Green Book*, p. 742, table 1.

20. The Parental Kidnapping Prevention Act of 1980 authorized the use of the PLS data for interstate child custody disputes. Krause, "Reflections on Child Support."

21. Garfinkel and McLanahan, *Single Mothers and Their Children*, p. 119.

22. Stouder, "Child Support Enforcement and Establishment of Paternity."

23. Mary R. Mannix, Henry A. Freedman, and Natarlin R. Best, "The Good Cause Exception to the AFDC Child Support Cooperation Requirement," *Clearinghouse Review* (August-September 1987): 339-348; James W. Johnson and Adele M. Blong, "The AFDC Child Support Cooperation Requirement," *Clearinghouse Review* (March 1987): 1388-1407. This would reduce the family benefit.

24. *Congressional Quarterly Weekly* (July 26, 1975): 1620.

25. Fleece, "A Review of the Child Support Enforcement Program."

26. Krause, *Child Support in America*, chapter 9.

27. For 1987 to 1988, a total of 4,587 good cause claims were allowed nationwide. Deborah Harris, "Child Support for Welfare Families: Family Policy Trapped in Its Own Rhetoric," *Review of Law and Social Change* 16 (1987-1988): 622, n. 12.

28. Stouder, "Child Support Enforcement and Establishment of Paternity."

29. Cited in Anne L. Radigan, "Federal Policy-making and Family Issues," in Elizabeth A. Mulroy, ed., *Women As Single Parents* (Dover, Mass.: Auburn House Publishing, 1988), p. 216.

30. Withholding was automatic for child support orders obtained through IV-D agencies; for non-IV-D cases, the custodial parent had to apply to the agency to begin the withholding process. The amount withheld, as provided by the Consumer Credit Protection Act, was limited to 50 percent of disposable earnings of an absent parent with a second family, and 60 percent of disposable earnings for a parent without a second family; employers were entitled to a fee as well. Committee on Ways and Means, U.S. House of Representatives, *Overview of Entitlement Programs, 1993 Green Book*, pp. 761-762; Harris, "Child Support for Welfare Families."

31. Paula Roberts, "Federal Income Tax Intercept," *Clearinghouse Review* (December 1985): 853-863; Douglas B. Neagli and Matthew B. Troutman, "Constitutional Implications of the Child Support Enforcement Amendments of 1984," *Journal of Family Law* 24 (1985-1986): 301-326. Limits on the government in the tax intercept procedure are discussed below.

32. A few states, such as Wisconsin, use the "percentage of income" method in which the courts fix the child support obligation as a percentage of the non-custodial

parent's income, varied by the number of children in the family. Irwin Garfinkel, *Assuring Child Support* (New York: Russell Sage Foundation, 1992), chapter 5; Goldfarb, "Child Support Guidelines."

33. Margaret Campbell Haynes, "Supporting Our Children: A Blueprint for Reform," *Family Law Quarterly* 27 (1993): 13.

34. *Congressional Quarterly Weekly* (August 11, 1984): 1965.

35. Harry O'Donnell, "Title I of the Family Support Act of 1988—The Quest for Effective National Child Support Enforcement Continues," *Journal of Family Law* 29 (1990–1991): 155; see also Paula Roberts and Mary Mason, "Promises, Promises: Child Support Enforcement in 1988," *Clearinghouse Review* (January 1989): 909–917.

36. In the 1993 Omnibus Budget Reconciliation Act, Congress required states to enact laws promoting voluntary acknowledgment of paternity in hospitals, and to raise their performance level in establishing paternity to 75 percent of out-of-wedlock births. 139 Cong. Rec. 6018–6019 (August 4, 1993).

37. Recent evidence indicates that states are still uncertain about allowing deviations from the numerical criteria and determining when it would be "inappropriate" or "unjust" to follow them at all. Additionally, because Title I made no mention of consistency across state lines, it had no impact on the variation among states. O'Donnell, "Title I of the Family Support Act of 1988," discusses the degree of variation among states.

38. Under Title IV-D women were allowed to seek federal court intervention in interstate IV-D cases involving arrearages after HEW certified that the originating state had not engaged to enforce the original support order within a reasonable time, and that federal court adjudication was the only reasonable method of enforcement. As of 1993, however, there was only one instance of application to the federal court for enforcement of an out-of-state child support award, suggesting the ineffectiveness of this interstate enforcement mechanism. Committee on Ways and Means, U.S. House of Representatives, *Overview of Entitlement Programs, 1993 Green Book*, p. 767; see Stouder, "Child Support Enforcement and Establishment of Paternity," for discussion of access to the federal courts in child support cases.

39. Haynes, "Supporting Our Children," p. 7; Committee on Ways and Means, U.S. House of Representatives, *Overview of Entitlement Programs, 1993 Green Book*, p. 765.

40. The due process clause often protects the out-of-state father who is delinquent in child support payments by barring suit against him in the state where the mother resides, requiring her to file suit in *his* home state. Supreme Court rulings on state long-arm statutes which try to circumvent this constitutional prohibition are discussed below.

41. Haynes, "Supporting Our Children," p. 12.

42. URESA is now called the Revised Uniform Reciprocal Enforcement of Support Act (RURESA).

43. Faye R. Goldberg, "Child Support Enforcement: Balancing Increased Federal Involvement with Procedural Due Process," *Suffolk University Law Review* 19 (1985): 687–714.

44. The Interstate Commission on Child Support heard evidence that some judges do not comply with the statute. See Haynes, "Supporting Our Children."

45. In August 1992 the National Conference of Commissioners on Uniform State Laws presented a new version of URESA, entitled the Uniform Interstate Family Support Act (UIFSA); it was approved by the American Bar Association in February 1993. The UIFSA would make it easier for custodial parents to enforce out-of-state support orders. Among other things, it would require a responding state to enforce the original support order and would prevent its modification. John J. Sampson and Paul M. Kurtz, "UIFSA: An Interstate Support Act for the twenty-first Century," *Family Law Quarterly* 27 (1993): 85–93.

46. Margaret Campbell Haynes, personal interview; see Haynes, "Supporting Our Children."

47. Laura Vogel, "Children in Poverty: Welfare and Work Together Can Make a Difference," *The Kansas Journal of Law and Public Policy* 3 (Spring 1994): 179.

48. Steven R. Miller, "Federal Law and the Enforcement of Child Support Orders: A Critical Look at Subchapter 4 Part D of the Social Services Amendments of 1974," *Review of Law and Social Change* 6 (1976): 35; see Harris, "Child Support for Welfare Families."

49. Harris, "Child Support for Welfare Families," p. 620. For discussion of the relationship between child support enforcement and AFDC policy, see Philip K. Robins, "Child Support, Welfare Dependency, and Poverty," *The American Economic Review* 76 (September 1986): 768–788; Brian L. Calistri, "Child Support and Welfare Reform: The Child Support Enforcement Provisions of the Family Support Act of 1988," *Journal of Legislation* 16 (1990): 191–201; Robert I. Lerman, "Child Support Policies," in Phoebe H. Cottingham and David T. Ellwood, eds., *Welfare Policy for the 1990s* (Cambridge: Harvard University Press, 1989).

Joel F. Handler, "The Transformation of Aid to Families with Dependent Children: The Family Support Act in Historical Context," *Review of Law and Social Change* 16 (1987–1988): 457–533, argues against forcing the father of an AFDC child to contribute.

50. Garfinkel, *Assuring Child Support*, p. 23.

51. Garfinkel, *Assuring Child Support*, p. 47.

52. Although Wisconsin had committed itself to a child support assurance scheme, it failed to implement the cornerstone of the plan—the assured benefit payment. Garfinkel, *Assuring Child Support*, pp. 116–118, discusses the Wisconsin experience.

53. David T. Ellwood, *Poor Support: Poverty in the American Family* (New York: Basic Books, 1988), p. 167. The Wisconsin CSAS has adopted the following scale: 17 percent of gross income for the first child, 25 percent for two children, 29 percent for

three, 31 percent for four, and 34 percent for five or more children. Tom Corbett, Irwin Garfinkel, and Nora Cate Schaeffer, "Public Opinion about a Child Support Assurance System," *Social Service Review* (December 1988): 634.

54. Irwin Garfinkel and Donald Oellerich, "Noncustodial Fathers' Ability to Pay Child Support," *Demography* 26 (May 1989): 230.

55. According to Paula Roberts, a CSAS program is more effective than the AFDC program because the latter offers the "illusion" of sufficient family income to survive on; under a CSAS, the dollar amount provided is too low to offer that illusion so women are immediately aware that they must find work. Paula Roberts, personal interview.

56. Obviously, if these poverty programs are cut, there would be little benefit in establishing a child support assurance system.

57. In addition to establishing a CSAS, Mary Jo Bane and David T. Ellwood, *Welfare Realities: From Rhetoric to Reform* (Cambridge: Harvard University Press, 1994), also support paying transitional benefits to single mothers for a limited period of time to allow them to cope with short-term problems. The benefits would include training and support services.

58. Bane and Ellwood, *Welfare Realities*, p. 155 (emphasis in the original).

59. Garfinkel, *Assuring Child Support*, pp. 68–69.

60. Under a CSAS, eligibility for the assured benefit would depend on identifying the father and establishing a child support award. Recognizing the problems that can result from identifying the father in some cases, Bane and Ellwood, *Welfare Realities*, nevertheless suggest phasing out the "good cause" exception.

61. Paula Roberts, personal interview.

62. To ensure discovery of all Supreme Court opinions relating to child support policy through 1993, a Lexis search of the GENFED library, US file, was conducted, using "Child w/5 Support or Title IV-D" as the search terms. This search yielded 105 decisions. Of these, there were 18 *relevant* opinions, that is, opinions in which the Court resolved disputes over state or federal child support policy by interpreting a state or federal law or regulation.

63. *Bowen v. Gilliard*, 483 U.S. 587 (1987) and *Sullivan v. Stroop*, 496 U.S. 478 (1990), two of the eighteen cases—both concerning the effect of child support payments on AFDC eligibility—are discussed in chapter 2.

64. 410 U.S. 614 (1973).

65. Stouder, "Child Support Enforcement and Establishment of Paternity," pp. 181–183, nn. 82–92; see Fleece, "A Review of the Child Support Enforcement Program," for a discussion of the lower court cases after Title IV-D.

66. 422 U.S. 391 (1975).

67. On remand, the lower court ruled that the Connecticut statute was not pre-empted by the 1974 act, but that the federal "good cause" exception had to be applied

before contempt charges could be brought against the women. The state appealed, claiming that the state could not apply the good cause exception because HEW had not yet adopted standards for determining it. In *Maher v. Doe*, 432 U.S. 526 (1977), the Supreme Court again vacated the lower court decision and remanded the case, asking the district court to consider whether Connecticut could adopt its own good cause standards. No further legal action was reported, and HEW eventually adopted good cause standards in 1978. See Fleece, "A Review of the Child Support Enforcement Program."

68. 420 U.S. 730 (1975).

69. 452 U.S. 1 (1981).

70. 424 U.S. 319 (1976). *Mathews* was a social security case in which the Supreme Court identified three factors to be balanced to determine the requirements of the due process clause.

71. 483 U.S. 574 (1987).

72. 455 U.S. 745 (1982).

73. 456 U.S. 91 (1982).

74. 462 U.S. 1 (1983).

75. 475 U.S. 557 (1986).

76. 486 U.S. 456 (1988).

77. 421 U.S. 7 (1975).

78. 429 U.S. 501 (1977).

79. 436 U.S. 84 (1978).

80. He was entitled to appear to challenge the jurisdiction question without conceding that the court had jurisdiction over him. Based on long-standing precedent, to enable courts to exercise personal jurisdiction over out-of-state residents there must be "minimum contacts" between the defendant and the state "such that the maintenance of the suit does not offend traditional notions of fair play and substantial justice." *International Shoe Co. v. Washington*, 326 U.S. 310, 316 (1945).

81. 467 U.S. 822 (1984).

82. 475 U.S. 851 (1986).

83. Due process requirements for proper notice were established in *Mullane v. Central Hanover Bank and Trust Co.*, 339 U.S. 306 (1950). See Roberts, "Federal Income Tax Intercept"; Neagli and Troutman, "Constitutional Implications of the Child Support Enforcement Amendments of 1984."

84. *Sorenson*, 475 U.S. at 866 (Stevens, J., dissenting).

85. 481 U.S. 619 (1987).

86. During these proceedings, Rose hired two men to burn his ex-wife's house; he was convicted of arson and sentenced to prison. Little damage was done to the house. American Bar Association, "Supreme Court Report: Child Support and Jail," *American Bar Association Journal* (August 1, 1987): 58–61.

87. The Women's Legal Defense Fund's brief also claimed that the fact that Rose married after he became disabled was evidence of his own intention to use his VA benefits to support his family. American Bar Association, "Supreme Court Report: Child Support and Jail."

88. *Rose*, 481 U.S. at 637 (O'Connor, J., concurring).

89. 485 U.S. 624 (1988).

90. As a matter of state law, which the Supreme Court could not alter, the appellate court had ruled on the question of whether proof of his inability to pay should be treated as an affirmative defense or as an element of the offense. The court also ruled on the issue of whether he bears the burden of proof or merely the burden of production in establishing his inability to pay. The court found that first, the inability to pay is an element of the offense, and second, that the parent bears the burden of proof.

91. *Hicks*, 485 U.S. at 642 (O'Connor, J., dissenting).

92. See Michael J. Dale, "The Evolving Constitutional Rights of Nonmarital Children: Mixed Blessings," *Georgia State University Law Review* 5 (1989): 523–555.

CONCLUSION

Amidst national debate over the allocation of resources devoted to them, this book has examined the role of the federal government in policymaking for children, concentrating particularly on the impact of the federal courts on policies relating to children. Its primary purpose was to determine the extent to which federal court decisionmaking has affected the legal, political, economic, and social status of children in the United States. Based on the notion that the federal courts are uniquely situated to provide relief to the less powerful, or disadvantaged, in society, this study was motivated by the desire to assess the Supreme Court's response to children's demands for rights and benefits across a number of policy areas and a range of statutory and constitutional issues.

There was an upsurge of litigation on behalf of children beginning in the 1960s and 1970s as leading children's advocacy groups in the United States followed the example of earlier social reform movements in seeking the intervention of the federal courts in the policymaking process. The children's advocates hoped that the federal courts would be receptive to the demands of children, who represent "one of the largest and most vulnerable minority groups [in the United States]."[1]

The litigation seeking to expand children's rights in the federal courts has revolved around a number of issues, ranging from the minor's right to privacy, limitations on the state's authority to discipline, train, and educate the child, permissible boundaries on a child's speech and access to information, and the state's responsibility to shield the child from harm. Cases in these categories typically raised two sets of questions: first, whether the Court should acknowledge children's rights to self-determination by granting independence from parental and state controls; second, whether their vulnerability requires children to be sheltered from the actions of parents and the state. The decisions in these cases were characterized by the Court's attempt to weigh the often competing interests of state, child, and parent in an effort to arrive at an appropriate balance between autonomy and protection. Through appeals to constitutional principles or the requirements of federal law, children's representatives also sought to enlist federal judicial authority to redress inequalities based on birth or wealth status and to increase children's access to public welfare assistance.

The Court was generally supportive of children's demands for self-determination in the expression of ideas and access to information, granting that children were entitled to engage in constitutionally protected speech. However, states were also permitted to regulate expression that was arguably improper, that is, expression declared to contain sexually explicit or otherwise inappropriate material. Eventually, based on later rulings, this exception began to swallow the rule as state officials were increasingly able to narrow the parameters of the types of speech considered proper for children. The Court began to give school officials greater latitude to declare material "unsuitable" and prevent student access to it, in large part, by requiring less proof that the speech interfered with the educational mission.

In decisions relating to a minor's right to privacy, beginning shortly after the Supreme Court handed down its landmark abortion rights decision, the Court determined that minors were entitled to some degree of privacy over reproductive decisionmaking; it stopped short, however, of according young people full adult privileges. Thus, while the Court refused to confer blanket authority on parents or the state to prevent a young woman from obtaining an abortion, it allowed states to retain some measure of control. And not surprisingly, when the Rehnquist Court began to permit states to impose more restrictions on the adult woman's right to privacy, it also allowed greater limitations on the minor woman's right to privacy. In its later rulings the Court permitted states to mandate parental involvement in a minor's abortion decision, even under circumstances when it seemed counterproductive to do so.

For the most part, the Court's decisionmaking in cases involving juvenile offenders was guided by the question of whether the practices of the juvenile courts, which often deprived minors of adult constitutional rights, served the intended purpose of rehabilitation rather than punishment. Because the Court determined that juveniles were often treated more harshly than adults by the juvenile court system, and deprived of many of the rights accorded adult offenders, it superimposed a number of adult constitutional guarantees on the state juvenile court structure.

With its record of support for individual rights in cases involving adult suspects, the Warren Court played a leading role in extending rights to juveniles; and as with adult defendants, the Burger Court did not reverse those decisions but generally refused to expand the range of constitutional guarantees for juveniles. The Rehnquist Court decisions were of a different type than the previous Courts; it was asked to recognize the immaturity of juvenile offenders and shield them from the consequences of their crimes by allowing them to escape the finality of the death penalty. It refused to do so and, with certain qualifications, allowed the state to impose the death penalty on minors. The *Stanford* decision arguably represents one of the Court's most stunning rejections of the protectionist principle.

Since the mid-1970s, children's legal representatives have sought to expand the parameters of the due process clause, primarily in matters concerning school discipline. However, beyond barring schools from suspending a student without a hearing, the Court placed few obstacles in the way of school officials administering corporal punishment or searching a student's property without prior judicial approval. Additionally, the Court found that state procedures for institutionalizing a mentally ill or mentally disabled child were constitutionally adequate, based on its assumption that the state and the parents were acting in the child's best interests despite the fact that there was no formal judicial ruling prior to the commitment.

In contrast to its position on procedural due process guarantees in juvenile offender cases, the Court was more hesitant to further children's rights in non-criminal cases and refused entirely to expand children's substantive due process rights. In adjudicating child welfare decisions generally, the Rehnquist Court was faced with the task of balancing the often competing interests of the parents' rights, the state's *parens patriae* authority, and the children's best interests. In most of these cases the Court assumed that either the parents or the state spoke for the children; for the most part the Court did not ascribe an independent interest to children and rarely examined their stake in the litigation.

Similarly, the Rehnquist Court refused to engage in fundamental rights analysis by holding that institutionalizing children accused of illegal immigration until their deportation hearings deprived them of a fundamental right. The Court reasoned that all children were in custody, and there was no constitutional significance to whether they were in the custody of their relatives or the state. Astonishingly, moreover, even in circumstances involving genuine harm to a child, the Rehnquist Court declined to hold the state responsible, dismissing a lawsuit that alleged that the state's negligence in failing to prevent serious injury to a small boy violated his Fourteenth Amendment liberty interest. Rather than adopting a far-reaching interpretation of the due process clause of the Fourteenth Amendment, the Court exempted the state from accountability for the child's injuries in federal court, raising questions about the effectiveness of the state's child protection system and child abuse reporting laws. The crucial issue for the majority was whether the state's liability for the child's injuries should be adjudicated in federal court.

The *DeShaney* opinion shows the extent to which the high court desired to shield the state from federal court oversight. Perhaps no other statement better illustrates the extent to which the Court was prepared to further this goal than the majority's pronouncement that the federal courts was an inappropriate forum for redressing the harm to Joshua. Declaring that the framers of the Constitution placed responsibility for protecting members of society from each other in "the democratic political processes," the Court rejected the injured child's federal damage remedy.

In *Suter*, the pivotal case requiring interpretation of the federal child welfare law, the Court construed the statutory mandate so narrowly that the state was able to escape responsibility for the slipshod administration of its foster care system. Thus, said the Court, compliance with the "reasonable efforts" clause in P.L. 96-272 was solely within the discretion of the state. Reflecting a constricted view of the legislative mandate to provide social services for abused and neglected children (as well as a tortured reading of existing case law), the Court said Congress never intended to allow children the right to seek a federal remedy for the state's failure to comply with the act. Indeed, said the Court, the only condition Congress imposed on the state in exchange for receiving federal funding was the requirement that the state file a plan with the federal authorizing agency.

Most of the constitutional cases decided over this forty-year span raised difficult questions about the proper role of the child in society and the appropriate balance between a child's need for freedom and the need for protection. The Court's decisionmaking in cases involving children's rights and welfare claims suggests that two generalizations may be made: first, on balance it appears the high court has been more amenable to children's demands for increased independence from state and parental authority than to claims for protection from the actions or inactions of state officials. Second, whether their claims sought greater protectionism or autonomy, over time the Supreme Court has become less willing to accede to the demands of children, in large part reasoning that this would require too much judicial interference with the authority of the state.

The Court responded most favorably to children's claims in cases involving challenges to state laws that assigned rights to them on the basis of their parents' marital status. As a group the rights of nonmarital children were greatly enhanced when the Court struck state illegitimacy classifications on constitutional equal protection grounds by imposing a stricter scrutiny on the laws. In deciding these cases the Court was principally motivated by the belief that legal classifications on the basis of birth status unjustly punished children for the actions of their parents.

Similarly, the Court's decisions in child support enforcement cases were for the most part decided in the children's favor, and undoubtedly were among the least difficult cases to decide. These cases involved balancing the interests of the child—which frequently converged with the interests of the state—against the interests of a private individual, chiefly an absent father. Not surprisingly, the Court was reluctant to provide a father with the opportunity to escape responsibility for supporting his child.

Overall these disputes were relatively easy for the Court to resolve: they involved little conflict with state authority—on the contrary, they reinforced the state's dominion over domestic policy issues—and, more important, they made no claims on the state's fisc—indeed they even promoted the state's interest in reducing the cost of public assistance programs. Because of the nature of these controversies, during the tenure of all three chief justices, the Court almost always supported the claims of nonmarital children and enhanced society's attempts to enforce parental obligations to their children.

In contrast to its willingness to rule for children in these areas, the Court was least supportive overall of claims brought by children seeking to compel a greater distribution of societal benefits: whether as demands for constitutional rights or statutory entitlements. Such cases, in which litigants appealed to the high court to intervene in state taxing and spending policy, illustrate the limits of litigation to attain social reform.

In the landmark *Rodriguez* case, litigants asked the Burger Court to accord a special status to laws relating to wealth and to impose a higher standard of review on the state's justification of its taxation policies. The Court rejected their demand for greater equity in the allocation of educational benefits and refused to bar states from funding their educational systems primarily through local property taxes.

As part of the litigation campaign on behalf of the poor—adults as well as children—children's advocates joined forces with poverty reform groups in seeking the aid of the federal courts in expanding access to benefits of the AFDC program. These cases raised questions of rules of eligibility, adherence to the federal statutory mandate, and access to the program's resources. And because the statutes were ambiguously worded and the intent of the legislature often unclear, the courts were left with a great deal of discretion in resolving conflicts over the state's responsibilities to the beneficiaries of the programs.

Initially the courts rewarded the efforts of litigants by interpreting the AFDC statute to effectuate its broad remedial purposes, prohibiting states from wrongfully limiting AFDC eligibility to needy children. Thus, the Supreme Court barred states from denying assistance to children who lived with unrelated men in the house as well as the children of military personnel. Such decisions often resulted in an expansion of the number of entitled beneficiaries.

Reflecting a determination to refrain from involvement in state economic policymaking, however, the Court steadfastly refused to intervene in disputes over the allocation of benefits, even when confronted with likely evidence of racial discrimination. Although the Court was, of course, constrained by the statutory language in which states were given a good deal of autonomy over such matters, it had the option—which it rejected—of declaring laws such as the Maryland flat grant unconstitutional as a violation of the equal protection clause of the Fourteenth Amendment.

In the latter part of the 1980s the Supreme Court became even less inclined to require states to broaden access to AFDC benefits, although here again the Court was somewhat confined within the bounds of the controlling federal law which reflected the efforts of the Reagan administration to save AFDC dollars. Thus, the Supreme Court was not *solely* responsible for the reverses suffered by the AFDC litigants during this time; more precisely, these reverses resulted from the confluence of legislative and executive policy—as well as judicial decisions—that led to constraints on public welfare programs. But contrary to the tenets of the "disadvantaged theory," the Court did not play a significant role in contravening the actions of the majoritarian branches of government.

In contrast to their significant impact on broadening rules of eligibility for AFDC beneficiaries, at least in the early years, the federal courts had little impact on the beneficiaries of programs designed to remedy nutritional and educational deficiencies—WIC and Head Start. Despite their enormous popularity on Capitol Hill and in the White House, these programs were subject to continual battles over authorizations and appropriations, leading at the extreme to a series of lawsuits against the executive branch. And although the federal court's ruling to spend the funds designated to WIC by Congress was a significant victory for plaintiffs, the remedy was quite limited, lasting only until the program was subject to re-authorization.

For a number of political and practical reasons both WIC and Head Start received enormous rhetorical support from policymakers and relatively consistent funding increases; yet, despite their ostensible popularity, the resources committed to them were insufficient to accommodate the needs of all those who were eligible. In large part because they never received entitlement status, beneficiaries had little recourse in the courts when denied access to the benefits of the programs. In the isolated cases when potential recipients filed lawsuits to secure greater access to the programs, the courts denied their claims, indicating that the judiciary was not properly suited to resolve disputes over the allocation of resources in such federal spending programs.

Thus, while these programs affected vital areas of children's lives, the legal issues in these federal court cases were largely confined to conflicts between employers and employees, challenges to federal administrative regulations, and intramural disputes among local governments, or between HHS and local governments, over the control of grantee agencies. The opinions were all rendered by the lower federal courts; none were reviewed by the Supreme Court. Taken together, the litigation over the WIC and Head Start programs suggests that litigation over programs that lack the funds to serve eligible beneficiaries is of little use to plaintiffs if the primary reason for their exclusion from the program is its limited financial resources.

Returning to the question raised at the outset of this analysis, overall to what degree have the federal courts supported children's demands for rights and benefits? Clearly litigation resulted in some victories for children's rights advocates, that is, Supreme Court rulings expanded the rights of children in several areas—allowing them to assume a greater degree of control over their lives, removing some legal disabilities, and providing added protection from arbitrary government action. But, increasingly over time the victories diminished as the Court became more unwilling to intrude into the policymaking role of the state and federal governments. Thus, spurred by a growing concern for principles of federalism and state autonomy, the Court refused to impose an affirmative obligation on the state to protect children from severe physical and emotional harm. Similarly, it rejected children's claims for a more equitable distribution of government resources and services, including education and public welfare assistance.

It is instructive to contemplate how contrary decisions in *Dandridge, Jefferson, Gilliard, Suter,* and *DeShaney* may have affected the quality of children's lives, that is, what if the Court had interpreted the Constitution and relevant federal statutes to require states to expand the quality of services and benefits in the AFDC and child welfare programs? The fact that these rulings were divided suggests that the results in these cases were not legally compelled. Similarly, consider if the federal judge in *Alexander* (the Philadelphia WIC case) had taken the opposite tack and granted litigants their injunction against the city as well as significant money damages.

Although the Court would not have reversed the life chances of all poor, abused, or minority children by ruling in their favor in these cases, at least it would have added its weight to efforts to force state and local governments to take more heed of the disadvantaged within their borders. Justice Blackmun's impassioned plea in *Suter*, reminding the Court that "after all, we are dealing here with children," calls on the judiciary not to abandon children such as these to their fate.

This review of public policymaking for children over the last sixty years— since the creation of the AFDC program in the Social Security Act of 1935—demonstrates that the federal government has largely taken the lead in advancing the interests of the nation's children by compelling or inducing states to act on their behalf. Although the federal role was not a panacea for children, federal initiatives have been responsible for the society taking an increasing interest in children and devoting more of the nation's resources to them. However, the actions of the 104th Congress in diminishing federal responsibility for children and, among other things, transforming individual entitlement programs into state block grant programs, will likely undo most of the federal government's past efforts on behalf of children.

The role of the Supreme Court in public policymaking for children over these years reveals that litigation is a fragile instrument for rectifying the problems of a "disadvantaged" group in the face of the Court's overriding concern for loosening the federal judiciary's supervisory role over the state and enhancing the state's autonomy in matters of public policy. Analysis of Supreme Court decisionmaking in the policy areas examined here suggests that attempts to enlist the power of the federal courts to enhance the federal government's role or impose national standards of behavior on states, in the absence of clearly specified mandates, will be largely futile. Thus, as many of the children's advocates interviewed for this study have already discovered, children must look elsewhere than to the courts for relief. However, given the recent initiatives of both national and state elected government officials, it may be that for children, especially poor and minority children, "elsewhere" is an elusive place.

Notes

1. Mary Kohler, "To What Are Children Entitled?" in Beatrice Gross and Ronald Gross, eds., *The Children's Rights Movement: Overcoming the Oppression of Young People* (Garden City, N.Y.: Anchor Books, 1977), p. 217.

APPENDIX 1: REHNQUIST COURT DECISIONS

Rehnquist Court Decisions

Name of Case	Year	Issue	Const'l. Provision
Reno	1993	Detention of Undocumented Juvenile Immigrants	Due Process
Casey	1992	Abortion/Parental Consent	Privacy
Akron Center	1990	Abortion/Parental Notification	Privacy
Hodgson	1990	Abortion/Parental Notification	Privacy
Stanford	1989	Death Penalty	8th Amendment
Stanglin	1989	Excluding Teenagers From Dance Hall	Free Expression
DeShaney	1989	State's Duty to Protect Child from Abuse	Due Process
Thompson	1988	Death Penalty	8th Amendment
Kadrmas	1988	Education and School Bus Fees	Equal Protection
Jeter	1988	Illegitimacy	Equal Protection
Kuhlmeier	1988	Student Newspaper	Free Expression

APPENDIX 2: BURGER COURT DECISIONS

Burger Court Decisions

Name of Case	Year	Issue	Const'l. Provision
Fraser	1986	Lewd Speech in High School	Free Expression
Campbell	1986	Illegitimacy	Equal Protection
TLO	1985	School Search	4th Amendment
Schall	1984	Pretrial Detention of Juveniles	Due Process
Ashcroft	1983	Abortion/Parental Consent	Privacy
City of Akron	1983	Abortion/Parental Consent	Privacy
Pickett	1983	Illegitimacy	Equal Protection
Martinez	1983	Residency Requirement for Public Schools	Equal Protection
McCluskey	1982	Suspension from School	Due Process
Pico	1982	Removing Books from School Library	Free Expression
Plyler	1982	School Tuition for Undocumented Immigrant Children	Equal Protection
Habluetzel	1982	Illegitimacy	Equal Protection
Eddings	1982	Death Penalty	8th Amendment
H.L.	1981	Abortion/Parental Notification	Privacy
Bellotti	1979	Abortion/Parental Consent	Privacy

Name of Case	Year	Issue	Const'l. Provision
Fare	1979	Confession by Juvenile	5th Amendment
Institut'lzd Juveniles	1979	Voluntary Commitment	Due Process
J.R.	1979	Voluntary Commitment	DueProcess
Lalli	1978	Illegitimacy	Equal Protection
Swisher	1978	Double Jeopardy	Due Process
Carey	1977	Access to Contraception	Privacy
Trimble	1977	Illegitimacy	Equal Protection
Ingraham	1976	Corporal Punishment in Schools	Due Process
Danforth	1976	Abortion/Parental Consent	Privacy
Lucas	1976	Illegitimacy	Equal Protection
Breed	1975	Double Jeopardy	Due Process
Goss	1975	Suspension from School	Due Process
Jimenez	1974	Illegitimacy	Equal Protection
New Jersey WRO	1973	Illegitimacy	Equal Protection
Rodriguez	1973	School Financing	Equal Protection
Gomez	1973	Illegitimacy	Equal Protection
Yoder	1972	Compulsory Education for Amish Children	Free Exercise
Weber	1972	Illegitimacy	Equal Protection
McKeiver	1971	Juvenile's Right to Trial by Jury	Due Process
Labine	1971	Illegitimacy	Equal Protection
Winship	1970	Burden of Proof in Juvenile Court	Due Process

APPENDIX 3: WARREN COURT DECISIONS

Warren Court Decisions

Name of Case	Year	Issue	Const'l. Provision
Tinker	1969	Protest in School	Free Expression
Levy	1968	Illegitimacy	Equal Protection
Ginsberg	1968	Obscenity Standard for Minors	Free Expression
Gault	1967	Right to Counsel	Due Process
Kent	1966	Waiver of Jurisdiction by Juvenile Court	Due Process
Gallegos	1962	Confession by Juvenile	Due Process

BIBLIOGRAPHY

Books

Abramovitz, Mimi. *Regulating the Lives of Women: Social Welfare Policy from Colonial Times to the Present.* Boston: South End Press, 1988.

Allen, MaryLee, Carol Golubock, and Lynn Olson. "Guide to the Adoption Assistance and Child Welfare Act of 1980." In Mark Hardin, ed. *Foster Children in the Courts.* Boston: Butterworth Legal Publishers, 1983.

American Bar Association. *America's Children at Risk: A National Agenda for Legal Action.* Washington, D.C.: American Bar Association 1993.

Bane, Mary Jo. "Household Composition and Poverty." In Sheldon H. Danziger and Daniel Weinberg, eds. *Fighting Poverty: What Works and What Doesn't.* Cambridge: Harvard University Press, 1986.

Bane, Mary Jo, and David T. Ellwood. *Welfare Realities: From Rhetoric to Reform.* Cambridge: Harvard University Press, 1994.

Bell, Winifred. *Aid to Dependent Children.* New York: Columbia University Press, 1965.

Berkowitz, Edward D., and Kim McQuaid. *Creating the Welfare State.* 2d ed. Lawrence: University Press of Kansas, 1992.

Berrick, Jill, and Neil Gilbert. *With the Best of Intentions: The Child Sexual Abuse Prevention Movement.* New York: Guilford Press, 1991.

Besharov, Douglas J. "The Misuse of Foster Care: When the Desire to Help Children Outruns the Ability to Improve Parental Functioning." In Douglas J. Besharov, ed. *Protecting Children from Abuse and Neglect: Policy and Practice.* Springfield, Ill.: Charles C. Thomas, 1988.

———. *Recognizing Child Abuse.* New York: Free Press, 1990.

Beyer, Margaret, and Wallace J. Mlyniec. "Lifelines to Biological Parents: Their Effect on Termination of Parental Rights and Permanence." In Douglas J. Besharov, ed. *Protecting Children from Abuse and Neglect: Policy and Practice.* Springfield, Ill.: Charles C. Thomas, 1988.

Bianchi, Suzanne M. "Children of Poverty: Why Are They Poor?" In Judith A. Chafel ed. *Child Poverty and Public Policy.* Washington, D.C.: Urban Institute, 1993.

Blasi, Vincent, ed. *The Burger Court.* New Haven: Yale University Press, 1983.

Block, Fred, Richard A. Cloward, Barbara Ehrenreich, and Frances Fox Piven. *The Mean Season: The Attack on the Welfare State*. New York: Pantheon Books, 1987.

Cassetty, Judith. *Child Support and Public Policy*. Lexington, Mass.: Lexington Books, 1978.

Chambers, David L. *Making Fathers Pay*. Chicago: University of Chicago Press, 1979.

Children's Defense Fund. *The State of America's Children*. Washington, D.C.: Children's Defense Fund, 1992.

Coontz, Stephanie. *The Way We Never Were*. New York: Basic Books, 1992.

Danziger, Sheldon. "Fighting Poverty and Reducing Welfare Dependency." In Phoebe H. Cottingham and David T. Ellwood eds. *Welfare Policy for the 1990s*. Cambridge: Harvard University Press, 1989.

Datta, Lois-ellin. "Another Spring and Other Hopes: Some Findings from National Evaluations of Project Head Start." In Edward Zigler and Jeanette Valentine, eds. *Project Head Start*. New York: Free Press, 1979.

Davis, Martha F. *Brutal Need: Lawyers and the Welfare Rights Movement, 1960–1973*. New Haven: Yale University Press, 1993.

Davis, Samuel M., and Mortimer D. Schwartz. *Children's Rights and the Law*. Lexington, Mass.: Lexington Books, 1987.

Edelman, Marion Wright. *Families in Peril: An Agenda for Social Change*. Cambridge: Harvard University Press, 1987.

Edelman, Peter B. "The Children's Rights Movement." In Beatrice Gross and Ronald Gross, eds. *The Children's Rights Movement: Overcoming the Oppression of Young People*. Garden City, N.Y.: Anchor Books, 1977.

Ellwood, David T. *Poor Support: Poverty in the American Family*. New York: Basic Books, 1988.

English, Abigail. "Litigating under the Adoption Assistance and Child Welfare Act of 1980." In Mark Hardin, ed. *Foster Children in the Courts*. Boston: Butterworth Legal Publishers, 1983.

Epstein, Lee. *Conservatives in Court*. Knoxville: University of Tennessee Press, 1985.

Friedman, Scott. *The Law of Parent-Child Relationships*. Chicago: American Bar Association, 1992.

Fryer, George E., Jr. *Child Abuse and the Social Environment*. Boulder: Westview, 1993.

Garfinkel, Irwin. *Assuring Child Support*. New York: Russell Sage Foundation, 1992.

Garfinkel, Irwin, and Sara S. McLanahan. *Single Mothers and Their Children: A New American Dilemma*. Washington, D.C.: Urban Institute Press, 1986.

Gaylin, Willard, and Ruth Macklin, eds. *Who Speaks for the Child: The Problems of Proxy Consent*. New York: Plenum Press, 1982.

Giovannoni, Jeanne M., and Rosina M. Becerra. *Defining Child Abuse*. New York: Free Press, 1979.

Goldstein, Joseph, Anna Freud, and Albert Solnit. *Beyond the Best Interests of the Child*. New York: Free Press, 1973.

Gordon, Linda. *Pitied but Not Entitled: Single Mothers and the History of Welfare*. New York: Free Press, 1994.

Greenberg, Jack. *Crusaders in the Courts*. New York: Basic Books, 1994.

Handler, Joel F. *Social Movements and the Legal System*. New York: Academic Press, 1978.

Hardin, Mark. *The Adoption Assistance and Child Welfare Act of 1980: An Introduction for Juvenile Court Judges*. Washington, D.C.: American Bar Association, 1983.

Hawes, Joseph M. *The Children's Rights Movement: A History of Advocacy and Protection*. Boston: Twayne Publishers, 1991.

Hewlett, Sylvia Ann. *When the Bough Breaks: The Cost of Neglecting Our Children*. New York: Free Press, 1991.

Joe, Tom, and Cheryl Rogers. *By the Few for the Few*. Lexington, Mass.: Lexington Books, 1985.

Johnson, Lyndon Baines. "Speeches by Lyndon B. Johnson." In Edward Zigler and Jeanette Valentine, eds. *Project Head Start*. New York: Free Press, 1979.

Kamerman, Sheila B. and Alfred J. Kahn. *Mothers Alone: Strategies for a Time of Change*. Dover, Mass.: Auburn House Publishing, 1988.

Kane, Thomas J. and Mary Jo Bane. "The Context for Welfare Reform." In Mary Jo Bane and David T. Ellwood. *Welfare Realities: From Rhetoric to Reform*. Cambridge: Harvard University Press, 1994.

Katz, Michael. *In the Shadow of the Poorhouse: A Social History of Welfare in America*. New York: Basic Books, 1986.

———. *The Undeserving Poor: From the War on Poverty to the War on Welfare*. New York: Pantheon Books, 1989.

Katzman, Robert. *Institutional Disability: The Saga of Transportation Policy for the Disabled*. Washington, D.C.: Brookings Institute, 1986.

Kfoury, Paul R. *Children before the Court: Reflections on Legal Issues Affecting Minors*. 2d ed. Salem, N.H.: Butterworth Legal Publishers, 1991.

Kluger, Richard. *Simple Justice*. New York: Alfred A. Knopf, 1976.

Kohler, Mary. "To What Are Children Entitled?" In Beatrice Gross and Ronald Gross, eds. *The Children's Rights Movement: Overcoming the Oppression of Young People*. Garden City, N.Y.: Anchor Books, 1977.

Kozol, Jonathan. *Rachel and Her Children*. New York: Ballantine Books, 1988.

Krause, Harry D. *Child Support in America: The Legal Perspective*. Charlottesville, Va.: The Michie Co., 1981.

Lawrence, Susan E. *The Poor in Court*. Princeton: Princeton University Press, 1990.

Lerman, Robert I. "Child Support Policies." In Pheobe H. Cottingham and David T. Ellwood, eds. *Welfare Policy for the 1990s*. Cambridge: Harvard University Press, 1989.

Levitan, Sar A. *The Great Society's Poor Law: A New Approach to Poverty*. Baltimore: Johns Hopkins University Press, 1969.

Lindsey, Duncan. *The Welfare of Children*. New York: Oxford University Press, 1994.

Lowry, Marcia. "Derring Do in the 1980s: Child Welfare Impact Litigation after the Warren Years." In Douglas J. Besharov, ed. *Protecting Children from Abuse and Neglect: Policy and Practice*. Springfield, Ill.: Charles C. Thomas, 1988.

Marmor, Theodore, Jerry Mashaw, and Philip L. Harvey. *America's Misunderstood Welfare State*. New York: Basic Books, 1990.

Mason, Mary Ann. *From Father's Property to Children's Rights: The History of Child Custody in the United States*. New York: Columbia University Press, 1994.

McCann, Michael W. *Taking Reform Seriously: Perspectives on Public Interest Liberalism*. Ithaca: Cornell University Press, 1986.

———. *Rights at Work: Pay Equity Reform and the Politics of Legal Mobilization*. Chicago: University of Chicago Press, 1994.

Mead, Lawrence. *The New Politics of Poverty*. New York: Basic Books, 1992.

Melnick, R. Shep. *Between the Lines: Interpreting Welfare Rights*. Washington, D.C.: Brookings Institute, 1994.

Mezey, Susan Gluck. *No Longer Disabled: The Federal Courts and the Politics of Social Security Disability*. Westport, Conn.: Greenwood Press, 1988.

Mnookin, Robert, ed. *In the Interest of Children*. New York: W. H. Freeman, 1985.

Myers, John E. B. *Legal Issues in Child Abuse and Neglect*. Newbury Park, Calif.: Sage Publications, 1992.

National Child Support Assurance Consortium. *Childhood's End: What Happens to Children When Child Support Obligations Are Not Enforced*. Uniondale, N.Y.: National Child Support Assurance Consortium, February 1993.

National Commission on Children. *Beyond Rhetoric: A New American Agenda for Children and Families*. Washington, D.C.: National Commission on Children, 1991.

Neier, Aryeh. *Only Judgment: The Limits of Litigation in Social Change*. Middletown, Conn.: Wesleyan University Press, 1982.

Nelson, Barbara. *Making an Issue of Child Abuse*. Chicago: University of Chicago Press, 1984.

O'Connor, Karen. *Women's Organizations' Use of the Courts*. Lexington, Mass.: Lexington Books, 1980.

Piven, Frances Fox, and Richard A. Cloward. *The New Class War*. New York: Pantheon Books, 1982.

————. "The Historical Sources of the Contemporary Relief Debate." In Fred Block, Richard A. Cloward, Barbara Ehrenreich, and Frances Fox Piven, eds. *The Mean Season: The Attack on the Welfare State*. New York: Pantheon Books, 1987.

————. *Regulating the Poor: The Functions of Public Welfare*. 2d ed. New York: Vintage Books, 1993.

Radigan, Anne L. "Federal Policy-making and Family Issues." In Elizabeth A. Mulroy, ed. *Women As Single Parents*. Dover, Mass.: Auburn House Publishing, 1988.

Richmond, Julius B., Deborah J. Stipek, and Edward Zigler. "A Decade of Head Start." In Edward Zigler, and Jeanette Valentine, eds. *Project Head Start*. New York: Free Press, 1979.

Robison, Susan. *Putting the Pieces Together: Survey of States Systems for Children in Crisis*. Denver: National Conference of State Legislatures, 1990.

Rodgers, Harrell R., Jr. *Poor Women, Poor Families*. 2d ed. New York: M. E. Sharpe, 1990.

Rosenberg, Gerald. *The Hollow Hope: Can Courts Bring About Social Change?* Chicago: University of Chicago Press, 1991.

Sard, Barbara. "The Role of the Courts in Welfare Reform." In Elizabeth A. Mulroy, ed. *Women As Single Parents*. Dover, Mass.: Auburn House Publishing, 1988.

Scarbrough, William H. "Who Are the Poor? A Demographic Perspective." In Judith A. Chafel, ed. *Child Poverty and Public Policy*. Washington, D.C.: Urban Institute, 1993.

Scheingold, Stuart. "The Politics of Rights Revisited." In Richard Gambitta, Marlynn May, and James Foster, eds. *Governing Through Courts*. Beverly Hills: Sage, 1981.

Schwartz, Bernard. *The Ascent of Pragmatism: The Burger Court in Action*. Reading, Mass.: Addison-Wesley, 1990.

Silver, Jessica Dunsay. "Baby Doe: The Incomplete Federal Response." In Douglas J. Besharov, ed. *Protecting Children from Abuse and Neglect: Policy and Practice*. Springfield, Ill.: Charles C. Thomas, 1988.

Skocpol, Theda. *Protecting Soldiers and Mothers: The Political Origins of Social Policy in the United States*. Cambridge: Belknap Press of Harvard University, 1992.

Stein, Theodore. *Child Welfare and the Law*. New York: Longman Publishing, 1991.

Stein, Theodore J., and Gary David Comstock. *Reasonable Efforts: A Report on Implementation by Child Welfare Agencies in Five States*. Washington, D.C.: American Bar Association, 1987.

Tushnet, Mark. *The NAACP's Legal Strategy against Segregated Education, 1925–1950*. Chapel Hill: University of North Carolina Press, 1987.

U.S. Advisory Board on Child Abuse and Neglect. *The Continuing Child Protection Emergency: A Challenge to the Nation*. Washington, D.C.: Department of Health and Human Services, Administration for Children and Families, 1993.

Vondra, Joan I. "Childhood Poverty and Child Maltreatment." In Judith A. Chafel, ed. *Child Poverty and Public Policy*. Washington, D.C.: Urban Institute, 1993.

Vose, Clement. *Caucasians Only*. Berkeley: University of California Press, 1959.

Wald, Michael, and Sophia Cohen. "Preventing Child Abuse—What Will It Take?" In Douglas J. Besharov, ed. *Protecting Children from Abuse and Neglect: Policy and Practice*. Springfield, Ill.: Charles C. Thomas, 1988.

Washington, Valora, and Ura Jean Oyemade. *Project Head Start: Past, Present, Future Trends in the Context of Family Needs*. New York: Garland Publishing, 1987.

Working Group on Welfare Reform, Family Support, and Independence. *Background Papers on Welfare Reform: Child Support Enforcement*. Washington, D.C.: Administration for Children and Families, Department of Health and Human Services, 1994.

Young, Leontine. *Wednesday's Children: A Study of Child Neglect and Abuse*. New York: McGraw-Hill, 1964.

Zarefsky, David. *President Johnson's War on Poverty: Rhetoric and History*. University, Ala.: University of Alabama Press, 1986.

Zigler, Edward, and Karen Anderson. "An Idea Whose Time Has Come: The Intellectual and Political Climate for Head Start." In Edward Zigler, and Jeanette Valentine, eds. *Project Head Start*. New York: Free Press, 1979.

Articles

Amar, Akhil Reed, and Daniel Widawsky. "Child Abuse As Slavery: A Thirteenth Amendment Response to *DeShaney*." *Harvard Law Review* 105 (1992): 1359–1385.

American Bar Association. "Supreme Court Report: Child Support and Jail." *American Bar Association Journal* (August 1, 1987): 58–61.

Areen, Judith. "Intervention Between Parent and Child: A Reappraisal of the State's Role in Child Neglect and Abuse Cases." *Georgetown Law Journal* 63 (1975): 887–937.

Atwell, Barbara. " 'A Lost Generation': The Battle for Private Enforcement of the Adoption Assistance and Child Welfare Act of 1980." *University of Cincinnati Law Review* 60 (1992): 593–645.

Barnett, W. Steven. "Benefits of Compensatory Preschool Education." *The Journal of Human Resources* 27 (Spring 1992): 279–312.

Baskin, Stuart J. "State Intrusion into Family Affairs: Justifications and Limitations." *Stanford Law Review* 26 (1974): 1383–1409.

Bennett, Michele K. "Native American Children Caught in the Web of the Indian Child Welfare Act." *Hamline Law Review* 16 (1993): 953–973.

Besharov, Douglas J. "A New Start for Head Start." *The American Enterprise* 3 (March-April 1992): 52–57.

Bigelow, Aileen M. "In the Ghetto: The State's Duty to Protect Inner-City Children from Violence." *Notre Dame Journal of Law, Ethics and Public Policy* 7 (1993): 533–567.

Buechner, Jay S., H. Denman Scott, John L. Smith, and Alan B. Humphrey. "WIC Program Participation—A Marketing Approach." *Public Health Reports* 106 (September-October 1991): 547–556.

Bussiere, Alice. "Federal Adoption Assistance for Children with Special Needs." *Clearinghouse Review* 19 (October 1985): 587–599.

Bussiere, Elizabeth. "The Failure of Constitutional Welfare Rights in the Warren Court." *Political Science Quarterly* 109 (1984): 105–131.

Caldeira, Gregory A., and John R. Wright. "Amici Curiae before the Supreme Court: Who Participates, When, and How Much?" *Journal of Politics* 52 (1990): 782–806.

Caldwell, Robert, G. Anne Bogat, and Willliam S. Davidson II. "The Assessment of Child Abuse Potential." *American Journal of Community Psychology* 16 (1988): 609–624.

Calistri, Brian L. "Child Support and Welfare Reform: The Child Support Enforcement Provisions of the Family Support Act of 1988." *Journal of Legislation* 16 (1990): 191–201.

Casey, Timothy J. "The Family Support Act of 1988: Molehill or Mountain, Retreat or Reform?" *Clearinghouse Review* (December 1989): 930–944.

Center for Law and Social Policy. *Family Matters.* Washington, D.C.: (April 1991).

Chafel, Judith A. "Funding Head Start: What Are the Issues?" *American Journal of Orthopsychiatry* 62 (January 1992): 9–21.

Corbett, Tom, Irwin Garfinkel, and Nora Cate Schaeffer. "Public Opinion about a Child Support Assurance System." *Social Service Review* (December 1988): 632–648.

Cortner, Richard. "Strategies and Tactics of Litigants in Constitutional Cases." *Journal of Public Law* 17 (1968): 287–307.

Costin, Lela B. "Unraveling the Mary Ellen Legend: Origins of the Cruelty Movement." *Social Service Review* (1991): 203–223.

Cowan, Ruth. "Women's Rights Through Litigation: An Examination of the American Civil Liberties Union Women's Rights Project, 1971–1976." *Columbia Human Rights Law Review* 8 (1976): 373–412.

Dale, Michael J. "The Evolving Constitutional Rights of Nonmarital Children: Mixed Blessings." *Georgia State University Law Review* 5 (1989): 523–555.

Dawson, Diann. "The Evolution of a Federal Family Law Policy under Title IV-A of the Social Security Act—The Aid to Families with Dependent Children Program." *Catholic University Law Review* 36 (1986): 197–218.

DiLeonardi, Joan. "Families in Poverty and Chronic Neglect of Children." *Families in Society* 74 (November 1993): 558.

Dobbs, Thomas. "The Domestic Relations Exception is Narrowed after *Ankenbrandt v. Richards*, 112 S.Ct. 2206 (1992)." *Wake Forest Law Review* 28 (1993): 1137–1166.

Doolittle, Fred C. "State-Imposed Nonfinancial Eligibility Conditions in AFDC: Confusion in Supreme Court Decisions and a Need for Congressional Clarification." *Harvard Journal on Legislation* 19 (1982): 1–48.

Dubowitz, Howard, et al. "A Conceptual Definition of Child Neglect." *Criminal Justice and Behavior* 20 (March 1993): 8–26.

Edelman, Peter B. "Toward a Comprehensive Antipoverty Strategy: Getting Beyond the Silver Bullet." *The Georgetown Law Journal* 81 (1993): 1697–1755.

Epstein, Lee, and C. K. Rowland. "Debunking the Myth of Interest Group Invincibility in the Courts." *American Political Science Review* 85 (1991): 205–217.

Failinger, Marie A., and Larry May. "Litigating against Poverty: Legal Services and Group Representation." *Ohio State Law Journal* 45 (1984): 2–56.

First, Curry. " 'Poor Joshua!': The State's Responsibility to Protect Children from Abuse." *Clearinghouse Review* 23 (August-September 1989): 525–534.

Fleece, Steven M. "A Review of the Child Support Enforcement Program." *Journal of Family Law* 20 (1981–1982): 489–520.

Fontana, Vincent J. "Child Abuse, Past, Present, and Future." *Human Ecology Review* 15 (1984): 2–23.

Food Research and Action Center. "Foodlines." *Social Policy* 20 (Winter 1990): 55.

Fried, Arlene. "The Foster Child's Avenues of Redress: Questions Left Unanswered." *Columbia Journal of Law and Social Problems* 26 (1993): 465–491.

Frye, Lisa. "*Suter v. Artist M.* and Statutory Remedies under Section 1983: Alteration without Justification." *North Carolina Law Review* 71 (1993): 1169–1205.

Galanter, Marc. "Why the 'Haves' Come Out Ahead: Speculations on the Limits of Legal Change." *Law and Society* (1974): 95–160.

Garfinkel, Irwin, and Donald Oellerich. "Noncustodial Fathers' Ability to Pay Child Support." *Demography* 26 (May 1989): 219–233.

Goldberg, Faye R. "Child Support Enforcement: Balancing Increased Federal Involvement with Procedural Due Process." *Suffolk University Law Review* 19 (1985): 687–714.

Goldfarb, Sally F. "Child Support Guidelines: A Model for Fair Allocation of Child Care, Medical, and Educational Expenses." *Family Law Quarterly* 21 (1987): 325–349.

Graham, George G. "WIC: A Food Program That Fails." *Public Interest* 103 (Spring 1991): 66–75.

Hafen, Jonathan O. "Children's Rights and Legal Representation—The Proper Role of Children, Parents, and Attorneys." *Notre Dame Journal of Law, Ethics and Public Policy* 7 (1993): 423–463.

Handler, Joel, F. "The Transformation of Aid to Families with Dependent Children: The Family Support Act in Historical Context." *Review of Law and Social Change* 16 (1987–1988): 457–533.

———. " 'Constructing the Political Spectacle': The Interpretation of Entitlements, Legalization, and Obligations in Social Welfare History." *Brooklyn Law Review* 56 (1990): 899–974.

Harris, Deborah. "Child Support for Welfare Families: Family Policy Trapped in Its Own Rhetoric." *Review of Law and Social Change* 16 (1987–1988): 619–657.

Haynes, Margaret Campbell. "Supporting Our Children: A Blueprint for Reform." *Family Law Quarterly* 27 (1993): 7–29.

Highlights from the Executive Summary. "WIC Participation and Program Characteristics, 1988." *Nutrition Today* (September-October 1990): 32–34.

Hirsch, Amy E. "Income Deeming in the AFDC Program: Using Dual Track Family Law to Make Poor Women Poorer." *Review of Law and Social Change* 16 (1987–1988): 713–740.

Johnson, James W., and Adele M. Blong. "The AFDC Child Support Cooperation Requirement." *Clearinghouse Review* (March 1987): 1388–1407.

Kamerman, Sheila B. "Women, Children, and Poverty: Public Policies and Female-Headed Families in Industrialized Countries." *Signs: Journal of Women in Culture and Society* 10 (1984): 249–271.

———. "Toward a Child Policy Decade." *Child Welfare* 68 (July-August 1989): 371–390.

———. "Doing Better by Children: Focus on Families." *The Journal of Law and Politics* 8 (1991): 75–88.

Kelly, Timothy G. "Protecting the Handicapped Newborn: Where the Courts Failed and the Legislature Succeeded—The Child Abuse Amendments of 1984." *John Marshall Law Review* 19 (1986): 397–429.

Kempe, C. Henry, et al. "The Battered Child Syndrome." *The Journal of the American Medical Association* 181 (July 7, 1962): 17–24.

Kobylka, Joseph. "A Court-Created Context for Group Litigation: Libertarian Groups and Obscenity." *Journal of Politics* 49 (1987): 1061–1078.

Krause, Harry D. "Child Support Enforcement: Legislative Tasks for the Early 1980s." *Family Law Quarterly* 15 (1982): 349–370.

———. "Reflections on Child Support." *University of Illinois Law Review* (1983): 99–119.

Krislov, Samuel. "The OEO Lawyers Fail to Constitutionalize a Right to Welfare: A Study in the Uses and Limits of the Judicial Process." *Minnesota Law Review* 58 (1973): 211–245.

Ku, Leighton. "Factors Influencing Early Prenatal Enrolment in the WIC Program." *Public Health Reports* 104 (May-June 1989): 301–306.

Law, Sylvia A. "Women, Work, Welfare, and the Preservation of Patriarchy." *University of Pennsylvania Law Review* 131 (1983): 1249–1339.

———. "Rethinking Sex and the Constitution." *University of Pennsylvania Law Review* 132 (1984): 955–1040.

Lee, Valerie E., J. Brooks-Gunn, and Elizabeth Schnur. "Does Head Start Work? A One-Year Follow-up Comparison of Disadvantaged Children Attending Head Start, No Preschool, and Other Preschool Programs." *Developmental Psychology* 24 (1988): 210–222.

Levy, Paul A. "The Durability of Supreme Court Welfare Reforms of the 1960s." *Social Service Review* 66 (June 1992): 215–236.

Malloy, Robin Paul. "Market Philosophy in the Legal Tension between Children's Autonomy and Parental Authority." *Indiana Law Review* 21 (1988): 889–900.

Mannix, Mary R., Henry A. Freedman, and Natarlin R. Best. "The Good Cause Exception to the AFDC Child Support Cooperation Requirement." *Clearinghouse Review* (August-September 1987): 339–348.

Meiss, Katherine E., and Ann VanDePol. "California's GAIN: Greater Avenues or a Narrow Path? The Politics and Policies of Welfare Reform and AFDC Work Programs in the 1980s." *Berkeley Women's Law Journal* 3 (1987–1988): 49–95.

Mezey, Susan Gluck. "Judicial Interpretation of Legislative Intent: The Role of the Supreme Court in the Implication of Private Rights of Action." *Rutgers Law Review* 36 (1983): 53–89.

———. "The Burger Court and *Younger* Abstention: Enhancing the Role of State Courts in Constitutional Adjudication." *Publius* 19 (1989): 25–40.

Miller, Laura Ariane. "Head Start: A Moving Target." *Yale Law and Policy Review* 5 (1987): 322–344.

Miller, Steven R. "Federal Law and the Enforcement of Child Support Orders: A Critical Look at Subchapter 4 Part D of the Social Services Amendments of 1974." *Review of Law and Social Change* 6 (1976): 23–42.

Moffitt, Robert. "Work Incentives in the AFDC System: An Analysis of the 1981 Reforms." *American Economic Review* 76 (May 1986): 219–223.

Murphy, Maryellen. "Domestic Relations Exception to Diversity Jurisdiction: *Ankenbrandt v. Richards*, 112 S.Ct. 2206 (1992)." *New England Law Review* 28 (1993): 577–601.

Neagli, Douglas B., and Matthew B. Troutman. "Constitutional Implications of the Child Support Enforcement Amendments of 1984." *Journal of Family Law* 24 (1985–1986): 301–326.

Nelson, Kristine E., Edward J. Saunders, and Miriam J. Landsman. "Chronic Child Neglect in Perspective." *Social Work* 38 (November 1993): 661–671.

Neuhardt, Michael. "The 1981 AFDC Amendments: Rhetoric and Reality." *University of Dayton Law Review* 8 (1982): 81–107.

O'Connor, Karen, and Lee Epstein. "The Rise of Conservative Interest Group Litigation." *Journal of Politics* 45 (1983): 479–489.

O'Donnell, Harry. "Title I of the Family Support Act of 1988—The Quest for Effective National Child Support Enforcement Continues." *Journal of Family Law* 29 (1990–1991): 149–170.

Olson, Susan. "Interest-Group Litigation in Federal District Court: Beyond the Political Disadvantage Theory." *Journal of Politics* 52 (1990): 854–882.

Oren, Laura. "The State's Failure to Protect Children and Substantive Due Process: *DeShaney* in Context." *North Carolina Law Review* 68 (1990): 659–731.

Oyemade, Ura Jean. "The Rationale for Head Start As a Vehicle for the Upward Mobility of Minority Families: A Minority Perspective." *American Journal of Orthopsychiatry* 55 (October 1985): 591–601.

Parnas, Raymond I., and Sherry Cermak. "Rethinking Child Support." *University of California, Davis Law Review* 22 (1989): 759–800.

Paterson, Andrea. "Between Helping the Child and Punishing the Mother: Homelessness among AFDC Families." *Harvard Women's Law Journal* 12 (1989): 237–259.

Pine, Barbara. "Child Welfare Reform and the Political Process." *Social Service Review* 60 (September 1986): 339–359.

Prasad, Ashish. "Rights without Remedies: Section 1983 Enforcement of Title IV-D of the Social Security Act." *University of Chicago Law Review* 60 (1993): 197–222.

Reich, Charles. "The New Property." *Yale Law Journal* 73 (1964): 733–787.

———. "Individual Rights and Social Welfare: The Emerging Legal Issues." 74 (1965): 1245–1257.

Reidinger, Paul. "Why Did No One Protect This Child?" *American Bar Association Journal* (December 1, 1988): 48–51.

Roberts, Paula. "Federal Income Tax Intercept." *Clearinghouse Review* (December 1985): 853–863.

———. "Additional Remedies under the Child Support Enforcement Amendments of 1984." *Clearinghouse Review* (May 1986): 17–22.

Roberts, Paula, and Suellen Lowry. "Benefiting AFDC Children by Counting Social Security Dependents' Payments toward Their Absent Parent's Support Obligations." *Clearinghouse Review* (April 1987): 1526–1536.

Roberts, Paula, and Mary Mason. "Promises, Promises: Child Support Enforcement in 1988." *Clearinghouse Review* (January 1989): 909–917.

Robins, Philip K. "Child Support, Welfare Dependency, and Poverty." *The American Economic Review* 76 (September 1986): 768–788.

Rodham, Hillary. "Children under the Law." *Harvard Educational Review* 43 (1973): 487–514.

Rose, Susan J., and William Meezan. "Defining Child Neglect: Evolution, Influences, and Issues." *Social Service Review* (June 1993): 279–293.

Rush, Sharon E. "The Warren and Burger Courts on State, Parent, and Child Conflict Resolution: A Comparative Analysis and Proposed Methodology." *Hastings Law Journal* 36 (1985): 461–513.

Ryan, Kevin. "Stemming the Tide of Foster Care Runaways." *Catholic University Law Review* 42 (1993): 271–311.

Sampson, John J., and Paul M. Kurtz. "UIFSA: An Interstate Support Act for the Twenty-first Century." *Family Law Quarterly* 27 (1993): 85–93.

Sard, Barbara. "The Role of the Courts in Welfare Reform." *Clearinghouse Review* 22 (1988): 367–388.

Schwartz, Ira, Martha Wade Steketee, and Jeffrey Butts. "Business As Usual: Juvenile Justice During the 1980s." *Notre Dame Journal of Law, Ethics and Public Policy* 5 (1991): 377–396.

Serratelli, Lori K., and Alvora Varin-Hommen. "The 1974 Child Support Provisions: Constitutional Ramifications." *Capital University Law Review* 6 (1976): 275–297.

Shotton, Alice C. "Making Reasonable Efforts in Child Abuse and Neglect Cases: Ten Years Later." *California Western Law Review* 26 (1989–1990): 223–256.

Skerry, Peter. "The Charmed Life of Head Start." *The Public Interest* 73 (1983): 18–39.

Smith, Leo. "Reducing State Accountability to the Federal Government: The *Suter v. Artist M.* Decision to Dismiss Section 1983 Claims for Violating Federal Fund Mandates." *Wisconsin Law Review* (1992): 1267–1297.

Songer, Donald R., and Reginald S. Sheehan. "Interest Group Success in the Courts: Amicus Participation in the Supreme Court." *Political Research Quarterly* 46 (1993): 339–354.

Staffs of the American Civil Liberties Union and the Food Research and Action Center. "Introduction to the WIC and CSFP Programs." *Clearinghouse Review* (December 1990): 820–828.

Stein, Theodore. "The Child Abuse Prevention and Treatment Act." *Social Service Review* 58 (June 1984): 302–314.

Stouder, Judith. "Child Support Enforcement and Establishment of Paternity As Tools of Welfare Reform—Social Services Amendments of 1974, pt. B, 42 U.S.C. §§ 651–60 (Supp. V, 1975)." *Washington Law Review* 52 (1976): 169–192.

Tjaden, Patricia G., and Nancy Thoennes. "Predictors of Legal Intervention in Child Maltreatment Cases." *Child Abuse and Neglect* 16 (1992): 807–821.

Vogel, Laura. "Children in Poverty: Welfare and Work Together Can Make a Difference." *The Kansas Journal of Law and Public Policy* 3 (1994): 173–183.

Wald, Michael. "State Intervention on Behalf of 'Neglected' Children: A Search for Realistic Standards." *Stanford Law Review* 27 (1975): 985–1040.

———. "State Intervention on Behalf of 'Neglected' Children: Standards for Removal of Children from Their Homes, Monitoring the Status of Children in Foster Care, and Termination of Parental Rights." *Stanford Law Review* 28 (1976): 623–699.

———. "Children's Rights: A Framework for Analysis." *University of California, Davis Law Review* 12 !1979): 255–282.

Washington, Valora. "Head Start: How Appropriate for Minority Families in the 1980s?" *American Journal of Orthopsychiatry* 55 (October 1985): 577–589.

Watkins, Sallie A. "The Mary Ellen Myth: Correcting Child Welfare History." *Social Work* 35 (November 1990): 500–503.

Wexler, Richard. "The Children's Crusade." *Chicago Reader* (March 24, 1995).

Wholey, Joseph S. "WIC: Against the Tide." *The Bureaucrat* (Summer 1986): 26–30.

Williams, Wendy. "The Equality Crisis: Some Reflections on Culture, Courts, and Feminism." *Women's Rights Law Reporter* 7 (1982): 175–200.

Zigler, Edward. "Assessing Head Start at Twenty: An Invited Commentary." *American Journal of Orthopsychiatry* 55 (October 1985): 603–609.

Government Documents

Committee on Ways and Means, U.S. House of Representatives. *Overview of Entitlement Programs, 1993 Green Book: Background Material and Data on Programs Within the Jurisdiction of the Committee on Ways and Means.* Washington, D.C.: Government Printing Office, 1993.

H.Rep. No. 778, 91st Cong., 1st Sess. (1969).

H.Rep. No. 671, 93d Cong., 1st Sess. (1973).

H.Rep. No. 159, 98th Cong., 1st Sess. (1983).

H.Rep. No. 213, 103d Cong., 1st Sess. (1993).

S.Rep. No. 1356, 93d Cong., 2d Sess. (1974).

S.Rep. No. 830, 93d Cong., 2d Sess. (1974).

S.Rep. No. 259, 94th Cong., 1st Sess. (1975).

S.Rep. No. 884, 95th Cong., 2d Sess. (1978).

S.Rep. No. 838, 96th Cong., 2d Sess. (1980).

S.Rep. No. 484, 98th Cong., 2d Sess. (1984).

S.Rep. No. 327, 99th Cong., 2d Sess. (1986).

S.Rep. No. 421, 101st Cong., 2d Sess. (1990).

CASE INDEX

Note: See chapter notes for citations of principal cases.

SUBJECT INDEX

Abramovitz, Mimi, 56n. 10
Aid to Families with Dependent
  Children: benefits of, 38–40, 44–45,
  46, 53, 55, 59n. 48, 60–61n. 69,
  63nn. 98, 99, 171; costs of, 38–40;
  and child support eforcement,
  136–40, 142, 144–46, 147–48, 155,
  158, 163n. 49, 164nn. 55, 63; and
  child welfare system, 103–4, 121; and
  constitutional claims, 42–47, 171, 173;
  eligibility, rules of, 33–37, 41, 42–43,
  47–54, 57n. 16, 60–61n. 69, 63nn.
  98, 99, 171, 172; and Family Support
  Act, 37–38; and food stamps, 35, 36,
  39; and Head Start, 76; and inflation,
  39; and litigation, 41–53, 171–72, 173;
  origins of, 32–33; and Personal
  Responsibility Act, 41; and racial
  minorities, 33, 34, 41, 46–47, 53–54,
  59n. 46, 171; and statutory claims,
  47–53, 134n. 113, 171; and WIC, 88n.
  1; work requirements, 34–35, 37, 48
Allen, MaryLee, 8, 13n. 31, 127n. 40,
  128nn. 49, 52
Amar, Akhil Reed, 131n. 85
American Bar Association, 5, 7, 12n.
  19, 97, 111, 119, 125n. 4, 126n. 20,
  159nn. 1, 4, 163n. 45, 166nn. 86, 87
American Civil Liberties Union, 5–6,
  8, 42, 43, 52, 62n. 89, 97, 112, 114,
  119, 151
Amicus curiae, 5, 8, 12n. 19; and
  AFDC litigation, 42, 43, 45, 46, 48,
  49, 50, 51, 52; and child welfare
  litigation, 110, 111, 112, 114, 119, 134n.
  118; and child support enforcement
  litigation, 148, 150, 151, 156, 157
Anderson, Karen, 91nn. 54, 58, 60, 61

Areen, Judith, 126n. 15
Ashish, Prasad, 134n. 114
Atwell, Barbara, 128n. 47
Autonomy v. protectionism, 2, 4, 16,
  26, 27n. 8, 167, 168, 170

Bane, Mary Jo, 57nn. 20, 23, 58nn. 27,
  39, 42, 59n. 55, 159n. 3, 164nn. 57,
  58, 60
Barnett, W. Steven, 90–91n. 49
Baskin, Stuart J., 27n. 6
Bauman, Robert, 139
Becerra, Rosina M., 56n. 11, 125n. 7
Bell, Winifred, 57n. 16
Bennett, Michele K., 128n. 46
Besharov, Douglas, J., 91n. 51, 97,
  124n. 2, 125n. 8, 126nn. 15, 18, 21,
  127n. 35
Best, Natarlin R., 161n. 23
Beyer, Margaret, 126n. 21
Bianchi, Suzanne M., 56n. 2, 59n. 52
Bigelow, Aileen M., 131–32n. 87, 132n. 95
Blackmun, Harry, 55, 63n. 112, 116,
  117, 120–21, 173
Blasi, Vincent, 28n. 23
Blong, Adele, 7, 8, 12n. 22, 13n. 33,
  161n. 23
Bogat, G. Anne, 125n. 13
Bond, Christopher, 106
Brennan, William, 47, 110, 116
Brooks-Gunn, J., 90–91n. 49
Buechner, Jay S., 88n. 4
Burger Court, 17–25, 28n. 23, 54, 168,
  171, 177–78
Burger, Warren, 26
Bush (George) administration, 69, 70,
  80–82, 105–6